Promoting Optimum Mental Health Through Counseling:

An Overview

Edited by

J. Scott Hinkle

PO Box 26171
Greensboro, NC 27402-6171

In association with the ERIC Counseling
and Student Services Clearinghouse

ISBN 1-56109-084-0

This publication was funded in part by the US Department of Education, Office of Educational Research and Improvement, Contract no. RR93002004. Opinions expressed in this publication do not necessarily reflect the positions of the US Department of Education OERI, or ERIC/CASS.

Blue Blook for Final - Marriage Family 9
Adults/Aged 6

Dr. Levy's Presentation

Here - 39, 40, 44, 45, 10, 11, 34, 35
History

Table of Contents

II. Client Focus in Mental Health Counseling

III. Multiculturism in Mental Health Counseling

IV: Special Emphases in Mental Health Counseling

Preface

Within the professional field of counseling, few specialties have assumed as much importance and grown as rapidly as mental health counseling (MHC). As Hinkle estimates in his overview (Chapter 1, page 1), 41,000 of an estimated 124,000 active counselors are practicing in a clinical setting. Further, it is variously estimated that close to one half of the members of ACA identify themselves as practicing mental health counselors. But numbers by themselves provide only a limited perspective of the increasingly important role that MHC plays within both the broad field of health and the specific field of mental health services. A moment's reflection on events covered by TV and the public press readily attest to the breadth and depth of issues relevant to mental health services in general and MHC in particular. Even knowledgeable mental health counselors will be both surprised and impressed by the range of topics selected by Dr. Hinkle for this publication as relevant to MHC.

In his discussion with me as to the need for this publication, Dr. Hinkle stressed the need for a publication that would assist readers new to MHC to grasp the breadth and dynamism of this relatively new counseling specialty and the contributions it is making to assisting thousands of people to more adequately cope with the stresses of contemporary life and to enjoy a rewarding life experience. Further, he sought to develop a publication which would provide practicing counselors (be they mental health counselors or other counseling specialties) a window into the myriad topical areas where MHC is a vital contributor. Further, we agreed that each chapter should, whenever possible, not only describe a mental health intervention or review a topical area, but offer specific ideas and information useful to practicing counselors of all counseling specialties.

Another important consideration was brevity. We all have long reading lists but only limited time in which to do our reading. There is an ongoing struggle we experience as to how to allocate our limited "discretionary" time. Dr. Hinkle has followed our recent emphasis on "packing a lot in a little space" by the use of a succinct essay format rather than the traditional longer journal article format. These articles have lost little in substance by their brevity, but lend themselves to electronic communication and, especially important, our being able to read them when we receive them rather than store them up for a hoped-for less busy time.

Recency is important to all of us. We all want the very latest research and information on the topics we are pursuing. It can be rather perplexing to be uncertain as to whether the information we are acting upon is comprehensive and up-to-date. We have responded to this special need for the newest and best information by including a short search of the ERIC database on mental health. It will not only provide some very recent information about mental health but also model how useful an ERIC search can be. Brief instructions on how to search the ERIC database online are included as well as URLs for one of ERIC/CASS's most innovative recent developments - topically targeted online virtual libraries.

In short, I believe that Dr. Hinkle has done an exceptional job in producing a highly cogent and succinct publication useful to counselors of ranging specialties and experience. It is truly a book that has the probability of quickly becoming dog-eared. You will use it!

Garry Walz
Director, ERIC/CASS

Promoting Optimum Mental Health Through Counseling: An Overview

I. Overview: The Evolution of Mental Health Counseling

CHAPTER ONE

Promoting Optimum Mental Health Through Counseling: An Overview

J. Scott Hinkle

Mental Health Counseling (MHC) has become increasingly viable within the helping professions during the past 20 years. Specifically, mental health counselor education, training, and practice is making its mark within the field of counseling as reflected by program accreditation offered by the Council for the Accreditation of Counseling and Related Programs (CACREP) and by specialty certification awarded by The National Board of Certified Counselors (NBCC). In addition, broader recognition is reflected in acceptance by third-party payers, including the federal government. In 1990, almost 20% of all health expenditures were for mental health, indicating that employment opportunities for competently trained mental health counselors will continue to be robust.

Definitively, MHC includes preventive, facilitative, rehabilitative, and remedial services and MHC strives to improve the quality of life for the people it serves (Hershenson & Power, 1987). According to Spruill & Fong (1990), MHC objectives include the advancement and maintenance of mental health, the prevention and treatment of mental disorders, the identification and modification of etiologic, diagnostic, and systems correlates of mental health, and the improvement of the mental health service delivery system. Additionally, Spruill (in press) has indicated that MHC has rapidly developed into a broad-based discipline which has struggled for recognition and identity among professionals and consumers. Moreover, MHC is a specialty within counseling that requires preparation in specific academic content areas, as well as extensive supervised clinical experiences (Dial et al., 1992). Unfortunately, this counseling specialty has a sparse but scholarly body of knowledge regarding specific educational, scientific, and professional contributions associated with the disciplines of counseling, education, and psychology (Hinkle, Kline, & Christensen, 1996).

This volume includes a broad selection of topics representing important aspects of mental health counseling. For example, MHC includes the diagnosis and treatment of mental disorders, which is covered by a series of papers on various aspects of the *DSM-IV.* The Certified Clinical Mental Health Counselor credential, now managed by NBCC, also is discussed herein. Furthermore, this volume contains articles concerning critical issues in the provision of MHC (e.g., adjunctive services, special populations, and multicultural counseling). In this overview, I present five major ideas concerning MHC. Namely, mental health associations, accreditation, certification, mental health counselor education, as well as some reflections on mental health counseling in general.

ACA and AMCHA

At present, an estimated 26,000 of the approximate 60,000 American Counseling Association (ACA) members identify themselves as practicing clinical counselors, operating in a variety of settings. Interestingly, the ACA division most relevant to clinical/therapeutic counseling, the American Mental Health Counselors Association (AMCHA), has only 9,000 members. Furthermore, approximately 124,000 counselors were working in the United States in 1988, according to the Occupational Outlook Handbook (1990-1991) and an estimated 41,000 of these counselors practice in a clinical setting. Furthermore, in 1990, graduates of master's training programs of a clinical nature totaled almost 5,000. Thus, there is a significant number of "clinical counselors" (Dial et al., 1992), many of which are not members of AMCHA or ACA.

It is important to keep in mind that MHC is a counseling specialty, not an organization or association. Professionals trained to perform MHC in a competent fashion may or may not be members of the American Counseling Association or the American Mental Health Counselors

Association. By deducting from previously stated data, it is clear that the majority of clinical counselors are not members of AMCHA or ACA. For the training and practice of MHC to flourish, there needs to be a broad recognition that MHC service providers first must have competent education and training. Training and associated professional issues should not be dependent on organizational politics. In fact, such politics can be a major hinderance to the development of any viable and essential counseling specialty.

CACREP and the CCMHC Specialty

Curricular experiences for MHC programs (60 semester hours), as defined by CACREP (1994), require preparation in specific knowledge and skills, along with requirements for supervised experiences in clinical settings that exceed the general counseling core. These standards not only require instruction in the foundations of MHC, they also promote the historical and philosophical dimensions of MHC.

We are approaching the end of the embryonic stage for this young counseling specialty. This means that although CACREP standards have matured, they will still need continual refinement. Such modifications should include *specific* information about the competencies needed to provide effective and efficient MHC services (e.g., mental status examination, crisis and trauma intervention, treatment planning, treatment strategies, psychiatric liaison, multidisciplinary networking, contextual and social network considerations, psychotropic medications, relationship counseling, etc.)(Hershenson & Strein, 1991; Hinkle et al., 1996).

Refinements in curricular experiences also need to reflect continuous changes in the clinical aspects of the counseling profession through ongoing research that can guide university instruction. For example, mental health practicum and internship experiences must include opportunities in managed care environments and faculty involved in this training need to verify clinical competence.

Clinical mental health counseling is considered the specialty area of professional counseling, requiring extensive clinical graduate course work and supervision. The Academy of Clinical Mental Health Counselors (ACMHC) of the NBCC requires a 60-semester-hour master's degree for the Certified Clinical Mental Health Counselor (CCMHC) credential. Course work includes at least one course in each of the following areas: Theories of Counseling, Psychotherapy, and Personality; Counseling and Psychotherapy Skills; Abnormal Psychology and Psychopathology; Human

Growth and Development Theory; Group Counseling and Psychotherapy; Professional Orientation and Ethics; Research; Testing and Appraisal; and, Social and Cultural Foundations (Hinkle et al., 1996). Clinical supervision, a taped and critiqued counseling sample, and a clinical examination that is based on a national work study of clinical mental health counselors also are required for the CCMHC certification (Dial et al., 1992; Hinkle et al.).

Mental Health Counselor Education

Counselors who practice MHC need expert training and support at the preservice stage. This includes competent curricular components (both didactic and experiential) and mentoring by professionals who are competent in the practice of MHC. To facilitate this, mental health counselor education needs to be endorsed not only by more educational units, but also by units that are *committed* to MHC. To lend additional support, NBCC's Clinical Mental Health Counseling Credential (CCMHC) is now available on a board-eligible basis for students graduating from CACREP/MHC programs.

In the past training practices and philosophies grew from the research efforts of faculty, resulting in an uneven diffusion of knowledge. For example, as diagnostic technology becomes increasingly sophisticated due to the increased knowledge regarding psychoemotional disorders, MHC educators will need to likewise keep pace. In the present, clinical training in diagnostic technology appears to be uneven across training centers and universities. Students will need to be integrated into updated diagnostic training; in some cases faculty will need retraining, and an introduction to this process in other cases (Dial et al., 1992). Externships will be helpful in facilitating this process among faculty.

In 1996, the ACMHC completed a work behavior study for the purpose of developing a clinical examination as part of the requirements for clinical mental health counselor certification (NBCC, 1996). The major themes that arose included diagnosis and treatment planning, assessment, counseling practice, and professional issues. The diagnosis and treatment planning theme addressed such problems as "medical" issues, assessing crises, diagnosis, monitoring progress, and making appropriate referrals and follow-ups. Crisis intervention, the most highly rated work behavior, was included in this thematic area. The assessment theme included performing and utilizing comprehensive biopsychosocial assessment data to determine clinical issues, conducting mental status examinations, and interpreting assessment results. Selecting, administering, scoring, and interpreting personality instruments, and interpreting intelligence tests also were significant assessment-related MHC work behaviors. The counseling practice themes encompassed crisis intervention, as well as individual, relationship, family, and group counseling. The professional issues theme highlighted informed consent, insurance payments, legal and ethical issues, continuing education, and understanding the credentialing process. Additionally, secondary themes emerged. These included operating as a member of an interdisciplinary team, psychoeducation and prevention, providing supervision and training, and consultation to individuals, groups, and organizations (Hinkle et al., 1996). These aspects of MHC should be included in mental health counselor education programs.

For MHC to have a viable future as a profession, accreditable mental health counseling curriculums must proliferate. For this to become a reality, it seems that counselor educators' perceptions of mental health counseling must be addressed and that refinements in the CACREP standards are necessary.

Reflections on MHC

MHC as a counseling specialty needs to engage in an examination of what it is and where it is going. For example, defining MHC only in terms of *prevention* and *development* does not tell one very much. Are psychologists and social workers not interested in preventing social and personal suffering? Are marriage and family therapists and psychiatrists not concerned with the development of their patients and clients? Differentiating MHC from other helping disciplines using these two variables will only end in argument and disbelief. Mental health counselors are concerned about pathology, but not from a myopic perspective. People develop difficulties (and in many cases pathology) at various times in their lives. This is a central aspect of the MHC perspective (Hershenson & Strein, 1991).

Steenbarger and LeClair (1995) have indicated that

> "Mental health counseling represents a conscious guidance of the evolutionary process, catalyzing the creation and selection of novel adaptations through are alignment of person-context relations. Thus, development does not follow a maturational blueprint, with predetermined stages constraining future outcomes. Rather, there is a fundamental open-endedness and even indeterminacy to development in which, over any span of time, an individual generates a range of novel adaptations that become the

building blocks from which future change can emerge" (p. 182-183).

Relatedly, an orientation of mental health counselors to health and wellness, as opposed to psychopathology (Brown & Srebalus, 1988) does not enable counselors to effectively deal with the burgeoning mental health concerns of our society. Surely, MHC has a rich perspective to offer, and it needs to be captured in the counseling literature (Hinkle et al., 1996), as well as in counselor education programs.

Relatedly, prevention is a good idea, but few mental health counselors are paid to do it (by out-of-pocket payment or insurance reimbursement). Personal and public incentives for wellness programs are obvious; however, the economic incentives to promote such programs have waned over the years. Therefore, there is less commitment to prevention. However, this does not mean that prevention is not important and should not be included in the conceptualization of cases and in treatment planning. For example, sharing a parenting technique with a family that already has significant problems (e.g., AD/HD) may prevent the development of another problem in the future (e.g., conduct disorder; dropping out of school; career problems)(Hinkle et al., 1996).

It is interesting to note that professionals are more alike in their treatment planning processes than different, regardless of training or therapeutic orientation (Falvey, 1992). Furthermore, "there may be relatively few distinctions in clinical judgment... across highly trained allied mental health professions" (Falvey, p. 487). In 1992 more than half of the counselor education faculty in combined master's and doctoral counselor education programs were licensed as psychologists (Zimpfer, Mohdzain, West, & Bubenzer, 1992). Moreover, almost 60% of NCCs with doctorates have degrees in fields other than counselor education (25% in counseling psychology). Obviously, consideration of the diversity in these academic backgrounds will be necessary for the future development of MHC.

Furthermore, there are substantial intra-counselor differences among the work behaviors and professional perspectives of nationally certified counselors (NCCs), or generalists (NBCC, 1993). For instance, clinical counselors rarely engage in career development, but it is a major task often performed by generalists. Similarly, the DSM has been widely used by CCMHCs, but is infrequently used by NCCs in general (Hinkle et al., 1996; NBCC, 1993).

The central questions that remain for MHC include: What distinguishes MHC from other helping disciplines? and, What can MHC offer that makes it an important and valuable contributing member of the mental health care environment? The papers in this Digest offer specific information to enable this important specialty to begin to answer these questions, as well as to pose new questions essential to the development of MHC.

Finally, and politically speaking, MHC needs to be organized by practitioners who are knowledgeable about the trends and issues in clinical counseling. For this to become a reality, one suggestion involves the reconfiguring of the organizational governing bodies associated with MHC to more accurately reflect the membership of professional clinical counselors. For example, if 80% of the membership are clinical counselors, then it would be wise for them to be administered or governed by other clinicians. This could be facilitated by paying organizational officers a modest honorarium to offset their loss of wages as they engage in governing business.

References

Brown, D., & Srebalus, D. J. (1988). *An introduction to the counseling profession.* Englewood Cliffs, NJ: Prentice Hall.

Council for Accreditation of Counseling and Related Educational Programs. (1994). *CACREP accreditation standards and procedures manual.* Alexandria, VA: Author.

Dial, T. H., Pion, G. M., Cooney, B., Kohout, K., Kaplan, K. O., Ginsberg, L., Merwin, E. I., Fox, J. C., Ginsberg, M., Staton, J., Clawson, T. W., Wildersmuth, V. A., Blankertz, L., & Hughes, R. (1992). Training of mental health providers. In R. W. Manderscheid & M. A. Sonnenschein (Eds.), *Mental health, United States, 1992* (pp. 142-162). Washington, DC: U. S. Government Printing Office.

Falvey, J. E. (1992). From intake to intervention: Interdisciplinary perspectives on mental health treatment planning. *Journal of Mental Health Counseling, 14,* 471-489.

Hershenson, D. B., & Power, P. W. (1987). *Mental health counseling: Theory and practice.* New York: Pergamon.

Hershenson, D. B., & Strein, W. (1991). Toward a mentally healthy curriculum for mental health counselor education. *Journal of Mental Health Counseling, 13,* 247-252.

Hinkle, J. S., Kline, W. B., & Christensen, T. M. (1996). *Issues in mental health counselor education and certification: Why are we doing what we are doing?* Paper submitted for publication.

National Board for Certified Counselors. (1993). *A work behavior analysis of professional counselors.* Muncie, IN: Accelerated Development.

Spruill, D. A. (in press). Definition of Mental Health Counseling: What is it? in J. S. Hinkle (Ed.). *Promoting optimum mental health through counseling: An overview,* 1998, p. 13. Greensboro, NC: ERIC.

Spruill, D. A., & Fong, M. L. (1990). Defining the domain of mental health counseling: From identity confusion to consensus. *Journal of Mental Health Counseling, 15,* 12-23.

Steenbarger, B. N., & LeClair, S. (1995). Beyond remediation and development: Mental health counseling in context. *Journal of Mental Health Counseling, 17,* 173-187.

Zimpfer, D. G., Mohdzain, A. Z., West, J. D., & Bubenzer, D. L. (1992). Professional identification of counselor preparation programs. *Counselor Education and Supervision, 32,* 91-107.

J. Scott Hinkle, Ph.D., NCC, CCMHC is Chair of the Academy of Clinical Mental Health Counselors, National Board for Certified Counselors, and Associate Professor of Community Counseling at the University of North Carolina at Greensboro.

CHAPTER TWO

Definition of Mental Health Counseling: What Is It?

David A. Spruill

Mental Health Counselors (MHCs) are increasingly called upon to explain to consumers, businesses, legislative bodies, and other mental health practitioners who they are and what they do. To compete effectively in the health care service delivery system, MHCs must be able to define their profession and practices. Because of the infancy of the profession, consumers and others may not be familiar with mental health counseling as a core mental health care discipline. This article presents information about defining mental health counseling so as to assist MHCs in promoting the profession.

Discussion

Historical Roots

Mental health counseling has its roots in education and the school guidance movement, beginning with the National Defense Education Act (NDEA) of 1958, which funded training for school counselors. Our origins, therefore, stem directly from education and educational counseling, and indirectly from psychology. In 1963, the Community Mental Health Centers Act funded the establishment of community mental health centers. These new centers utilized an interdisciplinary approach and provided new employment opportunities for NDEA counselors, who were primarily trained within Colleges of Education.

According to Weikel and Palmo (1989), counselors worked in community mental health centers under many titles in the 1960s and 1970s, utilizing treatment approaches which were effective in out-patient settings. Currently, the majority of community mental health agencies in the United States employ graduate level, non-medical MHCs (West, Hosie, & Mackey, 1987). Because of the many settings and roles performed by counselors, mental health counseling has lacked a common professional identity. Attempts have been made to define mental health counseling based on four components: counselor roles, settings, required knowledge and skills, and conceptual or theoretical base.

Components of Mental Health Counseling

A question frequently asked of the MHC is What do you do? Respondents typically state that they provide direct counseling services to clients and that they engage in consultation, case management, assessment, skill development, and prevention services. Regulations governing the practice of mental health counseling (e.g., licensing and credentialing boards) are a further way of defining counselor roles. Such regulations set minimum standards for academic training and supervised counseling experience for licensure as a MHC or for national certification. Counselor roles also can be defined by the settings in which they are performed.

MHCs are primarily employed in non-school settings, including private agencies, private practice, hospitals, community mental health centers, substance abuse centers, colleges and universities, business and industry, and employee assistance programs. MHC employment is influenced by the lack of recognition of MHCs as "core providers." Core provider status is "recognition and inclusion as qualified mental health providers in legislation and health care plans" (Picard, 1994, p. 7). Without core provider status, MHCs are unfairly denied access to the marketplace, and consumers are limited in their choices of qualified service providers.

The knowledge and skills necessary for mental health counseling form the third component in defining the profession. Standards for counselor training programs are found in accreditation standards such as those of the Council for Accreditation of Counseling and Related Education Programs (CACREP, 1994). In addition, state licensure and credentialing boards (e.g., National Board for Certified Counselors) set standards for knowledge and skills. Common to all standards are minimum academic coursework and supervised counseling experience requirements, although actual standards often vary across groups.

The fourth component in defining the profession is the foundation or model underlying mental health counseling. It is generally agreed that mental health counseling is based on a developmental model which emphasizes prevention and mental health rather than treatment of pathology or mental illness. In this context, mental health ranges from mental wellness to mental illness, with a goal of promoting personal development and potential. Fong stated that the term mental health "denotes a professional scope or continuum of services that is developmental, environmental, and ecological, as well as remedial" (1990, p. 108). This more inclusive model is a major difference between MHCs and other allied mental health providers, such as psychologists and psychiatrists who are primarily oriented toward diagnosis and treatment of mental illness and emotional disorders (i.e., a medical model vs. a developmental model).

Essential for the continued growth and viability of mental health counseling is a definition which encompasses the diversity within the profession, the variety of roles performed, and is based on a common historical and conceptual foundation, as well as the knowledge and skills needed for practice. Such a definition provides MHCs with a common professional identity and a unique and clear professional image. The literature generally supports a broad definition which applies the term *mental health counseling* to the profession as a whole, with specialties (e.g., gerontology, prevention, substance abuse, etc.) within this broad, interdisciplinary spectrum.

What Is It?

Although many definitions of mental health counseling have been suggested, until recently they reflected parts of the profession but did not contain all the elements necessary for a comprehensive definition. Spruill and Fong (1990) suggested a broad based and comprehensive definition which has been supported in the literature (Cowger, Hinkle, DeRidder, & Erk, 1991; Ginter, 1993; Hershenson, 1992; Steenbarger & LeClair, 1995).

Mental health counseling, a core mental health care profession, is the aggregate of the specific educational, scientific, and professional contributions of the disciplines of education, psychology, and counseling focused on promotion and maintenance of mental health, the prevention and treatment of mental illness, the identification and modification of etiologic, diagnostic, and systems correlates of mental health, mental illness, and related dysfunction, and the improvement of the mental health service delivery system (pp. 20-21).

It is important that the field of mental health counseling emphasize its diversity as a strength and focus on its developmental and preventive functions. As Hershenson (1992) pointed out, mental health counselors must distinguish themselves by promoting mental health and working with clients to develop personal resources and to learn and apply new skills and environmental supports.

Conclusion

Mental health counseling is an interdisciplinary field with roots in education and counseling. A relative newcomer to the helping profession, it has rapidly developed into a broad-based discipline which is struggling for recognition and identity in the professional and consumer arenas. Mental health counseling is defined by practitioner roles and settings, academic and experience standards, and its theoretical and conceptual foundations.

Unique to mental health counseling is the emphasis on developmental and preventive functions, as well as the remediation of mental illness. This distinguishes mental health counseling from fields based on the medical model and focus primarily on diagnosis and treatment of mental illness.

This digest has presented background information about the field, components of mental health counseling, and a comprehensive definition. Education, demonstration, and collaboration with consumers, allied health care professionals, legislators, and others will result in recognition of mental health counseling by other professions and will assist MHCs in achieving core provider status.

References

Council for Accreditation of Counseling and Related Educational Programs. (1994). *Accreditation procedures manual and application.* Alexandria, VA: Author.

Cowger, E. L., Hinkle, J. S., DeRidder, L. M., & Erk, R. R. (1991). CACREP community counseling programs: Present status and implications for the future. *Journal of Mental Health Counseling, 13,* 172-186.

Fong, M. L. (1990). Mental health counseling: The essence of professional counseling. *Counselor Education and Supervision, 30*(2), 106-113.

Ginter, E. J. (1993). A period of transition for the *Journal of Mental Health Counseling*: What we can learn from necker cubes and stones. *Journal of Mental Health Counseling, 15*(3), 221-227.

Hershenson, D. B. (1992). A genuine copy of a fake Dior: Mental health counseling's pursuit of pathology. *Journal of Mental Health Counseling, 14* (4), 419-421.

Picard, R. (1994, September). PPLC's directions and goals for 1994-95. *The Advocate*, p. 7.

Spruill, D. A., & Fong, M. L. (1990). Defining the domain of mental health counseling: From identity confusion to consensus. *Journal of Mental Health Counseling, 15*(1), 12-23.

Steenbarger, B. N., & LeClair, S. (1995). Beyond remediation and development: Mental health counseling in context. *Journal of Mental Health Counseling, 17*(2), 173-187.

Weikel W. J., & Palmo, A. J. (1989). The evolution and practice of mental health counseling. *Journal of Mental Health Counseling, 11*(1), 7-25.

West, J. D., Hosie, T. W., & Mackey, J. A. (1987). Employment and roles of counselors in mental health agencies. *Journal of Counseling and Development, 66* (3), 135-138.

David A. Spruill is an associate professor in the Department of Administrative and Foundational Services in the College of Education at Louisiana State University, Baton Rouge, LA.

CHAPTER THREE

The Evolution of Mental Health Counseling as a Core Mental Health Provider: Definition and Identity

William B. Kline

Wiggins (1980), in his commentary about early developments in mental health counseling, stated, "There are times of transition... "(p. 2). He continued, "Of course transitions never really end—they just enter new phases"(p. 3). Wiggins was prophetic. Since their inception, the American Mental Health Counselors Association (AMHCA) and the profession of mental health counseling have been continually involved in a turbulent evolutionary process. This article will examine the roles that the AMHCA and related organizations have played in mental health counseling as it evolved into core mental health provider status.

Mental health counseling, as reflected in the past 15 years of the *Journal of Mental Health Counseling* and other AMHCA publications such as *The Advocate,* demonstrates several re-emergent themes. Two of the primary themes have been the development of an adequate definition of mental health counseling and the establishment of the credibility and parity of mental health counseling with other masters' level providers by delineating exemplary training and certification standards.

Definition and Identity

Mental health counseling and the AMHCA were initially conceived because counselors working in "non-educational" clinical settings did not have a professional organization dedicated to representing them or a title that adequately described what they did or who they were. In retrospect, it appears clear that AMHCA was born from a need to establish a professional identity. It was obvious to AMHCA's founders that they were not guidance counselors who were by some quirk not working in school settings, but rather, they were clinicians providing mental health services along with traditional mental health service providers. The founding membership recognized that they were pressed between the conventional identity of guidance counselors and traditional definitions of who "should" be providing mental health services. It also was evident to them and their employers that their skills and philosophies offered an extremely useful and cost effective approach to helping (Weikel & Palmo, 1989). Presently, mental health counselors continue to be highly effective professionals in search of recognition and identity.

The development of a professional identity depends on the establishment of a clear definition of mental health counseling and a precise conception of who mental health counselors are. In 1978 AMHCA took a significant step toward this goal when it established the National Academy of Certified Clinical Mental Health Counselors. The Academy, now the Clinical Academy of the National Board for Certified Counselors (NBCC), defined from both functional and philosophical perspectives who Certified Clinical Mental Health Counselors (CCMHC) were.

The *definition* issue, however, is not over. It continues, in part, because AMHCA's membership quickly grew to include counselors with a highly diverse range of training and practice experience. These individuals perceive themselves as mental health counselors but they often are not qualified or motivated to become CCMHCs. Weikel and Palmo (1989) contend:

> It seems to us that the true MHC [Mental Health Counselor] is actually the certified clinical mental health counselor (CCMHC). Individuals possessing the CCMHC credential are certified by the NACCMHC; all others are not. This wholesale use of the MHC title would never occur in psychiatry or psychology (p. 11).

An indiscriminate and confusing presentation of the term "mental health counseling" and the title "counselor" is thus created because definitions of mental health counseling are utilized to represent certified, uncertified, and uncertifiable members of AMHCA, as well as other variously qualified counselors working in "non-educational" settings.

In order to resolve this problem, various attempts have been made to present alternative definitions. In spite of the admonition of such authors as Cowger, Hinkle, DeRidder, and Erk (1991) to develop consensus, the confusion continues. Sherrard and Fong (1991) describe nine different definitions of mental health counseling, ranging from very role specific definitions to one that includes the entire counseling profession. They conclude by endorsing the definition presented by Spruill and Fong (1990):

> Mental health counseling, a core mental health profession, is the aggregate of the specific educational, scientific, and professional contributions of the disciplines of education, psychology, and counseling focused on promotion and maintenance of mental health, the prevention and treatment of mental illness, the identification and modification of etiologic, diagnostic, and systems correlates of mental health, mental illness, and related dysfunction, and the improvement of the mental health service delivery system. (pp. 20-21).

This interdisciplinary and functional definition provides a solid description of mental health counseling. Unfortunately, the majority of AMHCA's members who call themselves mental health counselors are probably not qualified to perform these functions. This is reflected by the scarcity of mental health counselors certified as CCMHCs or who have graduated from the Council for the Accreditation of Counseling and Related Educational Programs (CACREP) accredited mental health counseling programs. In addition, there are no data available that can verify that the typical "mental health" counselor has been trained or can demonstrate competencies in these areas.

This discussion of mental health counseling as a core provider is continued in the next chapter which focuses on training and certification standards and provides recommendations for the future.

References

Cowger, E. L., Hinkle, J. S., DeRidder, L. M., & Erk, R. R. (1991). CACREP community counseling programs: Present status and implications for the future. *Journal of Mental Health Counseling*, 13, 172-185.

Sherrard, P. A. D., & Fong, M. L. (1991). Mental health counselor training: Which model should prevail? *Journal of Mental Health Counseling*, 13, 204-209.

Spruill, D. A., & Fong, M. L. (1990). Defining the domain of mental health counseling: From identity confusion to consensus. *Journal of Mental Health Counseling*, 12, 12-23.

Weikle, W. J., & Palmo, A. J. (1989). The evolution and practice of mental health counseling. *Journal of Mental Health Counseling*, 11, 7-25.

Wiggins, J. D. (1980). Editorial: Transitional times. *American Mental Health Counselors Association Journal*, 2, 2-3.

William B. Kline, LPC, NCC, CCMHC, CGP is a Professor of Counselor Education at Idaho State University where he coordinates the CACREP accredited Mental Health Counseling program.

CHAPTER FOUR

The Evolution of Mental Health Counseling as a Core Mental Health Provider: Training and Certification

William B. Kline

Much to its credit, the American Mental Health Counselors Association (AMHCA) continues its efforts to differentiate mental health counselors from other mental health professions. Its objective is to develop professional identity and credibility as a profession (Weikel & Palmo, 1989). This process has continued since the founding of AMHCA and sets the style for mental health counselors as they seek a credible identity and strive for parity with other mental health professions.

The means to accomplish a credible identity and parity with other professions does not seem to be a mystery to mental health counselors or AMHCA. In discussing a survey of AMHCA members conducted over 15 years ago, Anderson and Parente' (1980) predicted that individuals considering a future career in mental health counseling should consider a number of key issues as they plan ahead. Among these suggestions were that individuals should receive training in an accredited graduate program (to date there are less than 10 Council for the Accreditation of Counseling and Related Educational Programs (CACREP) accredited mental health counseling programs nationally), and they should regard certification as essential (to date there are less than 1800 CCMHCs). These suggestions have been offered consistently over the years and are yet to be accomplished tasks for AMHCA. This is the case even though the accrediting and certifying mechanisms necessary to reach these goals are in place.

Lamentably, for the development of the mental health counseling profession, the bulk of CACREP accredited programs offering degree programs for counselors who wish to work in mental health settings are accredited in community counseling and not mental health counseling. Counselors prepared in accredited or non-accredited community counseling programs are likely to receive variable training experiences. The fact that the bulk of individuals who identify themselves as mental health counselors are most likely trained in community counseling programs (Cowger, Hinkle, DeRidder, & Erk, 1991) further compounds the issue of definition. What exactly is a mental health counselor?

Unfortunately, AMHCA has not consistently encouraged counselor education programs to implement accreditable mental health counseling programs, and counselor educators and their primary organization—the Association for Counselor Education and Supervision (ACES)—have not shown any perceptible support or interest. This is a dilemma for individuals who want to become mental health counselors and for the profession's need for uniform training curricula. Since accredited mental health counselor training programs are not readily available, the only choice for most prospective mental health counselors is to enroll in community counseling programs. These programs may or may not meet the academic preparation requirements for accreditation as a mental health counseling program or provide the prospective counselor with the qualifications necessary for certification as a CCMHC. Given the current scenario, it seems that answers to definition and training issues will continue to recycle like the repetitious attempts at failed solutions in first order change.

AMHCA's recently published "Orlando Project" (Altekruse & Sexton, 1994), *National Training Standards for Mental Health Counselors Who Deliver Clinical Services* (Covin & Robinson, 1992), and numerous articles in AMHCA's newsletter, *The Advocate*, have endorsed the mental health counseling accreditation standards of CACREP and the certification standards for the CCMHC of the NBCC. These endorsements have been compromised by AMHCA's simultaneous presentation of essentially duplicate "equivalency" standards and alternative paths to meet these requirements. To date, AMHCA has not implemented a viable or recognized alternative means to meet certification and training standards.

AMHCA's efforts to develop and implement equivalency standards and alternative paths to meet these standards appear to encourage its membership to upgrade their qualifications. The remaining question is how many of AMHCA's members will invest the time and money necessary to meet these standards. Unless a large majority of its members meet CACREP's training and NBCC's certification standards or AMHCA's equivalents, AMHCA cannot argue that the qualifications of its members are comparable to other masters' level mental health care professionals (i.e., social workers). This also brings into question AMHCA's presentation of these standards to federal agencies and legislators, insurers, and managed care organizations as an argument that mental health counselors are as qualified as other mental health care providers. Success for mental health counseling, as Covin (e.g., 1995) repeatedly asserts, depends on fully implemented uniform education and certification standards. Consequently, it appears that the success of AMHCA as an organization, with its current membership configuration and political agenda, is not consistent with the forward movement of the profession of mental health counseling.

The fact that mental health counseling is not becoming a widely recognized mental health profession, lacking deserved recognition as a core provider, is not the fault of consumers, legislators, insurers, or managed care organizations who do not seem to understand who mental health counselors are and what they are capable of doing. We are the problem! Rather than being unified and consistent in the presentation of mental health counseling, we present a confusing image of what we want to become and who we are. Therefore, the following recommendations are offered:

Recommendations

1. AMHCA must establish a clinical membership. Only CCMHCs and members who meet AMHCA's equivalency standards would qualify. Members of AMHCA who do not meet these requirements would receive an alternative designation such as "affiliate." AMHCA should then focus its lobbying and advocacy efforts in support of its clinical members as core providers. This structure is consistent with the National Association of Social Worker's clinical registry and would be less confusing to consumers, federal agencies, insurers, and managed care providers. As a result AMHCA could more legitimately argue that its clinical members have comparable training and experience and that these members are adequately prepared to provide clinical services.

2. The counseling profession must acquire a shared vision of what counseling is to become in "non-educational" settings. A definition agreed upon by AMHCA, ACES, CACREP, and NBCC that differentiates mental health counseling from other counselors or mental health care professions is essential for the development of a viable professional identity. At present there is no common belief among these most essential organizations about the identity or future of counseling in the mental health arena. The result is an implicit agreement to sabotage the efforts of others. Only when counselor educators, AMHCA leadership, and accrediting and certifying bodies agree to a common purpose for mental health counseling will attempts to advance the profession of mental health counseling be more than "false starts."
3. By continuing accreditation standards for community counseling, CACREP does the future of mental health counseling a great disservice. Mental health counseling cannot move forward until "non-educational" training programs become mental health counseling training programs and identify themselves as such. AMHCA and ACES must achieve agreement in this area in order for the profession to be represented by a uniform national standard for training. By focusing accreditation efforts on training counselors to become mental health counselors, the profession would present a convincing, sanctioned, and unified belief about the training required for effective mental health counseling practitioners. Community counseling accreditation must be discontinued.
4. Counselor education departments must discontinue offering community counseling programs. Regardless of the "sound reasons" counselor educators offer to continue community counseling programs (e.g., mental health programs require too many credit hours; mental health counseling is not what counseling is supposed to be; community counseling prepares our students to do jobs other than clinical counseling, etc.), they damage the future and potential of the counseling profession. Their arguments focus on maintaining a historical definition of counseling and an avoidance of the changes necessary to maintain professional viability in a changing society that places ever increasing demands on counselors. Clearly, if counselor educators would become committed to the future of

mental health counseling, there is opportunity to establish counseling as a responsive, evolving, and essential mental health profession.

Conclusion

To present mental health counseling to others clearly and convincingly requires consistency in definition and training and certification standards. If these objectives are not attained, mental health counseling and the counseling profession in general will continue to be blocked in their attempts to move forward. Strategies that have produced growth to this point in the development of the mental health counseling profession and AMHCA are no longer useful; they have failed. Perhaps there is too much concern that progress will offend or exclude the individuals who block it.

References

Altekruse, M. K., & Sexton, T. L. (1994). *Mental health counseling in the '90s: A research report for training and practice.* Tampa, FL: The Commission for Mental Health Counselor Training.

Anderson, J. A., & Parente, F. J. (1980). AMHCA members forecast the future of the mental health profession. *American Mental Health Counselors Association Journal, 2,* 4-12.

Covin, T. M. (1995). Freedom of choice, mental health counseling and clinical social work. *The Advocate, 18,* 4.

Covin, T. M., & Robinson, G. (1992). *National training standards for mental health counselors who deliver clinical services.* Alexandria, VA: American Mental Health Counselors Association.

Cowger, E. L., Hinkle, J. S., DeRidder, L. M., & Erk, R. R. (1991). CACREP community counseling programs: Present status and implications for the future. *Journal of Mental Health Counseling, 13,* 172-185.

Weikle, W. J., & Palmo, A. J. (1989). The evolution and practice of mental health counseling. *Journal of Mental Health Counseling, 11,* 7-25.

William B. Kline, LPC, NCC, CCMHC, CGP is a Professor of Counselor Education at Idaho State University where he coordinates the CACREP accredited Mental Health Counseling program.

CHAPTER FIVE

Certified Clinical Mental Counselors: History, Development, and Future

Thomas W. Clawson and Kathryn K. Rhodes

A look at the history and development of clinical mental health counseling would not be complete without a brief review of the general history of the counseling profession. In the early years of the 20th century, professional counseling began with vocational counseling. At that time, counselors were likely to be found in governmental agencies dealing with vocational selection. Later, these positions were established in educational settings. Vocational counselors in agency settings and guidance counselors in educational settings prevailed as the defined specialties of counseling for the first half of the century.

In the late 1950s, the passage of the National Defense Education Act paved the way for scores of graduate schools of education to establish funded programs to train guidance counselors. The intent of the school counseling legislation was to establish a national cadre of counselors adept in helping students plan for post high school education. More specifically, Congress wanted talented math and science students to be identified and encouraged to further their education. Thus, the Soviet space and arms race gave rise to the establishment of counselor education programs across the nation.

By the end of the 1960s, more than 300 academic units housed counselor education postgraduate training programs. That number increased to 550 by 1980, and stabilized at about 500 during the mid 1980s. The late 1970s saw as many as 20,000 advanced degrees awarded in various specialties of counseling.

In the 1980s, many trained counselors found work in clinical settings where they received supervision and experience in "non-educational" therapy milieus. At that time, the number of advanced counseling degrees being granted annually in counseling stabilized at about 10,000. In 1990, 9401 master's graduates and 664 doctoral graduates earned degrees in counseling.

History of Mental Health Counseling

The large number of counselor education graduates was accompanied by an increased number of students seeking work in settings outside education. The intriguing nature of clinical work and the preponderance of clinically trained counselor educators gave rise to specialized degree concentrations in clinical mental health counseling, family counseling, community agency counseling, and rehabilitation counseling.

The evolution of certified clinical mental health counseling parallels the history of the organization that has contributed to the growth of this specialty area of professional counseling. The American Mental Health Counselors Association (AMHCA) was founded in 1976 and soon began to refine the image and further the progress of mental health counseling.

The Board of Directors of the AMHCA voted, in March of 1978, to establish a national certification for mental health counselors. A credentialing committee was appointed to accomplish the goal of assessing the need and interest of the general membership on credentialing and certification. Later, a certification committee was selected and began work on specified procedures. Careful review of existing certification bodies enabled the committee to establish a clear process of application and internal organizational structure.

Need for certification could be categorized in two areas during the late 1970s. First, professional counseling in general, and clinical mental health counseling specifically, were in need of establishing recognition and parity with other mental health professions and the public. State counseling licensure was in its infancy and leaders correctly assumed that certification would aid recognition.

Secondly, clinical mental health counselors were, at that time, entering diverse practice settings in great numbers. Since few states regulated counselors, national certification for clinical mental health counselors was an avenue to establish a sound record of professional self-regulation. Public protection catalyzed the establishment of a credential that had professional recognition. That is, the process was not self-serving, but had the public interest in mind.

Through the efforts of AMHCA, the National Academy of Certified Clinical Mental Health Counselors (NACCMHC) was organized in 1979. The academy was formed to establish and maintain a national credential in the field of mental health counseling. The first national testing for mental health counselors applying for certification was conducted on February 3, 1979.

The title selected for this specialty was, and remains, Certified Clinical Mental Health Counselor (CCMHC). Fifty-one counselors became members of the first certification group. In 1995, this group numbered 1,775. Clinical mental health counseling, a specialty area of professional counseling, requires extensive coursework and clinical preparation and supervision. The Academy of Clinical Mental Health Counselors (ACMHC) requires a 60 semester-hour master's degree, as well as clinical supervision, taped therapy samples, and an examination for certification as a clinical counselor. Those standards are considered the minimum entry level requirements for clinical counselors.

Current Development

Effective July 1, 1993, the ACMHC united its clinical mental health counselor certification program with the certification programs of the National Board for Certified Counselors (NBCC). The National Academy of Clinical Mental Health Counselors became the Academy of Certified Clinical Mental Health Counselors, and subsequently became the Academy of Clinical Mental Health Counselors within NBCC.

The Professionalization Directorate of the American Counseling Association (ACA) in meetings in 1989 and 1990 provided a positive forum for serious talk and negotiations to begin between the two boards. While both cautiously explored the issue, they had in mind the best interest of the profession.

Over the years, the CCMHC process has been used as a model for several state licenses, and the qualifying exam has been used in seven states. The NACCMHC board negotiated those contracts and fashioned the first recognition by the Office of Civilian Health and Medical Program of the Uniformed Services (CHAMPUS) of the counseling profession. To date, CCMHCs continue to be recognized by CHAMPUS for third party review with physician authorization.

Under the provisions of the agreement, existing CCMHCs became national certified counselors (NCCs) and new applicants were made subject to the requirement to become NCCs as a prerequisite for certification as a CCMHC. Otherwise, their requirements for certification have remained the same. This includes two years of post-master's clinical practice which involves 3000 hours of direct client contact in a supervised clinical setting.

Applicants must document 100 hours of face-to-face individual and group supervision of their clinical practice by an acceptable supervisor. A graduate degree in counseling from a regionally accredited institution is required, including or with added coursework, the equivalent of a minimum of 60 semester hours. Much of this coursework must represent identified areas of clinical knowledge and expertise.

Careful review of the CCMHC application requirements convinced NBCC that all CCMHCs met the minimum standards for NCC status. Applicants must pass the National Clinical Mental Health Counseling Examination (NCMHE) and submit a tape recording of a complete clinical counseling session for evaluation. Equivalent entry options are available for those who qualify.

It is important to note that the core requirements of the NCC have been raised to roughly equal the original CCMHC requirements and that the CCMHC requirements have been increased.

Future of Mental Health Counseling

In the summer of 1990, the Center for Mental Health Services (CMHS) of the Department of Health and Human Services invited the counseling profession to be part of the publication, *Mental Health United States 1992.* The National Institute of Mental Health, in essence, for the first time publicly recognized that counseling and certified clinical mental health counseling, properly belonged in the mental health care arena. The Center for Mental Health Services must accurately represent to Congress the care available to the population. The inclusion of mental health counselors has indicated that the profession of counseling is part of the important realm of decision and policy makers serving the public. As the population grows, more professionals will be needed to serve mental health needs. CCMHCs, along with other counselors, will be called upon to fill a variety of positions.

Growth of clinical mental health programs accredited by the Council for Accreditation of Counseling and Related Programs (CACREP) will no doubt continue as more and more states require similar degrees for licensed independent practice. The numbers of CCMHCs will likewise grow.

In the words of the many authors of *Mental Health United States 1992:*

> Perhaps the most critical variable in the future of quality public mental health services is fostering collaboration among disciplines, and between academics and service providers. The future care providers of public mental health services will of necessity learn new knowledge, new interventions and new service delivery models. Educational programs that collaboratively educate and train multiple professional mental health students (psychiatrists, psychologists, psychiatric social workers, psychiatric nurses, psychosocial rehabilitation and mental health counselors, and marriage and family therapists) with the most current knowledge about mental illness and effective interventions are likely to determine how public mental health care will be delivered in the next century.

We echo their futuristic thinking and look forward to a continued bright future for the certified clinical mental health counselor.

References

Center for Mental Health Services and National Institute of Mental Health. (1992). *Mental Health in the United States - 1992.* Washington, DC: U.S. Government Printing Office.

Thomas W. Clawson is the Executive Director of the National Board for Certified Counselors, Inc. in Greensboro, NC.

Kathryn K. Rhodes is Executive Projects Coordinator at NBCC and a doctoral student in the Department of Counseling and Educational Development at the University of North Carolina at Greensboro, Greensboro, NC.

CHAPTER SIX

Freedom of Choice Issues

Theron Michael Covin

Since 1980, mental health counselors have made gains in their efforts to be recognized as health providers from which consumers can choose to receive mental health treatment services. These breakthroughs occurred in spite of a late start, during a time of solidification in gains, major cutbacks in reimbursement for mental health services, and emerging alternative managed care systems. Statutory regulation of counseling in 41 states and the District of Columbia has contributed to this success. The freedom of choice issues that are briefly discussed in this paper include mandated inclusion in insurance contracts, extraterritoriality, self-insured health care, managed care, and the federal reimbursement systems.

Mandated Inclusion

Mental health counselors have been included in health insurance and related reimbursement systems in at least three major ways: administrative recommendation, licensure, and direct legislation. Upon recommendation of the State Insurance Commissioner or similar authority, mental health counselors can be included in state insurance mandates. By administrative rule implementation, it is possible for qualified mental health counselors to become vendors or approved providers with major insurance companies and health care organizations. In some states, the privilege of being included as approved providers by health insurance and health care organizations comes with the licensure of mental health counselors. Simply put, the insurance codes may already mandate that any qualified licensed mental health provider may be included as an approved provider by insurance companies and health care organizations. The third way in which mental health counselors have come under state insurance mandates is by legislative change. The existing freedom of choice law, which generally includes an already approved long listing of health care providers, is modified to include licensed counselors in a respective state.

Extraterritoriality

Some mental health counselors who have been successful in joining reimbursement systems via one or more of the above options have found that such mandates often do not insure inclusion in all reimbursement systems. For example, the absence of an "extraterritorial law" often creates exclusion. The issue of extraterritoriality arises when an health insurance policy is written in a state other than the state in which the client or policy holder receives mental health treatment. A good extraterritorial law, combined with a good consumer freedom of choice law, requires a third-party payor to pay for mental health treatment regardless of where the policy is written, where the client or policy holder lives in relation to the state of origin of the insurance company, or where the mental health counselor provides the service in relation to the insurance company.

Self-Insured Health Care Plans

Mental health counselors have found that consumer freedom of choice is often limited by health care plans classified as *employee welfare benefit plans* which are regulated exclusively by ERSIA or the Employee Retirement Income Securities Act. This type of health care plan is self-insured or self-funded by the employer and is usually administered by the employer. The insurance company or health care organization can be used as the administrator or fiduciary of a health care plan which has been developed or selected by the employer.

Self-insured plans often exclude certain types of mental health treatment and/or provide limited access to such treatment through reduced benefits. In addition, the provider pool can be limited to certain providers within a provider group while excluding others. Mental health care is now being regulated in some situations by various managed care systems. Health maintenance organizations (HMOs), preferred provider organizations (PPOs), employee assistance programs (EAPs), and business coalitions are among these managed care operations. Consumer freedom of choice in relation to mental health benefits is generally very restrictive. Provider choices are often determined by the managed care system and terms of treatment (actual provider or provider pool, number of sessions, etc.). Fortunately, mental health counselors are slowly gaining acceptance in various managed care systems.

Federal Reimbursement Systems

Mental health counselors are typically excluded from federal freedom of choice mandates/reimbursement systems. This applies to Medicaid, Medicare, and Federal Employees Health Benefits Plans. There are a few exceptions. For example, mental health counselors are recognized at the State level in Montana and Maine in the Medicaid system as providers outside of community mental health centers. Mental health counselors who are employed by community mental health centers can be recognized as approved providers by Medicaid if mental health services are a part of the overall Medicaid delivery system within the respective state and are delivered under the supervision of a psychiatrist. It also is possible for mental health counselors in private practice to contract with the community mental health center as an approved provider within the local community mental health center contractual arrangement with Medicaid.

Mental health counselors are included by the Office of Civilian Health and Medical Program of Uniformed Services (OCHAMPUS) as providers upon referral from, and supervision by, a physician. In order to qualify, the mental health counselor must have the credentials (i.e., CCMHC) equivalent to those required by the Clinical Academy of the National Board of Certified Counselors. In those states that are designated by the United States Office of Personnel Management (OPM) as being medically underserved, consumers can choose mental health counselors who are licensed as providers of psychotherapeutic services. These recognized states are subject to change from year to year.

As an individual provider group, mental health counselors are not recognized by Medicare. However, under certain conditions, the services of mental health counselors are reimbursable. Rules that apply include a mental health counselor employed by a medical doctor, or when the mental health counselor and medical doctor are employees of the same employer, such as a professional association, a facility operated by a non-profit organization, or one whose board of directors is substantially physician-constituted. For the services of the mental health counselor to qualify for reimbursement, the services must be "incident to" the professional services of the medical doctor and the physician must be present in the office suite and immediately available to provide assistance and direction throughout the time the mental health counselor is providing services.

Conclusion

Mental health counselors are among the last health care provider groups to seek and gain entry into various reimbursement systems. Therefore, the consumers' freedom to select mental health counselors is often limited by lack of inclusion of mental health counselors as an individual provider classification both at the state and national levels.

Despite gains in recognition and reimbursement among other provider groups and major cutbacks in reimbursement for mental health services, mental health counselors have been successful in obtaining some recognition as qualified providers of mental health services. Such recognition has been possible at the state level through administrative directives, passage of licensure laws, and legislative modification of consumer freedom of choice laws to include counselors among the approved health care provider groups whose services are mandated for reimbursement by health insurance and health care organizations. In addition, there has been some success in gaining entry into the Medicaid system, especially through community mental health centers and in some individual states. Under certain conditions, mental health counselors are recognized by both the Federal Employees Health Benefit Plan and Medicare. Mental health counselors are also recognized by CHAMPUS if services are rendered upon referral by, and under the supervision of, a medical doctor. Managed care systems also are recognizing and including qualified mental health counselors as direct providers to consumers. The consumer's freedom to choose mental health counselors has been limited at most state levels by the reluctance of state legislators to pass proper statutory regulations for licensure and/or counselor freedom of choice. Furthermore, the lack of good extra territoriality laws and/or self-insured plans often interfere with consumer choice at the state level.

Theron Michael Covin, Ed.D., is Executive Director, Center for Counseling & Human Development, Inc., Ozark, AL.

CHAPTER SEVEN

The State of Prevention in Mental Health Counseling and Counselor Education

David M. Kleist

The Council for Accreditation of Counseling and Related Educational Programs (CACREP) states in its accreditation and procedures manual that curricular experiences for mental health counseling and community counseling programs should include the training of counselors in the prevention (i.e., primary prevention) of mental health problems (CACREP, 1994). Prevention of mental health problems has received insufficient attention in mental health counseling and counselor education (I will use the term "mental health counseling" for both mental health counseling and community counseling program descriptions as others in the field have argued for such a broad, inclusive definition of mental health counseling e.g., Spruill & Fong, 1990). The purpose of this chapter is to highlight the current lack of emphasis on the prevention of mental health problems in mental health counseling and counselor education. I will do so by (a) briefly reviewing the literature on prevention in mental health counseling and counselor education; (b) stating the results of a content analysis I performed on the mental health counseling and counselor education literature; and (c) summarizing the variables influencing the lack of emphasis on prevention.

Prevention in Counselor Education

The field of counselor education is currently lacking an appropriate emphasis on preventive interventions as directed by the 1994 CACREP Standards. Hershenson & Strein (1991) stated that mental health counselor education programs need to place more central emphasis on prevention, as current programs are almost indistinguishable from master's degree programs in clinical psychology. Cowger, Hinkle, DeRidder, and Erk (1991) surveyed 33 community counseling program coordinators and found that great variation existed in course offerings. In this variety of courses, ranging from family law to psychopharmacology, *not one* program provided a specific course on preventive interventions. In his qualitative study using semi-structured interviews, Ginter (1991) gathered information from twelve experts in mental health counseling and counselor education regarding their perceptions of factors related to training. Ginter concluded that despite the experts' expressed opinion that prevention is a defining element of the discipline, in his opinion, preventive interventions were obviously lacking in counselor training. Others (e.g., Kiselica & Look, 1993) have made similar assertions. This lack of emphasis on prevention in counselor education has occurred despite the leadership of the profession steadfastly advocating the importance of prevention.

Prevention in Mental Health Counseling

In 1978, the American Mental Health Counselors Association (AMHCA), included prevention in the definition of a professional counselor. More recently, others (e.g., National Board for Certified Counselors, 1995) have acknowledged that preventive interventions are defining elements of the discipline; consequently, prevention is at the core of mental health counseling (Weikel & Palmo, 1989). Nevertheless, the fields of counselor education and mental health counseling have shown little or no tangible support for prevention as a core concept.

Counseling Literature and Prevention

Another way of assessing the tangible emphasis paid to prevention in counselor education and practice is to compare the frequency of articles on preventive counseling versus remedial counseling in the field's professional journals. I performed content analyses of the journals of the Association for Counselor Education and Supervision (ACES) and AMHCA (i.e., *Counselor Education and Supervision* and the *Journal of Mental Health Counseling*, respectively) from January 1990 through December 1994, to locate articles that addressed either preventive or remedial counseling.

Results

In the past five years, the *Journal of Mental Health Counseling* focused only 11% of its articles on preventive counseling (20 out of 181), whereas, 74% of the articles spoke to remedial counseling (134 out of 181). In *Counselor Education and Supervision*, only 2% of the articles on counselor education and supervision concentrated on preventive counseling (2 out of 128). Again, a much larger percentage of articles, 44%, emphasized remedial counseling in counselor education and supervision (56 out of 128). Clearly, the journals relevant to counselor training and practice have focused more attention on remedial than preventive counseling. Making the assumption that journals represent a profession's current interests and activities, it is obvious that a disparity exists between the philosophy of prevention and its inclusion in mental health counseling and counselor education.

Possible Explanations for the Disparity

Numerous authors in the field have conjectured explanations for the disparity between mental health counseling and counselor education's interest in prevention and their respective lack of emphasis on preventive interventions. These explanations have included a lack of interest in prevention by students and practicing mental health counselors (Wilcoxon & Puelo, 1992), confusion about the definition of prevention (Kiselica & Look, 1993), a lack of qualified educators to teach prevention (Shaw & Goodyear, 1984), a lack of societal demand for preventive services (Hershenson & Power, 1987), difficulty with the unique ethical concerns inherent in prevention (Linn, Yager, & Leake, 1988), a lack of financial remuneration for preventive interventions (Yager et al., 1989), and the lack of research on the efficacy of preventive interventions (Yager et al., 1989). Kleist (1995) examined counselor educators' agreement with these explanations and found that the perceived lack of societal demand for preventive interventions was the only explanation viewed as valid in understanding the lack of emphasis onprevention. If these results are even partially generalizable to counselor education and mental health counseling, serious reflection is needed to consider the implications for these fields.

Implications for Mental Health Counseling and Counselor Education

In these times of managed care, capitation, and the prospect of "even briefer" models of counseling, the economic marketplace appears to be directing the future of counselor training. Julian Rappaport (1992), speaking of the death of the community mental health movement from the perspective of psychology, argued that its "resurrection lay not in good business practices but in the rediscovery of spirit (p.88)." The fields of mental health counseling and counselor education also are in need of rediscovering their spirit. If prevention of mental health problems is at the core of these fields, then counselor training, practice, and professional literature should reflect this. If it is not, then let us acknowledge that we as a profession are evolving into passive reactors to the political and economic needs of the time.

Historically, the development of mental health and the prevention ofmental health problems have been the spirit of mental health counseling and counselor education. They should not be hostage to the current political and economic culture. Culture is a continuously interactive system where culture and the individuals comprising it mutually and simultaneously define one another (Harwood & Weissberg, 1992). If the current culture of mental health services emphasizes the remediation of human problems instead of the prevention of them, then counselor education and mental health counseling need to examine their contribution to the present state of affairs. However, if prevention is a defining element of the field, then counselor educators need to examine how to encourage the development of prevention skills and their implementation into mental health service systems.

References

Albee, G. W. (1959). *Mental health manpower trends.* New York: Basic.

Council for Accreditation of Counseling and Related Educational Programs. (1994). *Accreditation procedures manual and application.* Alexandria, VA: Author.

Cowger, E. J., Hinkle, J. S., DeRidder, L. M., & Erk, R. R. (1991). CACREP community counseling programs: Present status and implications for the future. *Journal of Mental Health Counseling, 13,* 172-186.

Ginter, E. J. (1991). Mental health counselor preparation: Expert's opinions. *Journal of Mental Health Counseling, 13,* 187-203.

Harwood, R. L., & Weissberg, R. P. (1992). A Conceptual framework for context-sensitive prevention programming: A symbolic interactionist perspective. *Journal of Primary Prevention, 13,* 85-113.

Hershenson, D. B., & Power, P. W. (1987). *Mental health counseling: Theory and practice.* New York: Pergamon.

Hershenson, D. B., & Strein, W. (1991). Toward a mentally healthy curriculum for mental health counselor education. *Journal of Mental Health Counseling, 13,* 247-252.

Kiselica, M. S., & Look, C. T. (1993). Mental health counseling and prevention: Disparity between philosophy and practice?. *Journal of Mental Health Counseling, 15,* 3-14.

Kleist, D. M. (1995). *Counselor educators' explanations for a disparity between a philosophy of prevention in mental health and prevention training and practice in counselor education.* Unpublished doctoral dissertation, Southern Illinois University, Carbondale.

Linn, L. S., Yager, J., & Leake, B. (1988). Psychiatrists' attitudes toward preventive intervention in routine clinical practice. *Hospital and Community Psychiatry, 39,* 637-642.

National Board for Certified Counselors, Inc. (1995). *Clinical Mental Health Counselor Job Analysis Survey.* Greensboro, NC: Author.

Rappaport, J. (1992). The Death and resurrection of a community mental health movement. In M. Kessler, S. E. Goldston, & J. M. Joffe (Eds.), *The Present and Future of Prevention* (pp.78-98). Newbury Park: Sage.

Shaw, M. C., & Goodyear, R. K. (1984). Introduction to the special issues on primary prevention. *Personnel and Guidance Journal, 58,* 444-445.

Spruill, D. A., & Fong, M. L. (1990). Defining the domain of mental health counseling: From identity confusion to consensus. *Journal of Mental Health Counseling, 12,* 12-23.

Weikel, W. J., & Palmo, A. J. (1989). The evolution and practice of mental health counseling. *Journal of Mental Health Counseling, 11,* 7-25.

Wilcoxon, S. A., & Puelo, S. G., (1992). Professional development needs of mental health counselors: Results of a national survey. *Journal of Mental Health Counseling, 14,* 187-195.

Yager, J., Linn, L. S., Leake, B., Goldston, S., Heinicke, C., & Pynoos, R. (1989). Attitudes toward mental illness prevention in routine pediatric practice. *American Journal of Diseases of Children, 143,* 1087-1090.

David M. Kleist is an Assistant Professor of Counselor Education at Idaho State University.

II. Client Focus in Mental Health Counseling

CHAPTER EIGHT

Mandated Clients in Mental Health Counseling

Richard J. Riordan

Mental health counselors face an increasing number of clients who are mandated by the courts to receive counseling. This increase in mandated clients can in part be traced to (a) prison overcrowding which dictates different alternatives to incarceration; (b) the popularity of counseling as being beneficial in cases of first-time offenders, individuals with histories of abuse, and individuals who are being released from prison; and (c) a rise in the use of outpatient treatment for individuals with ongoing mental health problems (Lehmer, 1986).

Mental health counselors are sometimes ambivalent about counseling mandated clients. They may not feel trained to handle such cases or doubt that forced counseling for clients who may not desire change can be effective (Larke, 1985). This paper outlines a framework for helping counselors understand the dynamics of counseling the mandated client and explores ideas for doing this most effectively. Suggestions for ways client reluctance can be leveraged and insights about integrating counseling perspectives with the criminal justice system are highlighted.

Discussion

The mental health system and the criminal justice system have drastically different primary missions. This difference in priorities is often at the heart of the tension that arises between clients, counselors, and members of the criminal justice system. For example, the criminal justice system is seen as a place of toughness, whereas the mental health system is viewed as forgiving. The mental health system promotes hope, whereas the criminal justice system tends to be pessimistic. The criminal justice system takes an adversarial stance, but the mental health system strives to be non-judgmental and a client advocate. The criminal justice system demands that the counselor interact with not only the client, but also with people such as probation officers, lawyers, and family members of the client. These issues sometimes put strains on the counselor's role in observing the client's confidentiality and also in maintaining appropriate boundaries (Riordan & Martin, 1993).

Such constraints need to be addressed in ways that will optimize a functional working alliance and successful counseling outcomes. Some helpful steps include

1. discussing the issue of confidentiality with the client in the first session and reaching agreement on what type of information will be shared with other parties and the ways it will be shared with them;
2. educating clients and others such as probation officers and lawyers about what mental health counseling is so that any misconceptions or biases can be addressed;
3. having a court representative in attendance at the first session for all parties to hear and understand court requirements and appreciate the separateness of the legal relationship from the counseling relationship; and
4. taking special care to check that clients understand the counselor's role and their own role in the counseling process.

While the value differences between the mental health counseling and the criminal justice systems can present new challenges, counseling mandated clients is not always different from counseling voluntary clients. Mandated clients are not the only ones who are extrinsically motivated. In fact, many counselors work with "voluntary" clients who have been referred or pressured by schools, employers or families to receive treatment. Also, the broader treatment goals for both voluntary and mandated clients share similarities, including a focus on increasing self-esteem and pride, enhancing acceptance of self and others, increasing patience and tolerance, and improving interpersonal functioning (Larke, 1985).

Most studies suggest a number of qualities that mental health counselors should possess if they hope to work effectively with mandated clients. Among these qualities are a belief in the goodness of people, a willingness to work within systems, using a systems perspective, and an ability to recognize and handle a client who wants to engage the therapist in a role complementary to his or her negative behavior. These qualities, combined with clear goals, will help the counselor develop a solid working relationship with the client. Thus, when initiating the relationship, it is a good idea for the two parties to review a comprehensive client psychosocial history and formulate a written treatment plan that the counselor and client have produced collaboratively (Riordan & Martin, 1993).

The mandated client will often be reluctant, even hostile at times and the client may possess extraordinary powers to provoke negative feelings in the counselor. The challenge for the mental health counselor is to understand the dynamics and origins of this resistance. The reluctance does not have to be viewed as an obstacle to the therapeutic process, but it can be framed as a sign that the client is trying to restore a severely eroded power base. This is a goal the counselor shares and wants to help translate into appropriate self-agency and a socially acceptable lifestyle. Two critical activities in dealing with reluctant clients are acknowledging and processing negative feelings and discussing all of the specifics of the counseling relationship including the court-mandated goals of therapy and the client's role in goal development. Through tactful guidance, the reluctance can be channeled to a sense of empowerment. This empowerment comes from helping the client discover a revised sense of motivation and a positive self-image, as well as through the emotional processing and validation of the client's negative experiences.

Instilling high levels of motivation is critical to succeeding with reluctant clients. Motivation can be fostered by helping the client:

1. understand and experience the power of self-determination,
2. discover intrinsically rewarding behavior, and
3. embrace structure and direction in life.

Additionally, the mental health counselor can help the client appreciate the power of success over failure, the importance of congruent behaviors, and the primacy of reward over punishment (Riordan, Matheny, & Harris, 1978).

Another important consideration supported in the literature is that the mandated client's treatment plan needs to facilitate a much more comprehensive therapeutic connection than just individual counseling. A combination of individual, group and marital/family counseling has been shown to be more effective. Support groups, bibliotherapy, scriptotherapy, and other adjuncts to counseling also can be key elements in making connections which supplement and can reinforce the work done in counseling (Larke, 1985; Lehmer, 1986; Riordan, et al., 1978).

Consensual Point of View

The literature suggests that there are several skills that are important to working with the mandated client. These are:

1. managing client anger and understanding how the client's needs have been met through deviant or criminal acts;
2. viewing the client's behavior in the therapy session as representative of how he or she behaves in the "real world";
3. being aware of and able to control one's own negative feelings in relation to the client;
4. maintaining contact with members of the criminal justice system, such as probation officers;
5. maintaining clear, professional boundaries and open methods of communication with all involved parties; and
6. having the knowledge and ability to use a multimodal approach in treating the client.

Conclusion

Court-ordered clients represent a special challenge for mental health counselors. Clear goals, which are developed collaboratively with the client and also meet the needs of the court system, are imperative. Managing heightened client reluctance,striving for open and consistent communication with all parties, and applying effective motivational principles are also key ingredients for success. Finally, the creative integration of psychoeducational approaches, group work, and other adjunctive techniques as part of the treatment plan can significantly enhance outcomes with mandated clients.

References

Larke, J. (1985). Compulsory treatment: Some practical methods of treating the mandated client. *Psychotherapy: Theory, Practice, and Research, 22*(2), 262-268.

Lehmer, M. (1986). Court ordered therapy: Making it work. *American Journal of Forensic Psychology, 4*(2), 16-24.

Riordan, R. J., & Martin, M. H. (1993). Mental health counseling and the mandated client. *Journal of Mental Health Counseling, 15*(4), 373-383.

Riordan, R. J., Matheny, K. B., & Harris, C. W. (1978). Helping counselors minimize client reluctance. *Counselor Education and Supervision, 18*, 6-13.

Richard J. Riordan, Ph.D. is a Professor in the Department of Counseling and Psychological Services at Georgia State University, Atlanta, Georgia.

CHAPTER NINE

Mental Health Counseling and Sexual Harassment in the Workplace

Azy Barak

The term "sexual harassment" has been used since the late 1970s as a label of a distinctive social phenomenon, as a title of legal codes, and as a subject for research. Recently, the topic has been dealt with extensively by governments, businesses, educational institutions, militaries, and scientific projects world-wide (Barak, 1995).

While numerous terms refer to sexual exploitation of one person (the victim) by another (the perpetrator)–including sexual abuse, sexual assault, or sexual offence–sexual harassment. Sexual harassment is the term that generally includes the framework within which the perpetration has taken place. Usually it refers either to a framework of the workplace, to study sites, or to military service. Another important aspect associated with SH is that it has many definitions which relate in various degrees to different aspects of the perpetration, including legal, moral, behavioral, and psychological dimensions. Sexual harassment entails a very broad spectrum of behaviors, from gender verbal harassment (e.g., sexual- or gender-related comments and remarks), to unwelcome sexual attention (e.g., leering, whistling, certain gestures, drawing talk into sexual matters), to sexual coercion (e.g., sexual bribery and blackmailing, physical assault). These behaviors are considered to be sexually harassing if they are unwanted or unaccepted by the recipient. One of the significant, yet debatable, factors associated with the definition, judgment, and interpretation of an incident as sexually harassing has to do with personal perceptions and labeling of an event as sexual harassment. The latter have been shown to be related to various perceiver characteristics (e.g., gender, ethnic group and culture, and personality factors).

Prevalence of Sexual Harassment in the Workplace

Virtually all prevalence data of SH in the workplace rely on surveys of employees in organizations. The numerous difficulties in using this method prevent us from having a valid estimate of the extent of this phenomenon. First, because of the illegal, immoral, embarrassing, and sometimes threatening behaviors and consequences involved, perpetrators, as well as victims, might fully or partially underreport incidents in responding to questionnaires or interviews. Second, personal interpretations of incidents have a lot to do with responding to questions on this subject. Third, various questionnaires, interviewing protocols, or interviewers have differences in content (including variable forms and definitions of sexual harrassment), differing types of response scale, and divergent instructions. Fourth, questions may refer to a different time frame in which sexual harrassment incidents might have occurred. Fifth, respondents might be influenced in their answers by their political agenda on this issue. Nonetheless, it seems that anonymous surveys have been used as the most standard way to gather information on sexual harassment.

Keeping in mind the above mentioned limitations, we find large-scale workplace studies which report that 30% to 90% of women experienced unwelcome sexual remarks, 15% to 60% were exposed to suggestive looks and gestures, 10% to 30% were deliberately but unwelcomely touched, 2% to 10% were pressured for dates, 1% to 10% were pressured for sexual favors or cooperation, (a similar proportion were sent written notes or received phone calls with sexual messages), and 0.5% to 1.5% reported actual sexual assault or attempted rape. Generally, research shows that 20% to 60% of women encounter any one type of sexual harassment; the incidence rate changes by survey, workplace (or unit thereof), or culture. In responding to a more general question, only 6% to 17% of working women admitted they had been sexually harassed. As indicated above, non-standard methodologies and the nature of the organization, department, or culture studied lead to frequent discrepancies among surveys related to the methodological reasons mentioned (see recent reviews by Barak, 1995;

Fitzgerald, 1993; Fitzgerald & Shullman, 1993; Koss, et al., 1994).

Victims of sexual harassment are typically women, in ratios of 5:1 to 20:1 women to men in different comparative studies. Among various characteristics examined, age and marital status have stood out as consistent individual correlates of sexual harassment. Although it has been repeatedly found that younger women tend to be sexually harassed more often than older women, it was suggested that sexual harassment experiences are similar in all age groups,—younger women tend to label or to interpret their experiences differently than older women. Also, it has been found that single women reported more sexual harassment experiences than non-singles, but this finding may be contaminated by age, or may reflect other moderating effects. Even though ethnicity has been connected to sexual harassment, most data refuted this speculation.

Explanatory Models of Sexual Harassment

Various theories have attempted to explain the origins and dynamics of sexual harassment. Early models concentrated on biological factors (i.e., behavioral instincts, hormonal activity, genetic determination), social and cultural influences (social norms and values which refer to the status of men and women, myths related to sexual imposition, stereotypes of women's and men's needs, rights and roles, direct education and lack thereof by family members or teachers, as well as by the media, and so on), organizational structure (which typically favors men over women in positions, responsibilities, and control of resources), role spillover (carry over of social-sexual behavioral patterns into irrelevant work situations), and the men's agenda to dominate society and subordinate women. Current theory incorporates various situational, as well as dispositional, variables in delineating sexual harassment (cf. Pryor, LaVite, & Stoller, 1993).

Consequences of Sexual Harassment

Sexual harassment in the workplace has a severe impact on the individual victim as well as on the organization. On a personal level, psychological (i.e., emotional) consequences, work-related behaviors, and health-related effects have been associated with sexual harassment. Psychological effects of sexual harassment include damage to a person's well-being, self-esteem, self-confidence, and sense of control. Sexual harassment also leads to specific disorders such as general anxiety, depression, fear of rape and crime, and sexual dysfunctioning; some effects may be covert at first and may resemble the process of post-traumatic stress disorder. Work-related effects include job loss (either by quitting or being fired, transferred, or reassigned), decrease in productivity, decrease in morale, satisfaction, motivation, and increased absenteeism. For example, Morrow, McElroy, and Phillips (1994) found that sexual harassment initiated by superiors had a devastating impact on work-related attitudes in both men and women, whereas sexual harassment initiated by co-workers had a more limited impact on women and no impact for men. Physiological and health-related effects include sleep disturbance, headaches, weight gain or loss, gastrointestinal disorders, nausea, and teeth grinding.

On the organizational level, sexual harassment is devastating in three separate ways. First, it causes severe losses both in terms of work productivity and in revenue. Second, damage to morale has second-order effects on other workers and creates a negative social atmosphere. Third, sexual harassment lawsuits, where liability laws apply, are very costly for organizations.

Combating Sexual Harassment in the Workplace

Different measures have been proposed to prevent sexual harassment in the workplace. The most common and accepted measure entails legislative initiatives on different levels. Included in this category are different laws and legal acts which refer to definitions of illegal behaviors considered to be sexual harassment. There are legal acts on federal, state, or city levels, as well as any specific organization's guidelines. In addition, numerous professional associations have addressed sexual harassment in their ethical codes. In many cases, legal acts (or their related guidelines) include some detailed form of specific sexual harassment-related policies and grievance procedures.

Another approach has focused on primary prevention, in that some organizational steps could be taken to change the organizational culture or climate in order to lower the likelihood of sexual harassment occurring. This includes, for instance, balancing the frequencies of male and female workers in a given workplace, since it has been shown that gender ratio in the workplace is highly related to prevalence of sexual harassment. A different approach is to try and identify potential harassers by previous employment and legal records, or by assessing their personality characteristics and attitudes. Prevention also is considered to be possible by educating employees about the nature of sexual harassment, through relevant legislation and guidelines, and by offering ways to handle sexual harassment-related situations (e.g., Barak, 1994).

Counseling Victims of Sexual Harassment

Sexual harassment experiences may cause severe psychological damage to victims. Several specific counseling models and emphases have been proposed to deal with this problem (e.g., Quina & Carlson, 1989; Spratlen, 1988). Similar to counseling rape or incest victims, it is generally recommended to allow clients to ventilate negative emotions and to help clients constructively cope with the problematic employment situation using rational and behavioral problem-solving principles. The need to include sexual harassment counseling in training programs also has been stressed (Frazier & Cohen, 1992).

Conclusion

Different forms of sexual harassment, with women usually being the victims, are widespread in the workplace and have a strong negative impact both on individual victims and organizations. There is still a great need to further examine the crucial elements of the phenomenon so as to understand its origins and dynamics. Various preventative measures might be undertaken to reduce sexual harassment prevalence and severity, from changing organizational culture, to implementation of legislation, to delivering intensive education programs to male and female workers. Mental health counselors should be trained to offer professional services to sexual harassment victims, using specific and effective therapeutic techniques.

References

Barak, A. (1994). A cognitive-behavioral educational workshop to combat sexual harassment in the workplace. *Journal of Counseling and Development, 72,* 595-602.

Barak, A. (1995). Cross-cultural perspectives on sexual harassment. In W. O'Donahue (Ed.), *Sexual harassment: Theory, research, and treatment.* Needham Heights, MA: Allyn & Bacon.

Fitzgerald, F. L. (1993). Sexual harassment: Violence against women in the workplace. *American Psychologist, 48,* 1070-1076.

Fitzgerald, L. F., & Shullman, S. L. (1993). Sexual harassment: A research analysis and agenda for the 1990s. *Journal of Vocational Behavior, 42,* 5-27.

Frazier, P. A., & Cohen, B. B. (1992). Research on the sexual victimization of women: Implications for counselor training. *Counseling Psychologist, 20,* 141-158.

Koss, M. P., Goodman, L. A., Browne, A., Fitzgerald, L. F., Keita, G. P., & Busso, N. F. (1994). *No safe haven: Male violence against women at home, at work, and in the community.* Washington, DC: American Psychological Association.

Morrow, P. C., McElroy, J. C., & Phillips, C. M. (1994). Sexual harassment behaviors and work related perceptions and attitudes. *Journal of Vocational Behavior, 45,* 295-309.

Pryor, J. B., LaVite, C., & Stoller, L. (1993). A social psychological analysis of sexual harassment: The person/situation interaction. *Journal of Vocational Behavior, 42,* 68-83.

Quina, K., & Carlson, N. L. (1989). *Rape, incest, and sexual harassment: A guide for helping survivors.* New York: Praeger.

Spratlen, L. P. (1988). Sexual harassment counseling. *Journal of Psychosocial Nursing and Mental Health Services, 26* (2), 28-33.

Azy Barak, Ph.D., is an Associate Professor in the Counselling Program, Division of Educational Psychology, Faculty of Education, The University of Western Ontario, London, Ontario, Canada.

CHAPTER TEN

Internalized Homophobia: Implications for Counseling Gay Men and Lesbians

Mary Frances Arnold

It is essential for counselors who work with gay men and lesbians to have an appreciation for the external factors surrounding their clients' life-long development. Counseling gay men and women requires counselors to work in relation to the realities of being gay or lesbian rather than simply using non-gay interpretations of gay lifestyles (Teague, 1992). Although Americans have progressed in their views about homosexuality, the National Gay and Lesbian Task Force Policy Institute (1992) found that gays and lesbians are still subjected to harassment, threats of violence, bomb threats, physical violence, police abuse, vandalism, arson, and homicide. Furthermore, harassment and violence against gays and lesbians is on the increase (Hunt, 1993).

Internalized Homophobia

Lesbians and gay men do not escape societal prejudices. Hunt (1993) reminds us that all Americans, due to societal views of homosexuality, are raised with some level of homophobia and heterosexism; this includes gay men and lesbians. How this heterosexism and homophobia takes form may be determined by each person. Many gays and lesbians adopt and accept societal antigay views (internalized homophobia), which then becomes the largest obstacle to their self-esteem and mental health (Gonsiorek, 1993). Their negative feelings about sexual orientation may be generalized into other aspects of their identity (Gonsiorek). Consequently, establishing a positive gay or lesbian identity is crucial to optimal identity development.

There are a wide variety of expressions of internalized homophobia. Symptom presentation of internalized homophobia may range from a tendency towards self-doubt to unmistakable, overt self-hatred (Shively & DeCecco, 1993). Covert homophobia appears to be the most common type of expression (Gonsiorek, 1993). An example of covert homophobia may be an appearance of acceptance of one's sexual orientation, yet sabotaging of the self. Such persons may abandon their personal goals or education. Gonsiorek further describes subtle symptoms of internalized homophobia, such as not standing up for oneself, accepting an inferior status, impulsive behavior, or disclosing one's sexual orientation at an inappropriate time or in an inappropriate manner. There also may be a tendency towards perfectionism in an attempt to legitimize the self. The result of internalized homophobia may be a loss of one's true identity, self-neglect, and a disregard for one's own needs (Gonsiorek).

The implications of internalized homophobia are significant to the developmental processes and the mental health of many gay men and lesbian women. Many gay men and lesbians feel overwhelmed by homophobia, heterosexism, and internalized homophobia; as a result, they may become psychologically disturbed for a period of time (Savin-Williams, 1995). Many who have grown up to be gay or lesbian have reported that as children they felt different in a negative manner (Gonsiorek, 1993). Therefore, feeling different has been a part of their entire development. According to Gonsiorek, understanding and limiting internalized homophobia is the key to mental health.

Implications for Counseling

With the appropriate professional, counseling can be beneficial to gay men and lesbians. Once in counseling, gays and lesbians tend to share some major treatment issues: 1. coming out, 2. antigay and other prejudice, 3. relationship issues, 4. concerns of lesbian and gay youth, 5. gay and lesbian parenting, 6. concerns related to family of origin, and 7. therapist issues (Hancock, 1995). O'Connor (1992) stressed the importance of helping clients become aware of their own homophobic development and the resulting effects of stigmatization. Furthermore, O'Connor cautioned counselors to be careful not to minimize the importance of the client's sexual orientation, to offer sound and complete information about sexuality, to help clients identify positive role models, and to include the client's family in the therapeutic process.

Perhaps one of the most healing agents for gays and lesbians is involvement in the gay and lesbian community. "Lesbians and gay men maintain self-esteem most effectively when they identify with and are integrated into a larger gay/lesbian community" (D'Augelli & Garnets, 1995, p. 302). Furthermore, Hunt (1993) reports that negative symptoms associated with internalized homophobia all but disappear when individuals are connected to a larger gay/lesbian community. It is critical, however, that experiences with other gay men and lesbians be positive, especially when initially coming out. Such experiences encourage further contact and are useful during identity formation, whereas negative experiences facilitate identity confusion and isolation (Teague, 1992). Therefore, counselors need to be aware of positive resources in their community in order to meet the many needs of their diverse lesbian and gay clients.

Prepared counselors are in a unique position to make a positive impact on the lives of their gay and lesbian clients. Understanding the unique developmental issues facing gay men and lesbians while also examining the realities of individual clients' lives is essential to effective and affirmative counseling for this population.

References

D'Augelli, A., & Garnets, L. (1995). Lesbian, gay, and bisexual communities. In A. R. D'Augelli, & C. J. Patterson (Eds.). *Lesbian, gay, and bisexual identities over the lifespan* (pp. 293-320). New York: Oxford University Press.

Gonsiorek, J. (1993). Mental health issues of gay and lesbian adolescents. In L. D. Garnets, & D. C. Kimmel (Eds.).*Psychological perspectives on lesbian and gay male experiences* (pp. 469-485). New York: Columbia University Press.

Hancock, K. (1995). Psychotherapy with lesbians and gay men. In A. R. D'Augelli, & C. J. Patterson (Eds.). *Lesbian, gay, and bisexual identities over the lifespan* (pp. 398-432). New York: Oxford University Press.

Hunt, B. (1993). What counselors need to know about counseling gay men and lesbians. *Counseling and human development, 26 (1),* 1-12.

National Gay & Lesbian Task Force Policy Institute. (1992). *Anti-gay/lesbian violence, victimization and defamation in 1991.* Washington, DC: Author.

O'Connor, M. (1992). Psychotherapy with gay and lesbian adolescents. In S. H. Dworkin, & F. J. Guiterrez (Eds.). *Counseling gay men and lesbians: Journey to the end of the rainbow* (pp. 3-22). Alexandria, VA: American Association for Counseling and Development.

Savin-Williams, R. (1995). Lesbian, gay male, and bisexual adolescents. In A. R. D'Augelli, & C. J. Patterson (Eds.). *Lesbian, gay, and bisexual identities over the lifespan* (pp. 165-189). New York: Oxford University Press.

Shively, M., & DeCecco, J. (1993). Components of sexual identity. In L. D. Garnets, & D. C. Kimmel (Eds.). *Psychological perspectives on lesbian and gay male experiences* (pp. 80-89). New York: Columbia University Press.

Teague, J. (1992). Issues relating to the treatment of adolescent lesbians and homosexuals. *Journal of mental health counseling, 14,* 422-439.

Mary Frances Arnold is a graduate student at the University of North Carolina at Greensboro.

CHAPTER ELEVEN

Counseling Male Couples

Tom Campbell

Male couples are similar to heterosexual couples in many ways and struggle with many of the same relationship problems. However, male couples also must contend with the effects of same-sex socialization and the oppression of an often homophobic society (Shannon & Woods, 1991). Consequently, Rudolph (1988) estimated that approximately 25% to 65% of gay men seek counseling. Although the number of journal articles published concerning general issues of lesbians and gay men have increased in recent years (Gluth & Kiselica, 1994), few articles address same-sex couples seeking therapy (e.g., Buhrke, Ben-Ezra, Hurley, & Ruprecht, 1992). In fact, Buhrke et al. found that after reviewing 6,661 articles from six major counseling psychology journals over a twelve-year period, only 43 articles (0.65%) focused on variables related to gay or lesbian orientation. Of the 43 articles that addressed gay and lesbian issues, only three dealt with the concerns of same-sex couples. Similarly, when searching for outcome research literature to determine what modes of counseling work effectively with gay and lesbian clients, Dunkle (1994) could find only six studies (with only one study dealing with couples counseling). This review will present the similarities and differences between male and heterosexual couples, an overview of counseling approaches for male couples seeking therapy, and recommendations to counselors working with male couples.

Similarities and Differences in Male and Heterosexual Couples

Male and heterosexual couples are similar in that both have like-attributes and seek counseling for many of the same reasons of conflict and stress in the relationship. As George and Behrendt (1987) note, couples in a healthy relationship, whether gay or heterosexual, exhibit similar characteristics, such as commitment, shared feelings, respect, intimacy, and capacity to resolve conflicts. Likewise, both male and heterosexual couples struggle with the same problems in developing and maintaining a relationship, such as communication, money, sex, intimacy, and parenting. Because of the similarities in male and heterosexual couples, many counselors assume that studies dealing with heterosexual couples apply to male couples; however, this may be an oversimplification or an erroneous assumption (e.g., Dunkle, 1994).

Differences between male and heterosexual couples lie primarily in the types of problems gay couples encounter. Male couples encounter problems dealing specifically with their same-sex orientation, which are often exacerbated because of societal disapproval and oppression of same-sex couples (Dunkle, 1994). For example, male couples generally have more sexually open relationships (i.e., an acceptance of sexual activity outside the relationship) and may separate more readily than heterosexual couples (Bryant & Demian, 1994; Ussher, 1990a, 1991). Male couples often practice "serial monogamy"; i.e., going from one long-term relationship to another long-term relationship, without the idea of "till death do us part"(Ussher, 1991), have a poor support network (Lee, 1990), and experience problems associated with shared gender training (Markowitz, 1991).

Group Counseling for Male Couples

Most information regarding group counseling and gay men deals with issues of "coming out" or with specialized groups such as gay parents, gay alcoholics, gay youth, and the aging (e.g., Hutchins, 1992). Dunkle (1994) has noted that male couples, in which one or both partners have a sexual dysfunction, may be more amenable to group counseling because they have less rigid attitudes toward sexual activity than their heterosexual counterparts and may be more open to discussing such issues. Dahlheimer and Feigal (1991) have suggested that multiple-family groups are the best treatment for gay parents because each subsystem has a peer group with which to identify and to compare notes without fear of judgment. Although each of these articles offers insight in addressing specific problems of male couples in a group setting, information regarding group counseling and the common concerns of gay couples (e.g., communication, money, intimacy, etc.) is lacking.

Individual and Couples Counseling for Male Couples

Individual counseling for male couples is used as a precursor to couples counseling when one partner has a problem that precedes the presenting problem of the couple, or when only one partner is willing to enter counseling. Fisher (1993) has suggested using individual counseling sessions early in the therapeutic process with the gay couple to obtain a more effective lifestyle assessment. She found that using an Adlerian theoretical framework and intervention technique provided a highly efficacious model for improving the quality of functioning in gay as well as lesbian relationships. Mencher (1993) has advocated individual counseling when one partner has a problem that precedes or is more pervasive than the presenting problem of the couple. Another example of individual counseling for male couples is when one partner refuses to attend couples counseling. Here, individual counseling would be more beneficial to the couple than no counseling at all. The lack of literature regarding individual counseling for male couples suggests that this mode of counseling is not typically used for male couples.

Although there is very little descriptive or empirical research on counseling male couples, most of the information that is available focuses on couples counseling. Shannon and Woods (1991) state that for male couples to have a healthy relationship, each partner must be able to accept and value his homosexuality, to relinquish rigid stereotypic male and sexual roles, and to commit to not abusing mood-altering chemicals or each other. Couples counseling can be effective in resolving difficulties of male couples by allowing the couple to work together to solve their specific concerns; e.g., aging, antigay violence, and HIV/AIDS (Shannon & Woods, 1991). Shannon and Woods advocate affirmative psychotherapy for counseling male couples that includes establishing a positive gay identity, integrating the gay identity within the larger context of their social/professional/familial lives, and developing full interpersonal relationships. Hall and Fradkin (1992) have suggested a developmental approach for male couples in order to develop the existing strengths and abilities of the couple, to affirm the couple as equals in the counseling experience, to encourage the use of these strengths and abilities in the resolution of developmental life tasks, and to emphasize preventive interventions by working through community and political groups. Ussher (1990a) applied cognitive-behavioral therapy to male couples referred for psychological problems in a unique setting. Although this study dealt with male couples in an AIDS setting, the findings (i.e., improved communication and relationship satisfaction) suggest that counselors may use cognitive-behavioral therapy with male couples in other settings.

Recommendations to Mental Health Counselors

Some gay and lesbian mental health counselors feel strongly that only homosexuals should counsel homosexuals (Markowitz, 1993); however, studies show that this is not necessarily the best approach (e.g., Hayes & Gelso, 1993). Regardless of the mode of counseling used for male couples, the values, beliefs, and stereotypes of the counselor are central to the efficacy of any intervention (Ussher, 1990b). Mental health counselors working with male clients must have an accepting, nonjudgmental attitude, must be aware of issues of gender and sexuality, and must be able to recognize and redress their own homophobia and heterosexual bias (Dahlheimer & Feigal, 1991). Many counselors perceive that all they have to do to work effectively with gay and lesbian clients is to avoid society's classic fear and loathing of this population (Markowitz, 1991). Although this is a step in the right direction, until the counselor understands the full extent to which all people internalize the belief that homosexuality is a perversion, character defect, or moral flaw, even the best-intentioned counselor will echo the negative messages that bombard lesbians and gay men daily (Markowitz, 1991).

In summary, male couples have many of the same attributes as heterosexual couples, such as commitment, respect, and intimacy. Likewise, male couples must deal with many of the same issues as heterosexual couples, such as problems with money, sex, and communication. Furthermore, both types of couples can benefit from group, individual, and couples counseling (although more research is needed to decide the efficacy of these modes for male couples). However, to work effectively with male couples, mental health counselors must be aware of the related issues, as well as their own feelings and attitudes toward homosexuality.

References

Bryant, A. S., & Demian. (1994). Relationship characteristics of American gay and lesbian couples: Findings from a national survey. *Journal of Gay & Lesbian Social Services, 1* (2), 101-117.

Buhrke, R. A., Ben-Ezra, L. A., Hurley, M. E., & Ruprecht, L. J. (1992). Content analysis and methodological critique of articles concerning lesbian and gay male issues in counseling journals. *Journal of Counseling Psychology, 39* (1), 91-99.

Dahlheimer, D., & Feigal, J. (1991). Bridging the gap. *Networker, 15* (1), 44-53.

Dunkle, J. H. (1994). Counseling gay male clients: A review of treatment efficacy research: 1975-present. *Journal of Gay & Lesbian Psychotherapy, 2* (2), 1-19.

Fisher, S. K. (1993). A proposed Adlerian theoretical framework and intervention techniques for gay and lesbian couples. *Individual Psychology: The Journal of Adlerian Theory, Research & Practice, 49* (3/4), 438-449.

George, K. D., & Behrendt, A. E. (1987). Therapy for male couples experiencing relationship problems and sexual problems. *Journal of Homosexuality, 14* (1/2), 77-89.

Gluth, D. R., & Kiselica, M. S. (1994). Coming out quickly: A brief counseling approach to dealing with gay and lesbian adjustment issues. *Journal of Mental Health Counseling, 16* (2), 163-173.

Hall, A. S., & Fradkin, H. R. (1992). Affirming gay men's mental health: Counseling with a new attitude. *Journal of Mental Health Counseling, 14* (3), 362-374.

Hayes, J. A., & Gelso, C. J. (1993). Male counselors' discomfort with gay and HIV-infected clients. *Journal of Counseling Psychology, 40* (1), 86-93.

Hutchins, A. M. (1992). Coming out in a men's group: Exploring some issues and concerns. In S. H. Dwokin & F. J. Gutierrez (Eds.), *Counseling gay men & lesbians: Journey to the end of the rainbow* (pp. 293-306). Alexandria, VA: American Association for Counseling and Development.

Lee, J. A. (1990). Can we talk? Can we *really* talk? Communication as a key factor in the maturing homosexual couple. *Journal of Homosexuality, 20* (3/4), 143-155.

Markowitz, L. M. (1991). Homosexuality: are we still in the dark? *Networker, 15* (1), 27-35.

Markowitz, L. M. (1993). Understanding the differences. *Networker, 17* (2), 50-59.

Mencher, J. (1993). Commentary number one: A gay-affirmative approach. In *Quandaries of a heterosexual therapist: When should sexual orientation be a focus of treatment?* Fishman, H. C. (Ed.), *Networker, 17* (1), 73-75.

Rudolph, J. (1988). Counselors' attitudes toward homosexuality: A selective review of the literature. *Journal of Counseling and Development, 67* (2), 165-168.

Shannon, J. W., & Woods, W. J. (1991). Affirmative psychotherapy for gay men. *The Counseling Psychologist, 19* (2), 197-215.

Ussher, J. M. (1990a). Cognitive behavioral couples therapy with gay men referred for counselling in an AIDS setting: A pilot study. *AIDS Care, 2* (1), 43-51.

Ussher, J. M. (1990b). Couples therapy with gay clients: Issues facing counsellors. *Counselling Psychology Quarterly, 3* (1), 109-116.

Ussher, J. M. (1991). Family and couples therapy with gay and lesbian clients: Acknowledging the forgotten minority. *Journal of Family Therapy, 13* (2), 131-148.

Thomas Campbell is a graduate student in the Department of Counseling and Educational Development at the University of North Carolina at Greensboro.

CHAPTER TWELVE

Helping Clients Cope With Infertility

Judith Daniluk

Approximately 3.5 million couples in the United States experience difficulty as they attempt the transition to biological parenthood. The etiology of infertility problems are shared relatively equally among both members of the couple. Male-and-female factor problems account for 30% to 35% respectively, of diagnosed fertility difficulties, whereas 20% are attributed to both partners, and 10% remain unexplained. Infertility for women is characteristically related to endocrine imbalances or anatomical impairments including blocked tubes or endometriosis. The most common diagnoses for men are oligospermia, a deficient amount of spermatozoa in the seminal fluid, or azoospermia, an absence or near complete absence of sperm. The investigation and treatment of fertility problems involves a difficult and protracted process, with only 50% of couples who seek expert medical care eventually succeeding in their attempts to produce a child (Leader, Taylor, & Daniluk, 1984).

The experience of infertility exacts a heavy toll on the couples who are unable to bear a child. Infertile men and women consistently demonstrate elevated levels of psychosocial distress in comparison to their fertile counterparts. Couples undergoing treatment for infertility commonly report feelings of anger, betrayal, powerlessness, isolation, depression, and hostility, as well as difficulties in their intimate relationships (Abbey, Andrews, & Halman, 1991; Berg & Wilson, 1991; Daniluk, 1988; Wright,

Allard, Lecours, & Sabourin, 1989). Infertility profoundly challenges an individual's basic assumptions regarding justice, fairness, and the meaning of life (Daniluk, 1991; Mahlstedt, 1985). Some men and women experience infertility as an assault on their masculinity or femininity. Most report acute feelings of loss and grief in response to this personal crisis.

Factors that appear to be associated with a more negative response to infertility include being the member of the couple identified as the source of the fertility problem, advanced age and longer duration of infertility, and receipt of an ambiguous diagnosis such as unexplained infertility (e.g. Abbey et al., 1991; Berg & Wilson, 1991; Daniluk, 1988, 1991; Mahlstedt, 1985; Wright et al., 1989). Women appear to experience more overt psychosocial distress, somatic difficulties, lower self-esteem, higher levels of depression, and greater interpersonal sensitivity related to their infertility than their male counterparts. These differences may be exaggerated by the disproportionate number of women who participate in infertility research and by the nature of the research methodology characteristically employed in examining psychosocial responses to infertility (Newton & Houle, 1993), or these responses may reflect variations in the way men and women are socialized to respond to stress (Mahlstedt, 1985). Results of the few studies conducted for the purpose of examining men's responses to their inability to father a child suggest that men also experience considerable distress in response to infertility, distress that is often characterized by emotional and physical withdrawal (e.g., Mason, 1993).

The experience of infertility and the pursuit of treatment may involve literally years of a couple's life together, with the needs of couples differing based on whether they are undergoing initial medical investigations, are involved in treatment, or are attempting to deal with the consequences of successful or failed treatment. A brief discussion of the salient counseling issues at each of these stages is presented below, with suggestions being provided for possible intervention strategies to help couples cope with the stress of infertility and to make informed and satisfying decisions regarding the available treatment interventions and the pursuit of alternate options for satisfying lives.

Mental Health Counseling Implications

Initial Medical Investigations

A couple is considered to be infertile after one year of regular, unprotected intercourse, with medical investigations being initiated after the couple has been coping with their inability to conceive for an average of one to two years. Research indicates that in most cases it is the woman who initiates the process of seeking medical solutions to the couple's inability to conceive or carry a viable pregnancy to term. Following a very detailed medical and sexual history (one that commonly includes questions about past abortions and pregnancies), investigations of the female partner usually include pelvic examinations, blood tests, basal body temperature charting, tubal x-rays, and a surgical procedure (a laparoscopy) to examine the uterus, tubes and ovaries. The male partner undergoes a physical examination and is required to produce several semen samples. These investigative procedures are often invasive, uncomfortable, and humiliating, leaving most infertile individuals feeling somewhat violated and exposed with the most intimate and private aspects of the couple's life together being subjected to examination and scrutiny.

While couples are frequently quite anxious about what might be required of them during the process of diagnosis (Berg & Wilson, 1991; Daniluk, 1988), their fears are usually balanced with optimism and hope, believing that the source of their problem will be identified and a medical solution will be forthcoming. At this stage in the process, support and information are particularly important. Mental health counselors can help couples become informed consumers of medical services and can support them in their efforts to find ways of ensuring that their needs are met and their rights are respected within a system that is foreign and intimidating. Strategies such as relaxation techniques, self-hypnosis, and visualizations are also useful aids for coping with the unpleasant and sometimes painful investigative procedures. Also, couples may need assistance in dealing with the disclosure of information regarding their past sexual and reproductive history, particularly in cases where this information has not previously been shared within the couple's relationship. From the outset it is important that mental health counselors encourage couples to view infertility as a "couple's problem," to reinforce a necessary solidarity and alliance between the couple prior to being faced with a diagnosis and various treatment options, and to reduce the tendency to place blame or instill feelings of guilt if one partner is identified as being the source of the couples fertility impairment.

Treatment

The analogy most frequently used by couples to refer to this stage in the infertility process is an emotional "roller coaster." The news of a diagnosis, if one is forthcoming, is initially met with relief ("We finally have an answer.") followed by a cycle of fear, hope, and disappointment as couples are faced with deciding between a host of often expensive, controversial, and time-consuming treatment options, each of which is accompanied by a set of statistically generated "success rates," the interpretation of which would prove challenging to even the most well-trained researcher. Depending on the diagnosis, the list of treatment options may include the use of synthetic hormones to induce ovulation or to diminish endometrial tissue; hours of micro-surgery to repair damaged or blocked tubes; insemination with the husband's sperm or donor semen, in-vitro fertilization with the wife's eggs and the husband's sperm, with donor eggs and the husband's sperm, with the wife's eggs and donor sperm, or with donor eggs fertilized with donor sperm. In some states surrogacy is also an option. Couples often progress from one treatment regime to another, facing numerous decisions throughout the process until they are either successful in achieving a live birth or until treatment options run out. Even those whose fertility impairment remains undiagnosed following extensive investigations (commonly referred to as "unexplained" or "normal" infertility) may undergo any number of these treatment procedures in an attempt to enhance their chances of a pregnancy. The process is often protracted, with many couples dedicating 8 to 10 years in the pursuit of medical solutions.

Mental health counselors can assist infertile couples during this stage in the process by helping them to make informed treatment decisions based on their unique needs and values and in consideration of their personal circumstances and emotional resources (Daniluk, 1991; Mahlstedt, 1985). Couples require validation of their feelings and support for their choices, even when these choices appear to have a remote probability of success. They may require assistance in coming to agreement about the most appropriate course of action, and they may need help in accessing sources of emotional support outside of their relationship rather than relying exclusively on their partner to help them cope with the considerable stresses associated with treatment. Infertile clients may need help in assuming control over their treatment choices and setting limits on the extent of treatment they are willing to undergo, as well as requiring assistance in extricating themselves from the medical system when they no longer have the emotional, financial, or personal resources to continue pursuing medical solutions to their infertility.

Post-Treatment

Whether couples have selected to reject further treatment, whether medicine no longer has treatment options to offer them, or whether they are finally successful in achieving a pregnancy, it is important for mental health counselors to be aware that the experience of infertility does not end when treatment ends. Rather, while couples often experience tremendous relief that their bodies and lives will no longer be invaded by medications, probes, and practitioners, the end of treatment also brings them face to face with the reality of their infertility (Daniluk, 1991).

The couples who are successful in making the transition to parenthood will feel blessed in their good fortune and grateful to those whose knowledge, skill, and caring have helped them achieve this precious "gift of life." However, following years of coping with infertility couples may still require assistance in coping with the stress of bringing a pregnancy to term and effectively parenting the child (or children in the case of multiple births) to whom they have invested so much time and energy in creating. Should they decide to increase their family size at some point in the future, they may need assistance and support as they are faced again with the reality of their infertility and contemplate the prospect of putting themselves through another stressful and potentially expensive medical process that may or may not result in a subsequent pregnancy.

More frequently, counselors are faced with helping the 50% of couples who have not been successful in achieving a pregnancy through medical intervention. These couples require assistance in coping with feelings of anger and frustration at having had this important life experience denied to them, and having been failed by a system they had put their lives and their trust into. They need help in coping with often intense feelings of grief associated with the loss of the son or daughter that they will never know, the loss of a meaningful life role, the loss of genetic continuity, and the loss of their lives together as it had been envisioned. Relationships with family members and friends may need to be repaired, and couples may need assistance in rebuilding the intimate ties in their relationship that have been fractured by the stress of invasive treatments and prolonged investigations. It is also important for counselors to help infertile couples look toward the future and set new goals, based on a reassessment of the importance of parenting in their lives and on the viability of parenting and non-parenting options.

Conclusion

The extent of emotional upheaval caused by the inability to produce a child and the prolonged pursuit of medical treatment should not be underestimated. While not all couples experience infertility as a "crisis"

(Menning, 1977), infertility represents a difficult and painful life experience for many men and women. Counselors working with adult clients need to be aware of the extent to which the investigation and treatment of infertility can invade all aspects of couples' lives, creating barriers to intimacy and causing a tremendous amount of interpersonal and intrapersonal distress. It is important for counselors to be aware of the differing needs of couples seeking solutions to their infertility and to provide support and assistance at all stages of the infertility process.

References

Abbey, A., Andrews, F. M., & Halman, L. J. (1991). Gender's role in response to infertility. *Psychology of Women Quarterly, 15,* 295-314.

Berg, B., & Wilson, J. F. (1991). Psychological functioning across stages of treatment for infertility. *Journal of Behavioral Medicine, 14*(1), 11-26.

Daniluk, J. C. (1988). Infertility: Intrapersonal and interpersonal impact. *Fertility & Sterility, 49,* 982-990.

Daniluk, J. C. (1991). Strategies for counseling infertile couples. *Journal of Counseling & Development, 69,* 317-320.

Leader, A., Taylor, P. J., & Daniluk, J. C. (1984). Infertility: Clinical and psychological aspects. *Psychiatric Annals, 14,* 461-467.

Mahlstedt, P. P. (1985). The psychological component of infertility. *Fertility and Sterility, 43,* 335-346.

Mason, M. C. (1993). *Male infertility - Men talking.* London and New York: Routledge.

Menning, B. E. (1977). *Infertility: A guide for the childless couple.* Englewood Cliffs, NJ: Prentice-Hall.

Newton, C., & Houle, M. (1993). Gender differences in psychological response to infertility treatment. *The Canadian Journal of Human Sexuality, 2,* 129-139.

Wright, J., Allard, M., Lecours, A., & Sabourin, S. (1989). Psychosocial distress and infertility: A review of controlled research. *International Journal of Fertility, 34,* 126-142.

Judith Daniluk, Ph.D., is an Associate Professor in the Department of Counselling Psychology, University of British Columbia, Vancouver, British Columbia, Canada.

CHAPTER THIRTEEN

Prevention With At-Risk Students

Lawrence M. DeRidder

Overview

Alcohol and drug abuse, teenage pregnancy, dropping-out, and violence are changing the nature of schooling in the United States. The future of students is at risk as they, and their families, face obstacles in their communities. Efforts to limit the emergence of these behaviors are badly needed. Fortunately, school counselors are in a unique position to prevent future problems by encouraging early identification and intervention. This paper presents a brief summary of research related to this problem and provides suggestions for school counselors.

Research Review

Since 1978 research studies have concluded that the behaviors of dropping out, drug abuse, teenage pregnancy, and delinquency have resulted from family backgrounds that are similarly dysfunctional (e.g., Finn, 1989; Jessor & Jessor, 1978; McLaughlin & Vacha, 1993; Mills, Dunham, & Alpert, 1988; Zigler, Taussig, & Black, 1992). Children from all socio-economic levels bring risk factors from their homes into the school, including child abuse, rejection or neglect; history of family conflicts, family anti-social behavior, or ethnic or racial background (Entwisle & Hayduk, 1988; Hawkins, Kishner, Catalano, & Howard, 1985; Jesness, 1987; Loeber & Dishion, 1987). Typically, these students become poor performers, progress slowly, are retained more often, participate minimally, are often truant, and may become alienated from the school and its purposes. How the school and its teachers respond to and assist these students determines school success.

Components of Prevention

School counselors are in a pivotal position to identify at-risk students and to provide them early and critical assistance. Because at-risk students can be identified as early as kindergarten, scales such as that developed by Spivack & Swift (1973), as well as the *Devereaux Elementary Behavior Scale,* are useful for detection in the elementary grades. These scales rate the behaviors of disrespect or defiance, impatience, classroom disturbances, blaming others, and irrelevant responses. Alternative approaches also should be used by school counselors; for example, other excellent indicators may include days absent during the last year, grade point average, number of grades repeated, and reading level (Weber, 1986). Another approach, used by Wiggins (1988) to identify students at-risk, obtained the student responses to a short self-esteem inventory a teacher rating of the student's study skills, self-discipline, dependency, and peer relationships.

Once students at-risk are identified, preferably within the first month of school for all grade levels, the school counselor, teachers, and parents should consult and collaborate to explore options. Successful learning interventions may involve tutoring, hands-on activities, computer-managed learning, family support services, and/or parent training in discipline and nurturing.

At-risk students must have a reasonable number of early academic and social successes to achieve the necessary bonding with the school and its purpose. An ungraded K-3 program would allow students to develop and to learn at their own speed, perhaps using a program of reading and arithmetic competencies that are hierarchically arranged. As an alternative, students may be organized into multi-age and multi-grade classrooms where students help other students. Because all students respond to expectation, homogeneous learning tracks have been found to severely limit the learning opportunities for at-risk students. Each child should have the opportunity to achieve adequate self-worth in the school setting.

Students at all levels learn best by applying what is learned to actual life functions. Consequently, because of counselors' training and knowledge of potential resources, they can provide teachers with materials to achieve this real-life linkage. In order to facilitate the social acceptance of at-risk students and to encourage cooperative learning, teachers could be encouraged to use small (4-5) member within-class heterogeneous groupings to accomplish specific tasks. By middle school all students, especially at-risk students, need to determine tentative career interests, to examine relevant literature, and to develop a proposed program of high school studies. Developing such interests improves attendance as well as completion.

Times of great risk to school completion are points of transition from home to elementary school, to middle school, and again to high school. Many students get physically lost or psychologically damaged during these transitions. Assisting students to move comfortably and competently from their known environment into a new setting, typically with different rules, values, expectations, and social norms, is an important school counselor responsibility.

At the middle and high school levels, at-risk students also need help in developing employability skills, work habits, and learning how to find and keep a job. A part-time work experience, preferably school supervised and time-controlled, helps students to recognize that social and academic skills are needed for employment in today's society. When opportunity exists, school counselors could encourage the responsible school to graduate all of the students it serves by providing an in-school alternative program for all truant, suspended, or expelled students. Cast-offs become an economic and social burden and create individuals who are increasingly alienated from society.

Because persistent student problems reflect the values and behaviors of their homes, the greatest opportunity to assist them is through their parents. School counselors can help teachers explore the various ways to make parent contacts: phone calls, early morning or evening conferences, instructions on how to tutor or where to find one, individualized teacher-parent notes, class newsletters, a school phone listing of daily homework assignments, and weekly school events. If given specific things to do, parents often will take the time to assist their children. Additionally, one of the most powerful interventions used to establish rapport and understanding of the family system is a home visit. Many parents feel unsure about their parent-child communication, the setting of reasonable and consistent limits, emphasizing the positive rather than negative, monitoring student activities, and ways to assist in problem-solving.

Support groups for parents of at-risk students, initiated by school counselors, can provide information and mutual assistance, preferably in settings convenient to work and family schedules. Responses to a questionnaire on parenting could be used as the base for discussions and planning for change. The use of *Active Parenting, Systematic Training for Effective Parenting,* or other programs can improve parent-student interaction and communication. Parents learn the value of listening to their children read, helping with math, checking homework, and participating in various school and out-of-school activities. The involvement of parents in schools, at all grade levels, improves the attitudes of their children toward school and in turn increases their academic achievement. Parents need to be invited and encouraged to be involved as school partners. Each counselor and teacher is encouraged to include parents as a legitimate part of a learning process that is positive and long lasting.

Conclusion

The destructive behaviors that emerge at adolescence can be prevented. Dropping out, drug abuse, teenage pregnancy, and delinquency are the result of various but related factors. Research has demonstrated that students at-risk can be identified in kindergarten as well as in each grade thereafter. Once identified, inappropriate student behaviors can be modified through counselor-teacher efforts using the resources of the school and family. If the array of at-risk behaviors experienced by principals and teachers are to be reduced or eliminated, school counselors must be proactive in establishing an identification process and remediation plan for these troubled students.

References

Entwisle, D., & Hayduk, L. A. (1988). Lasting effects of elementary school. *Sociology of Education, 61,* 147-159.

Finn, J. D. (1989). Withdrawing from school. *Review of Educational Research, 59(2),* 117-142.

Hawkins, J. D., Kishner, D. M., Catalano, R. F., & Howard, M. O. (1985). Childhood predictors of adolescent substance abuse. *Journal of Children in Contemporary Society, 18*(1-2), 11-48.

Jesness, C. F. (1987). Early identification of delinquent-prone children. In J. D. Burchard & S. N. Burchard (Eds.), *Prevention of delinquent behaviors* (pp. 140-158). Beverly Hills, CA: Sage Publications.

Jessor, R., & Jessor, S. L. (1978). Theory testing in longitudinal research on marijuana use. In D. B. Kandel (Ed.), *Longitudinal research on drug use* (pp. 41-71). New York: John Wiley & Sons.

Loeber, R., & Dishion, T. J. (1987). Antisocial and delinquent youths: Methods for their early identification. In J. D. Burchard, & S. N. Burchard (Eds.), *Prevention of delinquent behaviors* (pp. 75-89). Beverly Hills, CA: Sage.

McLaughlin, T. F., & Vacha, E. F. (1993). Substance abuse prevention in the schools: Roles for the school counselor. *Elementary School Guidance and Counseling, 28*(2), 124-132.

Mills, R. C., Dunham, R. G., & Alpert, G. P. (1988). Working with high-risk youth in prevention and early intervention programs: Toward a comprehensive wellness model. *Adolescence, 23(9),* 643-660.

Spivack, G., & Swift, M. (1973). The classroom behavior of children: A critical review of teacher-administered rating scales. *Journal of Special Education, 7*(1), 55-89.

Weber, J. M. (1986). *An evaluation of selected procedures for identifying potential high school dropouts.* Columbus, OH: Ohio State University, National Center for Research in Vocational Education.

Wiggins, J. D. (1988). *School achievement and self-esteem.* Unpublished manuscript. Lawrenceville, GA: Gwinnett County Public Schools, 1-13.

Zigler, E., Taussig, C., & Black, K. (1992). Early childhood intervention: A promising preventative for juvenile delinquency. *American Psychologist, 47*(8), 997-1006.

Lawrence M. DeRidder is Professor Emeritus, Counselor Education and Counseling Psychology at the University of Tennessee - Knoxville.

CHAPTER FOURTEEN

Mental Health Counseling for Children in the Aftermath of a Disaster

Michael E. Wells

In the past few years the United States has suffered an inordinately high number of disasters (e.g., Hurricanes Hugo, Andrew, and Iniki; rioting and destruction in Los Angeles; terrorist bombings in New York and Oklahoma City; the Northridge, California earthquake; flooding, first along the Mississippi River in 1993, and then again in Georgia and the Southeast in 1994). Many of these disasters were history-making in terms of the number of lives directly affected and the impact on local, as well as national, economies. These disasters were brought into every home in the country instantaneously by television. While the entire country suffers, the immediate and often most intense blows from a disaster are suffered by individual men, women, and children. It is these individuals who continue to suffer from a disaster long after the nation's attention has moved on to more current news. Bringing rapid, intense, and situation-specific mental health services to victims of disasters provide a benefit (Kalichman, 1994), however, how to go about doing so effectively is not as obvious as it might seem.

The Child's Response

The immediate aftermath of a disaster is filled with a rapidly shifting diversity of responses from survivors, often described as human stress response syndromes (Horowitz, Stinson, & Field, 1991; Scott, 1994). Scott (1994) points out that the adjustment process is a "natural and adaptive" one which should only be considered pathological when it is "prolonged, blocked, exceeds a tolerable level, or interferes with life functioning to a significant extent."

Recent researchers in the field of disaster counseling have identified four basic response categories observed in children who experience a disaster (Eth & Pynoos, 1985; Johnson, 1992; Scott, 1994). Those four responses are described as follows:

Disorganization: Symptoms include a lack of attending skills, the inability to focus on one topic in conversation, confusion, and a lack of overall response to surroundings.

Primitivization: Children may regress to earlier developmental stages characterized by enuresis or encopresis, clinging or separation anxiety, fearfulness, and other behaviors common to younger children. A loss of coping skills or problem solving strategies also may be evidenced.

Deverbalization: In keeping with developmental digression children may cease to use verbal language as a primary means of communication. Acting out behaviorally, or avoiding interactions with others, may serve to communicate distress. Saylor, Swenson, and Powell (1992) have reported that a significant number of children used thematic play as an adjustment response following Hurricane Hugo.

Somatization: Physical ailments such as muscle pain, upset digestion, loss of appetite, headache, and respiratory difficulties are commonly seen.

LaGreca, Silverman, and Wasserstein (1994) found that the psychological functioning of a child prior to experiencing a disaster, especially anxiety, inattention, and academic problems was a good predictor of post-disaster stress responses of children immediately after a disaster (up to 3 months). Children with persistent (more than 6 months) adjustment problems also tended to have more pre-disaster problems. Interestingly, this same study found that children appeared to show little evidence for exacerbation of prior problems, with the exception of social anxiety, brought on by having experienced a disaster, even among those children with high levels of Post Traumatic Stress Disorder (PTSD) symptomology.

Intervention

When providing mental health services to children in the aftermath of a disaster, it is important to pair the particular intervention strategy to be used with an understanding of the specific needs of the child and his or her family. All services provided in post-disaster settings should be narrowly focused, based in the present, and not too probing. Interventions will be intense and short term. Initial assessments will attempt to discover the current crisis situation, the presence of relevant stressors prior to the disaster, and problem-solving and coping skills (Scott, 1994).

Once basic physiological needs are met (e.g. food, clothing, injuries treated) it will be necessary to address security and safety concerns. This may be especially relevant if the children are being seen at an emergency shelter or are living in temporary housing. Predictability can be a first step in re-establishing the life schedules and rituals which make daily life routine and, therefore, safe. Development of a plan for reacting to any future threatening situations will help the child regain some sense of control. This may involve identifying specific actions; e.g. "run out the back door if I smell smoke", as well as identifying specific adults who may be sought for help; e.g., parents, law enforcement officers. The child should make these choices with support and guidance from the mental health professional. Rehearsing the plan also is a good idea.

Next, children will need to recount the events they have experienced in order to try and make some sense of the situation. Children's accounts will often be distorted or inaccurate. Correcting inaccuracies at this time may only tend to undermine trust. Listening may be the best plan. Young victims of the Northridge earthquake typically ended their recounts with some traumatic events; e.g. ",then the ceiling crashed down" (Shelby, 1994). The child should be encouraged to go beyond that point, at least up to the current time. Symbolic means such as re-enactment of an event, drawing or coloring pictures, or completing some art project can help. This "debriefing" may best be done in small groups and include activities which create a heightened sense of control (Johnson, 1992; Mitchell, 1983; Scott, 1994; Shelby, 1994). Providing a common play area for young victims can encourage debriefing. Overestimation of control is generally not inconsistent with many cognitive levels of childhood and is not problematic at this point.

Once some ventilation has occurred it is time to begin to correct some of the distortions or inaccuracies and restore a more realistic sense of power and control. This may include very specific educational interventions such as showing children how earthquakes or hurricanes occur. If the trauma resulted from the actions of people, such as terrorist bombings or shootings, it is equally important for children to understand that all people are not like those who perpetrated the traumatic event at hand. As the child returns to a more balanced psychological state, the child may need help to restore trust in parents and other adults. The professional should keep in mind that since families often relocate with little warning, contact with the child is often ended abruptly, without the opportunity to address the issue of termination. It is necessary throughout contact for the mental health counselor to encourage a return of trust to parents or other adults who may be perceived, and in fact may perceive themselves, as disempowered and ineffective in providing protection. Parents can be designated recipients of donated clothes, toys, or personal items so that they may in turn distribute these to their family. Other responsibilities given to parents may include disseminating daily information and news regarding re-building or re-location status from local officials to other family members, notifying children of special activities planned, or helping to decide when and where counseling or educational groups will be conducted. It is important to allow parents to reclaim the responsibility for their family's continuation.

Mental health counselors who are interested in helping to provide the kinds of services summarized herein are encouraged to contact the Disaster Response Network through The American Red Cross, the American Psychological Association, the American Counseling Association, or their respective state affiliations.

References

Eth, S., & Pynoos, R. (1985). Developmental perspective on psychic trauma in childhood. In C. R. Figley (Ed.), *Trauma and its wake, Vol. 1: The study and treatment of post traumatic stress disorder.* New York: Brunner/Mazel.

Horowitz, M.J., Stinson, C., & Field, N. (1991). Natural disasters and stress response syndromes. *Psychiatric Annals, 21,* 556-561.

Johnson, K. (1992). *School Crisis Management.* Alameda, CA: Hunter House.

Kalichman, S. C. (1994). Children who survive traumatic events. *The Child, Youth, and Family Services Quarterly, 17,* 1.

LaGreca, A. M., Silverman, W. K., & Wasserstein, S. B. (1994). Factors affecting children's reactions to a natural disaster. *The Child, Youth, and Family Services Quarterly, 17,* 2-5.

Mitchell, J. (1983). When disaster strikes: The critical incident stress debriefing process. *Journal of Emergency Medical Services, 8,* 36-39.

Saylor, C. F., Swenson, C. C., & Powell, P. (1992). Hurricane Hugo blows down the broccoli: Preschoolers' post-disaster play and adjustment. *Child Psychiatry and Human Development, 22*(3), 139-149.

Scott, R. T. (1994). Dealing with the aftermath of a crisis, trauma and disaster: an overview of intervention strategies for children. *The Child, Youth, and Family Services Quarterly, 17,* 6-9.

Shelby, J. (1994). Psychological intervention with children in disaster relief shelters. *The Child, Youth, and Family Services Quarterly, 17,* 14-18.

Michael E. Wells, Ph.D. is the Director of Foothills High School, Mt. Airy, North Carolina.

CHAPTER FIFTEEN

The Treatment of Choice for Adolescent Anorexics: Family Therapy

Caroline S. Booth

Anorexia nervosa is an eating disorder that is very prevalent in our culture, especially among women. As the idealized body continues to get smaller, the incidence of anorexia and other eating disorders increases. Anorexia is characterized by a refusal to maintain body weight due to an intense and overpowering fear of becoming fat (Bastiani, Rao, Weltzin, & Kaye, 1995). Sufferers have a distorted body image. To combat an overweight body image, anorexics engage in a marked reduction of food intake to the point of self-starvation, as well as a tendency to exercise excessively (Bastiani et al., 1995). This extreme behavior usually results in substantial loss of body mass, amenorrhea, and an exaggerated interest in food (McNab, 1983).

It was once thought that anorexia was a problem found only in upper socio-economic groups, but it is now known that this is not true (Gard & Freeman, 1996). Anorexia can occur in almost anyone, even children (Sanchez-Cardenas, Mammar, Venisse, & Robin, 1995). Most health care professionals consider anorexia to be most common in white populations, but it has been suggested there may be a failure to recognize the symptoms where it is not expected (Gard & Freeman, 1996). Unfortunately, one group where anorexia nervosa is extremely common is among adolescents.

Adolescence is a stressful time in our culture. It is the stage when children change into young adults and begin to seek individuation from their parents and struggle to establish autonomy and a new self (Sanchez-Cardenas et al., 1995). This also is the time when young bodies are undergoing developmental changes that result in a loss of the shapeless child figure. Adolescence is a vulnerable time for the development of eating disorders such as anorexia.

It has been suggested that the adolescent anorexic is suffering from low self-esteem and seeks to control his or her body and create changes in the parental environment (McNab, 1983). Others believe that understanding family dynamics and parent-child relationships are the keys to understanding the development and pathogenesis of anorexia in adolescents (Shugar & Krueger, 1995). Shugar and Kruegar described several common features that exist in the family structure of adolescent anorexics.

- Mothers have been found to be overprotective and domineering.
- Family members are described as enmeshed, not permitting privacy or autonomy for individual members.
- Discipline and achievement in children are valued more than their maturation or independence.
- Interactional patterns are said to be rigid.
- The maintenance of apparent family harmony has been considered to be an essential feature by which families preserve stability (p. 24).

Anorexia nervosa is a disorder that reflects familial dysfunction or a parental problem. This belief is further substantiated by research that has shown that parents tend to project their own unresolved issues, such as grief, onto the child. The child in turn expresses the problem for the parent through anorexic symptoms (Sanchez-Cardenas et al., 1995). Another family hypothesis suggests that anorexia is born out of an inadvertent desire to protect the mother from depression and an "empty nest" syndrome that can occur when a child matures into an adult (Mirkin, 1985). Whatever the cause of adolescent anorexia, it appears that it is a problem that develops within the family and, therefore, needs to be treated within the family. The importance of the family in healing is more evident when you consider that some adolescent sufferers are as young as 11 or 12 years old.

Family Therapy

Before beginning family therapy, it is important to know that treating adolescent anorexia (or anorexia at any age) can be very difficult. This is because anorexic practices create and confirm the anorexic way of life (Garrett, 1997). Anorexics display rigid and obsessive behaviors that are very resistant to change. These behaviors are fueled by a self-imposed drive for perfectionism that can persist even after weight level is restored (Bastiani et al., 1995; McNab, 1983). In addition, sufferers set unrealistic standards and are overly critical of their successes and over generalize their failures (Hewitt & Flett, 1991). No weight loss is great enough. Anorexics are so successful at losing weight that many reach the point of death and are still obsessed with becoming fat. In fact, it is estimated that from 5% to 20% of anorexics ultimately die from metabolic collapse, circulatory failure, or suicide (Neumarker, 1997). For these reasons, it is imperative that the anorexic receive effective and comprehensive treatment and that the entire family be committed to the healing process.

Family therapy for anorexia nervosa is the most effective mode of treatment for adolescent sufferers (Le Grange, Eisler, Dare, & Russell, 1992; Robin, Siegel, & Moye, 1995; Shugar & Krueger, 1995). Since its creation in the 1970s, family therapy has been described and modified through various methodological changes (Shugar & Krueger). However, all family therapy approaches seem to emphasize an understanding of the way the family functions as a whole (Le Grange, et al.). Anorexia is treated as a severe symptom of a "family sickness" and the anorexic is treated as the overt manifestation of the problem. Two of the more common and successful family therapy approaches are systemic family therapy and a symptom-oriented family therapy.

Systemic family therapy involves treating anorexia by eliminating dysfunctional behavioral patterns in the family and by changing the family style to a direct and open interactional pattern (Shugar & Krueger, 1995). The goal is to replace covert aggression and indirect communications with conflict resolution skills, teaching the family to be understanding of each other's individuality. Along the same lines, symptom-oriented family therapy teaches parents to manage the adolescent's self-starvation. After this has been accomplished, the mental health counselor (MHC) focuses on changing the family's behavioral dysfunctions and the way the family organizes itself around the anorexic child (Le Grange et al., 1992).

It seems that the symptom-oriented approach might work best for younger adolescents while the systemic therapy might be the better choice for older adolescents because the child retains more autonomy. Both family therapy variations seek to correct family problems as a means to heal the eating-disordered child. The MHC must remember not to blame parents or to cause them to feel responsible for their adolescent's disorder, but to emphasize family strengths and resources (Le Grange et al., 1992).

Before beginning any type of family therapy for an anorexic child, the MHC needs to have an extensive understanding of family systems and the eating disorder itself. It is suggested that the MHC take a strategic approach and customize the therapy to fit the family. There are several things to keep in mind and factors to consider when selecting treatment components.

First, MHCs must be aware of the persistence of eating disorders and the tendency for anorexics to move to another type of eating disorder. The obsessive and compulsive characteristics common in anorexia tend to persist along with the desire for thinness, even after successful treatment (Bastiani et al., 1995). One study conducted a seven year follow-up and found that 44% of the subjects "still fulfilled DSM-III-R criteria for some kind of eating disorder" (Herpertz-Dahlmann, Wewetzer, Hennighausen, & Remschmidt, 1996, p. 467). Other eating disorders include bulimia, bulimia nervosa and EDNOS (Eating Disorder Not Otherwise Specified). This finding seems to be common in follow-up studies of adolescent anorexics (Herpertz-Dahlmann, Wewetzer, Schulz, & Remschmidt, 1996). The clinical implications for this are clear. The MHC and the family need to be aware of the possible long-term nature of successful treatment. Recovery should be described as an ongoing process rather than as a final point (Garrett, 1997). Even after the adolescent has moved into adulthood or the family has lost interest in therapy, further treatment for the recovering anorexic may be needed in the form of individual counseling.

Another consideration while treating the adolescent anorexic is the comorbidity anorexia shares with other psychiatric disorders, most commonly anxiety and affective disorders (Herpertz-Dahlmann, Wewetzer, Hennighausen, & Remschmidt, 1996). Anorexics are known to have very high rates of depression and social phobias. These disorders tend to develop parallel to or after the onset of the eating disorder (Herpertz-Dahlmann, Wewetzer, Schulz, & Remschmidt, 1996). MHCs should be aware of this and watch for signs of other disorders. To complicate matters even further, the anorexic client is not the only one to suffer from comorbid disorders. MHCs must pay attention to parental pathology, particularly maternal anxiety and somaticizing and paternal depression (Robin et al., 1995). Ignoring these parental symptoms could unnecessarily complicate the treatment for the anorexic and hinder the treatment.

Finally, it is meaningful to note a study of sociological interviews with recovering anorexics. The factors they believed contributed most to their recovery were the strong relationships in their lives (Garrett, 1997). This supports the necessity of successful family communication and behavior modifications through family therapy. In cases where clients felt the treatment had been successful, the success was not attributed to the counseling, but to the strength of the client/therapist relationship. The successful MHC should always be mindful of the power inherent in the counselor/client relationship and use this to aid the recovery of the family and the anorexic.

In summary, adolescent anorexia nervosa is an extremely complicated problem born from a culture that idolizes thinness and a family system that lacks effective communication and conflict resolution. Treatment should focus both on the anorexic and the family. It is important to consider the age of the adolescent and the unique family dynamics present when choosing specific family treatment components. MHCs should use their judgment and incorporate the specific treatment aspects that they feel would be most effective. While healing the family, the MHC can help adolescent anorexics restore weight and find a sense of peace within themselves and a oneness with other people (Garrett, 1997).

References

Bastiani, A., Rao, R., Weltzin, T., & Kaye, W. (1995). Perfectionism in anorexia nervosa. *International Journal of Eating Disorders, 17* (2), 147-152.

Gard, M., & Freeman, C. (1996). The dismantling of a myth: A review of eating disorders and socioeconomic status. *International Journal of Eating Disorders, 20* (1), 1-12.

Garrett, C. (1997). Recovery from anorexia nervosa: A sociological perspective. *International Journal of Eating Disorders, 21,* 261-272.

Herpertz-Dahlmann, B., Wewetzer, C., Henninghausen, K., & Remschmidt, H. (1996). Outcome, psychosocial functioning, and prognostic factors in adolescent anorexia nervosa as determined by prospective follow-up assessment. *Youth and Adolescence, 25* (4), 455-471.

Herpertz-Dahlmann, B., Wewetzer, C., Schulz, E., & Remschmidt, H. (1996). Course and outcome in adolescent anorexia nervosa. *International Journal of Eating Disorders, 19* (4), 335-345.

Hewitt, P., & Flett, G. (1991). Perfectionism in the self and social contexts: Conceptualization, assessment, and association with psychopathology. *Journal of Personality and Social Psychology, 60*, 456-470.

Le Grange, D., Eisler, I., Dare, C., & Russell, G. (1992). Evaluation of family treatments in adolescent anorexia nervosa: A pilot study. *International Journal of Eating Disorders, 12* (4), 347-357.

McNab, W. (1983). Anorexia and the adolescent. *Journal of School Health, 53* (7), 427-430.

Mirkin, M. (1985). The Peter Pan Syndrome: Inpatient treatment of adolescent anorexia nervosa. *International Journal of Family Therapy, 7* (3), 205-216.

Neumarker, K. (1997). Mortality and sudden death in anorexia nervosa. *International Journal of Eating Disorders, 21*, 205-212,

Robin, A., Siegel, P., & Moye A. (1995). Family versus individual therapy for anorexia: Impact on family conflict. *International Journal of Eating Disorders, 17* (4), 313-322.

Sanchez-Cardenas, M., Mammar, N., Venisse, J., & Robin, D. (1995). Complications of bereavement as seen in infant anorexia and adolescent anorexia nervosa. *International Journal of Eating Disorders, 17* (1), 39-44.

Shugar, G., & Krueger, S. (1995). Aggressive family communication, weight gain, and improved eating attitudes during systemic family therapy for anorexia nervosa. *International Journal of Eating Disorders, 17* (1), 23-31.

Caroline S. Booth is a graduate student at the University of North Carolina at Greensboro.

CHAPTER SIXTEEN

Marsha Linehan's Dialectical Behavior Therapy: A Treatment Summary

David C. Jones

Dialectical Behavior Therapy (DBT) is a highly specialized treatment tailored to meet the therapeutic needs of people suffering from Borderline Personality Disorder (BPD). The development of DBT has primarily been the work of Marsha Linehan and has evolved from her study and practice of Cognitive Behavioral Therapy (CBT) (Linehan, 1993), and her subsequent study of dialectics, a branch of classical Western philosophy articulated by Hegel and popularized by Marx. Although DBT is considered a type of Cognitive Behavioral Therapy, it has several important points on which it differs. Standard CBT functions upon the basic assumption that rationality is the paramount criterion for healthy thought. In the evolution of DBT Linehan found certain instances when employing paradox was the desired technique to further and/or stabilize the client's growth. Linehan also places a high value on "intuitive" thinking which is not considered a "rational" mode of thought. Another major difference between DBT and standard CBT is Linehan's appropriation of traditional dialectical theory. Linehan (1993) applies dialectical theory to her brand of behavior therapy in two contexts: (a) as a fundamental understanding of the nature of reality (world view), and (b) as a form of therapeutic dialogue and relationship.

Dialectics

Linehan (1993) summarizes the dialectical world view into three basic characteristics, or principles:

1. The Principal of Interrelatedness and Wholeness, meaning that all of reality is one great, interrelated, closed system. The self is relationally defined by its interaction with others. Socially speaking, this perspective would deny the existence of the completely individuated self. Linehan argues that the borderline client is an "emotionally vulnerable" relational self living in an environment that unrealistically demands a completely individuated self, which is an impossibility, in the context of the dialectical world view.
2. The Principle of Polarity, meaning that reality is not static, but is comprised by internal opposing forces (thesis & antithesis) out of whose integration (synthesis) evolves a new set of opposing forces (a new thesis & antithesis). It is here that one can see the validity and importance of accepting paradox, as we have two truths vying with one another, seeking integration. This presents the mental health counselor (MHC) with a new insight into understanding the borderline client. Within the borderline client's dysfunction there is function; within distortion, accuracy; within destruction, creation.
3. Thesis, Antithesis, Synthesis: The Principle of Continuous Change, meaning the interconnected, oppositional and irreducible nature of reality leads to a wholeness continually in the process of change. Change is produced by the tension between opposing internal forces. Change is a continual process, never fully resolved. It is imperative to realize that there is no "absolute" truth in this world view. The truth, like life itself, is temporary. This is a crucial goal in DBT. The acceptance that there is no absolute truth, but only a relative one, and indeed, more than one, is to be gradually achieved. Eventually, the borderline, in the process of dialectical change, may leave the thesis, "All therapists are jerks," behind and arrive at the synthesis "Some therapists are jerks," or, better yet, "Sometimes, therapists can be jerks."

Borderline Personality Disorder

Gunderson (1984) characterizes clients presenting BPD in the following manner: Borderlines often (a) engage in intense unstable personal relationships, (b) enact manipulative suicide attempts (Linehan doesn't like the term "manipulative," as it perpetuates a negative sense of self, which is part of the client's presenting problem), (c) present an unstable sense of self, (d) present a highly negative affect (angry, bitter, demanding, sarcastic, etc.), (e) exhibit a high degree of impulsivity, and (f) underachieve.

Linehan (1993) approaches BPD as a case of "dialectical failure," and divides this failure into three categories. First, she observes that borderline individuals frequently vacillate between rigidly held yet contradictory points of view (thesis-antithesis) which they are unable to successfully resolve (synthesize). This rigid cognitive style limits their ability to consider thoughts that might lead to change and growth, resulting in feelings of being in an interminable painful situation. For example, a borderline typically has trouble assessing him or herself as being either a "good" or "bad" person. If there is one iota of what is considered "bad" located within the self, then one cannot possibly be "good." Such is the borderline's painful dilemma. This dichotomous thinking is called "splitting" in the psychoanalytic community. Linehan understands the borderline's splitting dialectically, framing it as the client's tendency to get stuck in either the thesis or antithesis, unable to move towards synthesis. The resolution is brought about in mental health counseling and therapy by recognizing the polarities, entertaining the paradoxical notions that one can be both "bad" and "good," and can even be neither "bad" nor "good." Accepting these paradoxical possibilities, the borderline individual has a better chance of transcending the conflict.

The second instance of dialectical failure occurs in regards to identity. Borderline individuals fail to experience themselves as essentially related with others. They also fail to experience the relationship of the moment as comparable to previous relationships. It is as if they are trapped in an existential vacuum, isolated from knowledge of the past, or hope for the future. The borderline's identity is defined by the singular relationship of the moment and changes with each new relationship, creating a prolonged instability of identity. For a borderline individual, another person's anger is not buffered by other relationships (community) or by other points in time when this person is not angry with him or her. That person's anger becomes "infinite reality" to the borderline individual. Recovering this sense of essential relatedness and recovering (re-constructing) a memory of other relations becomes a crucial part of treatment.

The third example of dialectical failure relates to interpersonal isolation and alienation. Isolation, alienation, feelings of being out of contact or not fitting in—all characteristics of borderline individuals—are dialectical failures resulting from the construction of a self/other opposition. Borderlines often seek a sense of unity and integration by suppressing the development of self-identity (beliefs, desires, attitudes, etc.), rather than by the dialectical strategy of synthesis and transcendence. The borderline individual tenaciously maintains the opposition between person (part) and environment (whole), and in doing so fails to nurture personal growth and development.

The etiology of BPD is understood in the light of bio-social theory. According to Linehan, BPD forms within an emotionally vulnerable individual. Linehan proposes that being emotionallyvulnerable is directly related to the biological constitution of the individual. Her theory proposes that the borderline individual has an autonomic nervous system that reacts excessively to low levels of stress and takes longer to return to normal functioning once the stress has been removed. Emotional vulnerability alone does not necessitate the development of BPD. In order for BPD to develop, this innate characteristic must be met with what Linehan calls an invalidating environment. This term refers to a situation in which the personal experiences and responses of the growing child are disqualified or "invalidated" by the significant others in his or her life. The child's beliefs, perceptions, and/or attitudes are not accepted as an accurate indication of "true" feelings. An invalidating environment also is characterized by a tendency to place a high value on self-control and self-reliance. Should the child fail to accomplish a certain task in accordance with the invalidating environment's standard, then the fault is attributed to the child's character and hence ... the genesis of this particular character disorder.

An emotionally vulnerable individual in a invalidating environment often fails to understand and control emotions; that is, the individual fails to acquire the skills necessary for emotional modulation. This failure in turn creates a state of emotional dysregulation within the budding personality. Emotional dysregulation is exacerbated by the invalidating environment and is the fundamental dynamic that generates the borderline personality.

The Treatment

Linehan offers eight assumptions that need to be born in mind by the MHC when helping this desperate and exasperating population.

1. Clients are doing the best that they can.
2. Clients want to improve.
3. Clients need to do better, try harder, and be more motivated to change.
4. Clients may not have caused all their own problems, but they have to solve them.
5. The lives of suicidal, borderline individuals are unbearable as they are currently being lived.
6. Clients must learn new behaviors in all relevant contexts.
7. Clients cannot fail in therapy; the therapy or the MHC fails.
8. MHCs treating borderline clients need support.

At the outset of treatment, there are several agreements that need to be made between the MHC and the client. The client needs to commit to at least one year of continuous DBT. There is an attendance agreement in which the client agrees to come to all scheduled individual therapy sessions *and* skills training "classes." There is a suicidal behaviors agreement (including parasuicidal behavior; i.e., without intent to die). The client agrees to work on reducing this behavior, recognizing that it is a primary goal of the treatment. The final agreement is the "therapy-interfering behaviors" agreement, in which the client simply agrees to work on any problems that interfere with the progress of therapy. On the other hand, the MHC signs similar agreements, guaranteeing that the MHC will make "every reasonable effort" to conduct counseling competently; that the MHC will behave ethically; that the MHC will come to every scheduled session and give the client ample warning should the MHC need to reschedule; that the MHC will respect the rights and integrity of the client; that the MHC will maintain confidentiality with the client's informed consent to consult with other involved professionals.

With these assumptions in mind and the agreements in hand, DBT is ready to begin.

Linehan insists that the success of this treatment depends upon the quality of the relationship between the MHC and the client. A strong, positive interpersonal relationship needs to be established at the outset. Because of the high rate of burnout among MHCs working with this population, support and consultation with others MHCs is an integral part of the treatment. Indeed, Linehan recommends a team approach to treatment.

(Oftentimes there is no other choice given the high rate of hospitalization among this population).

There are two core strategies to the treatment: validation and problem solving. Validation is subdivided into two types. The first type of validation affirms the wisdom, correctness, and value of the client's behavioral, emotional, and cognitive responses. The second type of validation affirms the client's inherent ability to rise above the current misery and build a life worth living. In short, validation consists of believing the client and believing in the client.

Problem solving divides into five sub-strategies of change:

1. behavioral analysis of a targeted behavioral problem;
2. performing solution analysis, in which alternative behavioral solutions are developed;
3. orienting the client to proposed treatment solutions;
4. eliciting a commitment from the client to engage in the recommended treatment procedures; and
5. applying the treatment.

The MHC relates to the client in two dialectically opposed styles. The initial mode of relating, "reciprocal communication," involves responsiveness, warmth, and genuineness on the part of the MHC. The alternative mode, "irreverent communication," is more confrontational in tone and seeks to alert the client to deal with situations where therapy seems to be stuck.

Linehan, Armstrong, Suarez, Allmon, & Heard (1991) recommend four primary modes of treatment be offered concurrently.

1. Individual out-patient psychotherapy is the primary mode of treatment and occurs at least once a week, twice a week at the outset, and during crisis periods.
2. Skills training is to be conducted in open groups once a week.
3. Supportive process group therapy is made available to the client after successful completion of skills training.
4. Telephone consultations are a vital part of DBT as they provide continuous support while the borderline individual's dysfunctional behavior patterns improve and the client learns appropriate methods for seeking help.

In terms of accountability, Linehan conducted a study comparing the effectiveness of DBT to treatment as usual (Linehan et al., 1991). The study had three main objectives:

1. To reduce the frequency of parasuicidal behavior;
2. To reduce behaviors that interfere with the progress of therapy;

3. To reduce behaviors that interfere with the client's quality of life, operationally defined as a reduction in the number of days hospitalized.

Forty-four clients meeting the DSM-III-R criteria for BPD were selected and randomly assigned either into a control group or into an experimental group. The experimental group received DBT. The control group received treatment as usual, which consisted of individual psychotherapy, inpatient hospital services or outpatient hospital services. Clients were assessed on number of parasuicide attempts *and* on spectrum of mood. These assessments were made before treatment began, 4, 8, and 12 months into treatment, and 6 and 12 months beyond the termination of the one year of treatment. It was found that at all points of assessment, the control group engaged in more parasuicidal acts than the DBT group. It also was found that clients in the DBT group were more likely to start and remain in therapy than the control group. It was found that clients in the control group had significantly more inpatient psychiatric hospitalization time than those in the DBT group. However, regarding the questionnaires accounting for mood and suicidal ideation, there were no significant differences found between the groups during the course of the treatment.

References

Gunderson, J. (1984). *Borderline personality disorder.* Washington: American Psychiatric Press.

Heard, H., & Linehan, M. (1994). Dialectical behavior therapy: An integrative approach to the treatment of borderline personality disorder. *Journal of Psychotherapy Integration, 4,* 55-82.

Keher, C., & Linehan, M. (1996). Interpersonal and emotional problem solving skills and parasuicide among women with borderline personality disorder. *Journal of Personality Disorders, 10,* 153-163.

Layden, M., Newman, C., Freeman, A., & Morse, S. (1993). *Cognitive therapy of borderline personality disorder.* Boston: Allyn and Beacon.

Linehan, M. (1993). *Cognitive behavioral treatment of borderline personality disorder.* New York: Guilford.

Linehan, M., Armstrong, H., Suarez, A., Allmon, D., & Heard, H. (1991). Cognitive behavioral treatment of chronically parasuicidal borderline patients. *Archives of General Psychiatry, 48,* 1060-1064.

Linehan, M., Tutek, D., Heard, H., & Armstrong, H. (1994). Interpersonal outcome of cognitive behavioral treatment for chronically suicidal borderline patients. *American Journal of Psychiatry, 151,* 1771-1776.

Rockland, L. (1992). *Supportive therapy for borderline patients: A psychodynamic approach.* New York: Guilford.

Shearin, E., & Linehan, M. (1992). Patient-therapist ratings and relationship to progress in dialectical behavior therapy for borderline personality disorder. *Behavior Therapy, 23,*730-741.

Waldinger, R., & Gunderson, J. (1987). *Effective psychotherapy with borderline patients.* Washington: American Psychiatric Press.

David C. Jones is a graduate student at the University of North Carolina at Greensboro.

CHAPTER SEVENTEEN

Stress Counseling in Mental Health Practice

John Wagenaar and Jan La Forge

Overview

Stress has been postulated to be a major factor in personal health and well-being. However, our ideas about stress remain vague and unclear. This chapter summarizes basic trends in the literature and outlines practical clinical consequences for counselors. The goal is to introduce rationality into treatment of stress, which is the aim of psychological science.

There have been two basic trends in stress counseling therapy: The first involves the simplistic approach of a reputed "miracle cure" (Roskies, 1983). The basic example here is the universal application of relaxation therapy in the form of biofeedback for a wide range of stress-related conditions, including headache, gastrointestinal distress, hypertension, insomnia, cardiovascular problems, Raynaud's disease, dental problems, hyperactivity, anxiety, phobic reactions, Type A behaviors, and physiological tension.

Of course, there *is* no panacea. Relaxation will neither resolve difficult situations, remedy interpersonal conundrums, nor cure arcane physiological disorders; good nutrition, exercise, and basic satisfaction with life are far more crucial for general health. Moreover, a growing body of research has; (a) questioned the rationale for biofeedback therapy; (b) noted that very simple relaxation methods, preferable on a cost-benefit basis, work as well as biofeedback or hypnosis; and (c) concluded that biofeedback relaxation therapy only works within the context of a total effective therapy program, which suggests that placebo may be the crucial therapeutic agent.

At the other extreme of simplistic relaxation applications are those which are portrayed as eclectic, employing a range of complex assessment procedures without empirical foundation, and favoring comprehensive multivariate approaches for multifaceted problems. Such eclecticism lacks a rational basis for constructing a particular therapeutic program, or it needs a justification of procedures based on the battery of assessment techniques employed. Such complex interventions may, perhaps, be better characterized by a kind of "grab-bag" mentality, apparently rationalized on the assumption that "each case is different" and "something might work."

The challenge for stress counselors in the midst of these two popular mindsets is to become more knowledgeable about what they do and why. A good way to begin is to focus on being as clear and as effective as possible in therapeutic work. Today we know that more psychotherapy is not always better, and that, on balance, simpler procedures are preferable to more complex ones. The professional commitment to counseling means that the counselor can articulate a rational intervention strategy based on explicitly stated models of coping with stress according to the durable findings of the literature, and the counselor can argue the merits of an approach in terms of efficacy of results on a cost-benefit basis. This will become increasingly important for counselors in this era of professional accountability and financial constraints.

The Constructionalist Orientation

While medicine focuses on the diagnosis of disease and relieving suffering, professional mental health counselors teach people to cope effectively with the more or less normal stresses and strains of life. This constitutes a fundamental difference between psychiatric and instructional models for counseling practice. While the stress literature remains by and large preoccupied with the failure of the pathological model, a constructional approach focuses on identifying client strengths to help solve problems and to achieve personal goals (Antonovsky, 1987; Goldiamond, 1975). We learn far more from how people cope than from their failures. This means that counselors who wish to offer the greatest therapeutic effect must focus on "the individual life story" rather than rely on standardized assessment and treatment protocols.

A Stress Theory Review

There have been three major developments in the history of stress theory: Selye's work on the physiological stress response system served as a paradigm for a generation of stress researchers. Both the Holmes-Rahe Life Events and Lazarus' Hassle scales are based on an objective environmental approach. They assessed the nature of stress in terms of required life change or persistent daily problems.

However, as it became apparent that not everyone responded in the same way to a given situation, researchers increasingly focused on how people interpret their situation rather than on how they view the environment as such. Some people respond well to change; others become more vulnerable. The key question is whether they believe they can cope. Researchers concluded that a much better predictor of health or illness than life events or hassles per se is whether someone goes through a stage of "giving up."

Recently, mental health researchers have begun to focus on the protective function of personal belief systems, especially evident in tragic situations such as a death in the family, terminal illness, or the Oklahoma City Bombing, which often cannot be resolved through problem-solving or rational thinking. Here we must acknowledge the adaptive function of defensive mechanisms and personal values in the face of obvious vulnerability we all feel in response to the crises of the real world.

Stress Counseling Practice

The voluminous stress-coping literature falls into the three major domains of problem solving, cognitive reappraisal, and relaxation training. Because strategies for resolving stressors are more effective than strategies for tolerating them, the counselor should begin with a step-by-step problem-solving approach using behavioral analysis and social skills training. For example, can the client learn to express emotions appropriately to co-workers and spouse to enhance social support patterns? Can the client learn to manage time effectively or control spending?

However, some situations cannot be changed. Therefore, it is necessary to consider ways to facilitate positive change in the client's *construal of his or her situation* to produce adaptive problem-solving styles that enable effective coping responses. The aim is to increase the client's sense that she or he can manage. Basic strategies developed by Bandura, Ellis, Beck, and Michenbaum include refuting *irrational thinking* patterns, counter-acting *negative thinking styles*, or *positive coping imagery training.*

If problem-solving and reappraisal methods fail, try relaxation for emotional control. However, beware of indiscriminate application: The client who cannot get along with people would likely benefit little from a relaxation program. Keep in mind that relaxation constitutes mere symptomatic relief in contrast to problem-solving or reconstruing the stressor. Research shows that relaxation benefits are usually temporary and limited to the period of actual practice.

Finally, the life perspective modality which is related to both cognitions and coping responses in the redesign of psychological and behavioral environments is far more resistant to change. This is why the counselor is advised to assess this existential domain, helping the client make sense of life, only after having found behavior analysis, reappraisal, and relaxation ineffective in resolving the stressor. Does the client believe himself or herself to be victimized by life on the one hand, or to have total mastery over life on the other? Both are extreme defensive personal beliefs, expressed in the popular self-help literature of our time, which may lead ultimately to demoralization. The more balanced one's coping life philosophy is, the stronger the conviction than one is a *co-creator* of one's destiny (Burt, 1984).

Conclusion

Counselors must resist simplistic treatment fads for a diverse array of problems, and they must also avoid esotericism in their work under the flag of "eclecticism." This article outlines primary domains in a sequence of interventions according to the logic in the stress-coping literature summarized above: If problem-solving and environmental change using behavioral analysis works, therapy ceases; if not, then try cognitive reconstrual. If this works, therapy ceases; if not, try relaxation, *if* it appears the client may benefit. Finally, if relaxation fails, try the existential perspective to assess whether the client is entertaining a maladaptive philosophy of life based on victimization or absolute mastery beliefs. If there is no discernible progress at this point, recycle through the sequence once again.

The goal is to produce maximum significant results with minimal intervention and to unambiguously demonstrate a cost-effective basis of counseling interventions for stress problems. Increasingly, this will become the challenge for stress-reduction counselors in this third-party payer environment.

References

Antonovsky, A. (1987). *Unraveling the mystery of health: How people manage stress and stay well.* San Francisco, CA: Jossey-Bass.

Burt, J. J. (1984). Metahealth: A challenge for the future. In J. D. Matarazzo, S.M. Weis, J.A. Herd, N.E. Miller, & S.M. Weiss (Eds.), *Behavioral health: A handbook of health enhancement and disease prevention* (pp. 1239-1245). New York: Wiley.

Goldiamond, I. (1975). Toward a constructional approach to social problems. In C. M. Franks & G. T. Wilson (Eds.), *Annual Review of Behavior Therapy and Practice , Vol 3.* New York: Brunner Mazel.

Roskies, E. (1983). Stress management: Averting the evil eye. *Contemporary Psychology, 28*(7), 542-544.

Wagenaar, J. & La Forge, J. (1994). Stress counseling theory and practice: A cautionary review. *Journal of Counseling and Development, 73*(1), 23-31.

John Wagenaar, Ph.D., LPC, Health Counseling Associates, Yellow Springs, Ohio.

Jan La Forge, Ph.D., LPC, CRC, is Associate Professor and Chair, Department of Human Services, Wright State University.

CHAPTER EIGHTEEN

Mental Health Counseling with Adult Survivors of Childhood Sexual Abuse

Quinn M. Pearson

Given the prevalence of sexual abuse in our society, mental health practitioners are faced with adult clients who were sexually abused as children. Estimates among adults who were sexually abused before age 18 range from 25% (Joy, 1987) to 38% for women and 3% to 31% for men (Finkelhor et al., 1986). Many experts (e.g., Roland, 1993) have contended that these estimates may under-represent the actual cases. Therefore, mental health counselors who feel unprepared to work with survivors will likely see clients who disclose a history of sexual abuse only after a strong therapeutic alliance has been established. Such a situation is best avoided through adequate preparation to work with survivors, whether or not one chooses it as a specialty.

A critical aspect of preparing to work with survivors is recognizing common symptoms associated with a history of sexual abuse. Not only is depression the most common symptom, but suicidal and self-destructive tendencies tend to be more pronounced in survivors than in depressed nonabused individuals (Browne & Finkelhor, 1986). Distinguishing survivors from other clients who suffer from anxiety and depression is a crucial therapeutic task because many survivors do not connect the abuse to their current problems and, therefore, fail to report it. To help practitioners more readily identify problems commonly presented by sexual-abuse survivors, Ratican (1992) delineated symptoms that tend to be indicative of a sexual-abuse history. These indications include, but are not limited to the following: (a) suicidal thoughts or attempts, (b) frequent feelings of anger/rage for no apparent reason, (c) phobias (especially fear of dark/being alone), (d) fear of intimacy, (e) sexual dysfunction, (f) sexual abuse of others, (g) flashbacks or dissociation during sex, (h) amnesia for parts of childhood, (i) dissociative personalities, and (j) compulsive behaviors (i.e., eating disorders, substance abuse, sexual compulsions).

Discussion

Given the potential severity and variety of symptoms commonly associated with sexual abuse, the brevity of this chapter allows for only a cursory review of relevant counseling strategies. As such, several treatment factors are highlighted. They include facilitating disclosure, addressing ethical considerations, establishing the therapeutic atmosphere, releasing repressed memories and feelings, dealing with intrusive symptoms, and developing life-skills.

Facilitating disclosure of the abuse is often the first step in treatment because many survivors enter counseling for the problems caused by the abuse rather than for the abuse itself (Courtois, 1988). Repression, guilt, shame, and negative reactions to previous disclosures may contribute to clients' reluctance to disclose. Additionally, they may not realize or admit that current difficulties are directly related to the abuse. To facilitate disclosure, Josephson and Fong-Beyette (1987) suggested that counselors ask about sexual abuse directly or indirectly as a matter of routine or that they point out that clients' symptoms are common to sexual abuse survivors.

Once a history of sexual abuse has been established, mental health counselors are often faced with numerous ethical dilemmas (Daniluk & Haverkamp, 1993). Most of these considerations center around counselor competence, limits of confidentiality, and risks associated with treatment options and clients' decisions. Daniluk and Haverkamp assert that counselor competence should be assured through adequate preparation and supervision, as well as continuing education and consultation. In terms of the limits to confidentiality, they suggested that counselors warn clients of situations in which counselors are obligated to breach confidentiality, before such ethical dilemmas actually arise. Clients need to be warned, for instance, that confidentiality may not apply when the perpetrator poses a current danger to others. Additionally, clients also should be informed of the likely emotional consequences and/or legal ramifications of specific counseling interventions.

When establishing the therapeutic environment, counselors are urged to take a trauma-based approach. As children, survivors often learned that the world is an unsafe place in which they are powerless. For incest survivors, their ability to trust is often shattered because they were hurt by those that they loved and depended upon the most. In a trauma-based approach clients are given control over the pace and direction of therapeutic interventions. While promoting client autonomy and independence, mental health counselors create an environment of safety by setting boundaries and "behaving in ways that clients perceive as accepting, validating, encouraging, and knowledgeable" (Josephson & Fong-Beyette, 1987, p. 478). Finally, current symptoms are viewed as trauma-based rather than client-based. Many survivors fail to connect current problems to the abuse and instead blame themselves. By helping them to conceptualize current symptoms as direct effects either of the abuse or of old strategies developed to cope with the abuse, survivors can begin to confront the abuse directly and with less shame.

Confronting the abuse directly is an essential part of therapy and often involves helping survivors access repressed memories and feelings. Because of the pain associated with the specifics of the abuse, many survivors either have difficulty recalling the abuse or are reluctant to dredge up feelings associated with vivid memories. Guided imagery and concrete reconstructions of physical surroundings and/or events from childhood (i.e., drawing a house or a neighborhood) have been effective in accessing blocked memories and feelings (Roland, 1993). Similarly, hypnotherapy is another technique used to uncover memories, but Calof (1993) cautioned practitioners to warn survivors that if they decide to take legal action against the perpetrator, the use of hypnosis may preclude them from testifying.

Even when memories are not blocked, survivors tend to have difficulty either expressing repressed feelings or managing intense feelings. It is not uncommon for survivors to vacillate between numbness and emotional flooding. On the one hand, several techniques can be useful for helping clients experience and work through abuse-related emotions. These techniques include role-playing, empty-chair, psychodrama, letter writing, journaling, guided imagery, drawing, and inner child work (Pearson, 1994). On the other hand, once intense emotions do begin to surface, survivors may feel overwhelmed and out of control. In instances where clients become suicidal or in other ways self-injurious, crisis intervention is necessary

(Courtois, 1988). Other techniques used for helping survivors cope with emotional flooding, flashbacks, or other intrusive symptoms include the following: grounding techniques, grief work, stress inoculation training, relaxation training, guided imagery, anger management, and dosing exposure to painful stimuli in tolerable increments. Therefore, to facilitate the exploration of and management of abuse-related feelings, counselors need to balance expressive and containment techniques to avoid re-traumatizing the client.

As survivors begin to integrate these emotions, as they start to recognize current problems as related to the abuse, and as they place responsibility for the abuse on the perpetrator(s), they often need assistance in rebuilding their lives and relationships. Because many survivors feel little sense of control and power in their lives, training in problem-solving and decision-making may be indicated. Additionally, Norris (1986) recommended that mental health counselors train survivors in several other areas: communication, social skills, parenting, assertiveness, and anger control.

Conclusion

In summary, the widespread incidence of sexual abuse almost guarantees that mental health counselors who work with adults will see survivors in their practices. Because many adult clients do not readily disclose childhood sexual abuse, counselors need to know enough about the common symptoms in order to facilitate disclosure. For practitioners who plan to provide further interventions, several treatment considerations were introduced. Counselors should be alert to the unique challenges of assisting adult survivors through the healing process and should seek ongoing specialized training, supervision, and/or consultation.

References

Browne, A., & Finkelhor, D. (1986). Impact of child sexual abuse: A review of the research. *Psychological Bulletin, 99*(1), 66-77.

Calof, D. (1993). Facing the truth about false memory. *The Family Therapy Networker, 17,* 38-45.

Courtois, C. A. (1988). *Healing the incest wound: Adult survivors in therapy.* New York: W. W. Norton.

Daniluk, J. C., & Haverkamp, B. E. (1993). Ethical issues in counseling adult survivors of incest. *Journal of Counseling and Development, 72,* 16-22.

Finkelhor, D., Araji, S., Baron, L., Browne, A., Peters, S. D., & Wyatt, G. E. (1986), *Sourcebook on child sexual abuse.* Newbury Park, CA: Sage.

Josephson, G. S., & Fong-Beyette, M. L. (1987). Factors assisting female clients' disclosure of incest during counseling. *Journal of Counseling and Development, 65,* 475478.

Joy, S. (1987). Retrospective presentations of incest: Treatment strategies for use with adult women. *Journal of Counseling and Development, 65,* 317-319.

Norris, T. L. (1986). *Victim therapy with adult survivors of child sexual abuse* (Report No. CG020400). Paper presented at the annual conference of the American Association for Marriage and Family Therapy, Orlando, FL. (ERIC Document Reproduction Service No. ED 289 133)

Pearson, Q. M. (1994). Treatment techniques for adult female survivors of childhood sexual abuse. *Journal of Counseling and Development, 73,* 32-37.

Ratican, K. (1992). Sexual abuse survivors: Identifying symptoms and special treatment considerations.*Journal of Counseling and Development, 71,* 33-38.

Roland, C. B. (1993). Exploring childhood memories with adult survivors of sexual abuse: Concrete reconstruction and visualization techniques. *Journal of Mental Health Counseling, 15,* 363-372.

Quinn M. Pearson, Ph.D., is an Assistant Professor at the University of North Alabama who specializes in working with adults and adolescents.

CHAPTER NINETEEN

Four-Phase Mediation for the Victim/Offender Treatment Process

Linda H. Mortenson

Victim-offender mediation illustrates the emerging and alternative paradigm of restorative justice, which addresses the needs of the victim, offender, and community. The traditional, retributive model of justice emphasizes punishing the offender for violating the rules of society. Restorative justice, by comparison, gives offenders the opportunity to take responsibility for their actions and to make concrete and symbolic amends to the victim. Victims become actively involved in the process of justice, and the emphasis is on the restoration of emotional and material losses. Victim-offender mediation fills the void that exclusive concerns with guilt and punishment in the criminal justice system creates, a void exacerbated by the failure to address the interpersonal needs resulting from the violation of crime. It also offers challenging and exciting opportunities for MHCs to apply their skills and serve their clients in an expanding field.

Victim-offender mediation employs a four-phase process: intake, preparation, mediation, and follow-up (Umbreit, 1993, Umbreit & Coates, 1993). The intake phase begins with a court referral of the offender. Though a formal admission of guilt has been entered with the court in most cases, some cases are referred before there is a formal admission of guilt as part of a deferred prosecution effort.

During the second phase, preparation for mediation, the assigned mediator meets separately with the offender and victim. In these individual sessions, the mediator listens to the story of each party, explains the program, and encourages participation. Usually, the mediator first meets with the offender, and if he or she agrees to mediation, then meets with the victim. Since mediation is meant to empower both parties by presenting them with choices, mediators encourage, but do not coerce, both parties to participate. Building trust and rapport with the offender and victim, as well as gaining valuable information, are critical to the success of the later joint meeting.

The mediation phase brings the victim and offender together. The mediator explains his or her role, the communication ground rules (for example, no interrupting of each other), and identifies the agenda. The first part of the session focuses on the facts and feelings related to the crime. Victims express their feelings directly to the offender, and receive answers to such lingering questions of "Why me? Were you stalking me and planning to come back? How did you get into our house?" Victims often experience relief in finally seeing the offender, who usually bears little resemblance to the frightening character envisioned.

Offenders are in the uncomfortable and difficult position of facing the people they violated. Yet, this is a rare opportunity to exhibit a more human dimension of their character and to express remorse in a personal manner. This open, non adversarial discussion of feelings allows both parties to relate with each other as people rather than objects or stereotypes.

The second part of the session focuses on the discussion of losses and the negotiation of a mutually acceptable restitution agreement that serves as a focal point for the offender's accountability. Though mediators do not impose a restitution settlement, in 95% of all mediations, a written restitution agreement is negotiated and signed by the victim, offender, and mediator at the end of the meeting (Umbreit, 1991). When agreements cannot be reached, the case is returned to the court for determination of restitution. These joint meetings usually last one hour, although they can be extended to two hours.

The follow-up phase consists of monitoring completion of the restitution agreement; intervening if additional conflict develops; making monthly telephone calls to the victim to monitor fulfillment of the restitution agreement; contacting the probation officer concerning compliance by the offender; if appropriate, scheduling a follow-up meeting with the victim and offender; and completing paper work to close the case.

Mediating Crimes of Severe Violence

Although not a replacement for incarceration in crimes of severe violence such as rape or murder, victim-offender mediation has an enormous potential for facilitating a greater sense of healing and closure for both victim and offender (Umbreit, 1995b). These cases are usually mediated at the request of the traumatized surviving family members. Advanced mediator training focuses less on the techniques of mediation and more on comprehending the painful process experienced by the participants. This training emphasizes how to facilitate frank and open dialogue between the two parties, the journey of grief experienced by the victim's family members, and strategies for closure and healing (Umbreit, 1996).

This process of mediation is less mediation in the traditional sense of negotiation and more a process of facilitating a dialogue between those who have been traumatized and the person responsible for the pain. According to Umbreit (1996), mediating these cases involving unimaginable loss and pain is "ultimately a spiritual journey, an opening of the heart, a process in which the involved parties help each other heal" (p. 153). With extensive preparation and coaching of the parties prior to mediation, the mediator can "tap into the reservoir of strengths in the victim and offender, despite their pain" (p. 153), encourage direct dialogue, and facilitate a healing process grounded on mutual assistance in responding to informational and emotional needs.

Umbreit (1996) identifies the paradox of forgiveness, which is critical to understanding victim-offender mediation, especially in severe violent crimes. For victims, words such as forgiveness and reconciliation are too judgmental and tend to devalue the victim's legitimate anger and rage. Too often these words trigger resistance and anger in victims. If safe and less judgmental language is used, it is likely that elements of forgiveness and perhaps reconciliation will result spontaneously. But these results must emerge as a natural by-product of the mediation process. "Therein lies the paradox: the more one talks about forgiveness and reconciliation while encouraging parties to participate, the less likely it is that victims will participate and have the opportunity to experience elements of forgiveness and reconciliation" (Umbreit, 1996, p. 154).

Victim-offender mediation enriches the alternatives available to victims, offenders, and the community when dealing with the ravages of crime. Mediation helps to integrate the offender back into the community. The offender is treated with respect, is able to tell his or her own truth, and negotiates an agreement of reparation with the victim. Because the offender listens and is listened to by the victim, the interpersonal connection creates a bond with the community. In contrast, when treated with lack of respect as inferior and not fit to live within the community, offenders carry a stigma which continues to separate them from others. If a person is not accepted by the community, there is little incentive to follow its rules. Mediation provides the vehicle for offenders to redress their wrongs and make a positive connection and contribution to society (Joseph, 1996).

Research confirms high levels of client satisfaction with mediation, as well as perceptions of fairness for both victims and offenders. Although the possibility of receiving restitution motivates victims to enter mediation, meeting the offender and being able to talk about what happened proves to be more satisfying than receiving restitution. Mediation humanizes the criminal justice experience for both victims and offenders. Fear among victims is significantly reduced, restitution completion rates are higher, and future criminal behavior is reduced with victim-offender mediation (Coates & Gehm, 1989; Galaway, 1988, 1989; Gehm, 1990; Marshall & Merry, 1990; Umbreit, 1991, 1994, 1996; Umbreit & Coates, 1993).

Implications for Mental Health Counselors

Victim-offender mediation offers two significant contributions to the discipline of counseling. First, expanded professional opportunities are available to MHCs wanting to broaden their skills and services. MHCs interested in entering this type of mediation naturally bring many of the necessary skills for effective victim-offender mediation. Second, by examining one's personal concept of justice and questioning the influence of the inherent cultural bias toward retributive justice, MHCs can expand their concept of justice to include the facilitative characteristics of restorative justice.

In the growing field of mediation, therapists are often shouldered aside by lawyers whose claim to technical experience in legal issues gives them a distinct advantage. This has been the case, for example, in the field of divorce mediation. The field of victim-offender mediation, however, rightfully belongs to therapists. This endeavor does not involve legal or technical issues. However, it does call forth all the MHCs' skills in managing complex emotional processes. Both the victim and the offender are emotionally needy and require the insight and interventions of an informed and experienced therapist. Not only must each party be supported, but an interaction between the two that could easily go awry must be firmly orchestrated and managed. This is no place for amateurs. It is a field in which only the more skilled MHCs should consider practice. It also is a field that could grow to significance and offer new and challenging opportunities for therapists to expand their professional horizons.

The second contribution of victim-offender mediation is found in the challenge to MHCs to examine their personal concepts of justice. Retributive justice addresses the legitimate needs of the society to enforce its rules through punishment and deterrence and to protect its safety needs by incapacitating dangerous offenders. It leaves a void, however, in addressing the interpersonal damage of crime, a void that can be redressed by the therapeutic profession.

Conclusion

Comparing the concepts of retributive and restorative justice in the context of victim-offender mediation breaks the constraints inherent in the retributive paradigm. Such comparison reveals the capacity of the restorative justice paradigm to expand and enhance the opportunities for creating communication and acceptance of responsibility, and to facilitate healing. Virginia Satir regarded "authentic human connection as a fundamental to change processes" (Umbreit, 1996, p. 209). Victim-offender mediation creates for victims of crime an opportunity to talk, connect, grow, and heal.

Note: Information, books, and materials about victim-offender mediation are available through the Center for Restorative Justice and Mediation. Courses and training opportunities in victim-offender mediation also are offered through the Center. Requests should be addressed to:

Center for Restorative Justice and Mediation
School of Social Work
University of Minnesota
386 McNeal Hall - 1985 Buford Avenue
St. Paul, MN 55108
(612) 624-4923, FAX (612) 625-4288
e-mail: CTR4JM@CHE2.CHE.UMN.EDU

The author expresses appreciation to J. Scott Hinkle, Ph.D., and to Sam Margulies, J.D., Ph.D. for their editorial comments.

References

Bazemore, G. (1994). Developing a victim orientation for community corrections: A restorative justice paradigm and a balanced mission. Special Issue, American Probation and Parole Association. *Perspectives,* 19-24.

Coates, R. B., & Gehm, J. (1989). Victim meets offender: An evaluation of victim-offender reconciliation programs. In M. Wright & B. Galaway (Eds.), *Mediation and criminal justice* (pp. 251-263). London: Sage.

Galaway, B. (1988). Crime victim and offender mediation as a social work strategy. *Social Service Review, 62,* 668-683.

Galaway, B. (1989). Informal justice: Mediation between offenders and victims. In P. A. Albrecht & O. Backes, (Eds.), *Crime prevention and intervention: Legal and ethical problems* (pp. 332-348). Berlin: de Gruyter.

Gehm, J. (1990). Mediated victim-offender restitution agreements: An exploratory analysis of factors related to victim participation. In J. Hudson & B. Galaway (Eds.), *Criminal justice, restitution, and reconciliation* (pp. 177-182). Monsey, NY: Criminal Justice Press.

Joseph, K. L. (1996). Victim-offender mediation: What social and political factors will affect its development? *Ohio State Journal on Dispute Resolution, 11* (1), 207-225.

Marshall, T. F., & Merry, S. (1990). *Crime and accountability: Victim offender mediation in practice.* London: Home Office.

Umbreit, M. S. (1989). Victims seeking fairness, not revenge: Toward restorative justice. *Federal Probation, 53* (3), 52-57.

Umbreit, M. S. (1991, July). Having offenders meet with their victims can benefit both parties. *Corrections Today,* 164-166.

Umbreit, M. S. (1993). Crime victims and offenders in mediation: An emerging area of social work practice. *Social Work, 38,* 69-73.

Umbreit, M. S., (1994). *Victim meets offender: The impact of restorative justice and mediation.* Monsey, NY: Criminal Justice Press.

Umbreit, M. S. (1995a). The development and impact of victim-offender mediation in the United States. In J. Mika (Ed.), *Mediation Quarterly, 12* (3), 263-276.

Umbreit, M. S. (1995b, Winter). Mediating homicide cases. *Interaction,* 7-10.

Umbreit, M. S. (1996). *Mediating interpersonal conflicts: A pathway to peace.* West Concord, MN: CPI Publishing.

Umbreit, M.S., & Coates, R. B. (1993). Cross-site analysis of victim-offender mediation in four states. *Crime and Delinquency, 39* (4), 565-585.

Umbreit, M. S., & Niemeyer, M. (1996, Summer). Victim-offender mediation: From the margins toward the mainstream. *Perspectives,* 28-30.

Wright, M. (1991). *Justice for victim and offenders.* Philadelphia: Open University Press.

Zehr, H. (1985). *Retributive justice, restorative justice.* Elkhart, IN: Mennonite Central Committee Office on Criminal Justice.

Zehr, H. (1990). *Changing lenses: A new focus for criminal justice.* Scottsdale, PA: Herald Press.

Linda H. Mortenson, M.S., Ed.S. is a counselor in private practice in Greensboro, North Carolina.

CHAPTER TWENTY

Developmental Counseling for Men

Kevin R. Kelly & Alex S. Hall

Overview

Widespread discussion of gender issues by mental health professionals over the past three decades has spawned an embryonic examination of men's issues. However, the mental health needs of men have not yet become the focus of significant empirical inquiry and the practice of counseling men has outstripped our knowledge of men. The development of therapeutic skills to assist men in their efforts to change behaviors is needed. In this chapter, we will introduce the reader to the basic elements of a developmental model for counseling men (Kelly & Hall, 1992); specifically, the assumptions and counseling focus of the developmental model will be introduced in order to orient counselors to a set of constructive goals for counseling men.

A Developmental Model for Counseling Men

We advocate the adoption of a positive, developmental approach to mental health counseling with men. A developmental orientation is consistent with the goals of both the American Mental Health Counselor's Association and the American Counseling Association. There are four assumptions supporting the developmental approach. First, mental health counselors (MHCs) recognize that men need to develop latent abilities rather than being required to cure their masculinity. Male clients are given the opportunity to develop behavioral, cognitive, and affective skills that will raise their self-esteem and enable them to make more vital contributions to their families, friends, and communities. Second, MHCs recognize that men come to counseling with strengths and assets. Respect for male clients is demonstrated by viewing their skill deficits in light of their strengths. MHCs succeed in communicating their awareness of the difficulties of being a man in contemporary society. Third, MHCs understand the need for preventive interventions. Greater efforts are needed to develop men's psychological and behavioral skills in the educational and recreational institutions in which men participate. For instance, MHCs and high school counselors can work together to teach parenting skills to young men in health and home economics classes. Finally, MHCs do not blame men for their reluctance to participate in mental health counseling. Rather than seeing men as resistant to counseling, the lack of male participation in counseling is attributed to a failure on the part of the counseling profession to invite and welcome men to counseling and arises from a lack of value in the counseling that is provided.

Focus Areas for Developmental Counseling for Men

Using this developmental perspective, the focus of the counselors shifts from the individual in isolation to the individual in the context of family, cultural, and work systems. MHCs are aware that problematic male behaviors cannot be fully understood apart from a systemic perspective. Consider, for example, the man who is over-involved in work. From a pathology perspective, the man is selfishly indulging in career pursuits for his own gratification and he denies support and affection to his wife and children. From the systemic perspective, the man can be seen as attempting to provide emotional support for his family by being a good economic provider; or, he may be fulfilling an intergenerational legacy and is striving to bring honor or vindication to his family of origin through outstanding career achievement. The fact that the man is not providing sufficient emotional sustenance to his family does not change with the systemic perspective. However, effective behavior change interventions cannot be implemented until we understand the complex of factors that motivate male behavior. From the systemic perspective, counselors also become more receptive to hearing and identifying the abuse and childhood victimization their male clients may have experienced. This understanding moves conceptualization of the problem and treatment strategy from the individual to the family system. The systemic perspective necessitates change by all family-system members, not solely by the male client.

Respect and appreciation of the strengths and assets of men can be demonstrated when MHCs refrain from the use of negative descriptors of men and male behavior. For example, mental health professionals commonly describe men as inexpressive. This descriptor is based on the observation of male reticence in counseling situations in which men feel defensive and misunderstood. Rather than jumping to the conclusion that the quiet male client is inexpressive, the MHC attempts to identify if the man is verbally expressive in other contexts and the extent to which the man favors nonverbal expressions of affect. MHCs recognize that a man may express affection through instrumental actions such as washing his wife's car or coaching his children's athletic teams.

The counselor takes the time to ask the man what he is trying to communicate through his actions and is aware that men may value behaviors that are labeled as problematic by others. Consider the example of inexpressiveness. Many men grew up emulating the John Wayne "strong and silent" form of masculinity and remain quiet because that is what they think is expected of them by their mates and families. Under-involvement with children is another example of men attempting to fulfill perceived expectations. Many men, both in intact marriages and following divorce, feel they are best serving the needs of their children by allowing their spouse to be the dominant emotional provider and caretaker for their children. Again we see that behaviors that appear to be negative can have positive and constructive motivations. Before attempting to set behavior change goals with men, MHCs have to be aware of the meaning of male behaviors and they must understand the strengths and skills that are demonstrated in these behaviors even if the behaviors have reached the point of diminishing returns in the family system.

MHCs also are aware that many of the problems presented by male clients could have been prevented through psychoeducational programs. In reviewing the empirical literature regarding sex differences in socialization practices, the differential training provided to boys and girls is striking. Boys are taught to be competitive, dominant, aggressive, and independent and are made aware that competing and winning in athletic contests is a requisite for manhood. Our society prepares boys for competition in the world of work and the possibility of going to war. Girls are taught to be nurturing, compliant, and oriented to the needs of others.

They are prepared to be the emotional center of their family and for the responsibility of keeping family and relationships together. Given these socialization practices, it is no surprise that extraordinary efforts have to be made by counselors to teach young women the skills necessary to succeed in the world of work.

Young women now are being taught an appropriate level of career aspiration, are being encouraged to express their potential in the occupational world, and are being shown that they can meet their material needs and the financial demands of raising children through independent employment. Parallel efforts are necessary to teach young men to raise their level of aspiration as participants in the home-world of their spouses and children. Men need to learn that they have the ability to provide for their own emotional needs and the emotional needs of others and can acquire the skills necessary to raise their level of functioning in relationships. MHCs can develop and implement these programs for boys and young men in a way that parallels the career counseling programs for young women. We recognize that men cannot be held accountable for skills that they were never taught.

Finally, counselors need to ask themselves if they enjoy and value working with men. The lack of participation in mental health counseling elicits the question: Why don't men come to counseling? Lack of participation in counseling by men has more to do with our lack of knowledge and skill than it does with flaws in men. Counselors need to experiment with different formats (e.g., shorter counseling sessions), different methods (e.g., less of a focus on affect, use of a problem-solving orientation), and different attitudes (e.g., assuming that problems are not the sole responsibility of our male clients) in order to create a counseling environment and process that is more conducive to male participation.

Conclusion

Men have the same goals as women: to participate in the world of work and the private world of home and relationships and to be appreciated and respected for their efforts in these two domains. Effective mental health counseling for men is developmental, uses a systemic perspective for interpreting individual behavior, and validates the strengths and assets of men. A developmental approach to counseling can help men attain positive-growth goals and can enhance the quality of relationships men have with their mates, children, friends, and colleagues.

References

Farrell, W. (1986). *Why men are the way they are.* New York: McGraw-Hill.

Kelly, K. R., & Hall, A. S. (1992). Toward a developmental model for counseling men. *Journal of Mental Health Counseling, 14,* 257-273.

Levant, R. F. (1990). Coping with the new father role. In D. Moore & F. Leafgren (Eds.), *Problem-solving strategies and interventions for men in conflict* (pp. 81-94). Alexandria, VA: American Association for Counseling and Development.

Macchietto, J. G. (1992). Aspects of male victimization and female aggression: Implications for counseling men. *Journal of Mental Health Counseling, 14,* 375-392.

Moore, D., & Leafgren, F. (1990). *Problem-solving strategies and interventions for men in conflict.* Alexandria, VA: American Association for Counseling and Development.

Kevin R. Kelly is an Associate Professor of Counseling and Development at Purdue University.

Alex S. Hall is an Associate Professor of Psychology at St. Joseph's College.

CHAPTER TWENTY-ONE

Counseling Teenage Parents

Mark S. Kiselica

Overview

The growing number of adolescent girls having children out of wedlock is a major social issue in the United States. Approximately two-thirds of all births to teenage girls occur out of wedlock (Moore, Snyder, & Halla, 1992). These youths are at-risk to be poor and dependent on public welfare (Vera Institute of Justice, 1990). In addition to these economic hardships, unmarried adolescent mothers and their male partners are at-risk for a host of adjustment difficulties, including failure to complete school, unemployment, inadequate parenting skills, and a variety of problems in their interpersonal relationships (see Kiselica & Pfaller, 1993). Clearly, teenage mothers and fathers can benefit from supportive counseling during the transition to parenthood. This digest highlights the role of the mental health counselor in helping this population with the developmental challenges associated with unplanned, out-of-wedlock childbearing and parenthood.

Program Development Considerations

The first task that must be achieved in helping teenage parents is to develop service programs that address the needs of this population. Teenage parents require a wide range of services: child care, transportation, child development and parenting skills training, nutritional counseling, health care for the young parents and their child; individual, couple, and family counseling; teenage parent support groups, family life education and family planning; educational and career counseling, job training and cooperative education, and legal counseling (Kiselica & Pfaller, 1993).

In order to provide these services, it is recommended that mental health counselors work cooperatively with other professionals, such as school counselors, social workers, educators, lawyers, dietitians, nurses and physicians. Interdisciplinary collaboration enables professionals to develop full-service programs that permit teenage parents to do "one-stop shopping" (Kiselica, 1995).

While mental health counselors work with other professionals to develop teenage parent programs, it is important that the needs of adolescent fathers are not ignored (Kiselica, Stroud, Stroud,and Rotzien, 1992). Historically, service programs for teenage parents have neglected to include assistance for young fathers in spite of the fact that research on adolescent fathers indicates that they express an interest in receiving help with the demands of unplanned paternity (Kiselica & Sturmer, 1993). By including services for teenage fathers in teenage parenting programs, mental health counselors will promote responsible paternal behaviors and will enhance the experience of fatherhood for young men.

Pregnancy-Resolution Counseling

Expectant teenage parents require crisis-oriented, decision-making counseling to assist them in resolving the pregnancy. Throughout this process, the pros and cons of each of the possible options for resolving the pregnancy (i.e., abortion, adoption, marriage, and single-parenthood), must be reviewed. In reviewing each of these options, mental health counselors must be careful not to impose their own values on the couple. Instead, the counselor's role is to help the clients to define their values as they relate to each of the pregnancy-resolution options and to estimate the likelihood that any particular option is feasible.

When possible, the parents of the teenagers should be included in this process to ascertain the potential sources of influence and support the family might provide during the crisis; for example, in some families, strong religious prohibitions against abortion may preclude the termination of the pregnancy as an option. In other families, the provision of financial assistance to the young couple might make marriage a viable option. By working with the families of the parents during this period of crisis, the stage is set for engaging the family in long-term counseling.

Family Counseling

An unplanned, out-of-wedlock pregnancy occurs within the contexts of two existing families. The news of the pregnancy usually sends shock waves throughout both families. Besides helping the families to resolve this crisis, mental health counselors must help both the family of the mother and that of the father to establish a new homeostasis after the pregnancy is resolved. If the decision has been made to abort or place the baby for adoption, one or both families may need supportive counseling to help them mourn the loss of the baby. If the couple decides to keep the baby, the family needs assistance in negotiating whether of not the couple will marry, where the young parents will live, how they will support themselves, who will care for the baby, and what the teenage parents will do regarding school and/or work. Throughout the process of settling these issues, new family boundaries must be defined and old, unresolved issues among family members may resurface. Thus, the mental health counselor must help the family to attend both to the present practical needs of the family (e.g., who will care for the baby at which time of day) and to ongoing family conflicts (e.g., preexisting resentment between parent and child that might be exacerbated in the wake of the unplanned pregnancy). By addressing these many issues, the mental health counselor will remove obstacles that might prevent the family from maximally enjoying the new baby (Kiselica, 1995).

Preparation for Parenthood

Caring for the new baby is the most important responsibility that teenage parents face. Because adolescents tend to have inadequate knowledge of child development, parenting skills training is essential. This training should include information about infant and child development, proper parenting behaviors, and actual practice at caring for young children. In addition, it is recommended that expectant, young mothers participate in peer discussion groups to clarify their attitudes and feelings regarding femininity and motherhood, while expectant, adolescent fathers clarify their views on masculinity and fatherhood. Also, preparation for the childbirth process is recommended to help allay the fears of the expectant parents regarding childbirth and to help each parent to regard the other as a vital source of support (Kiselica, 1995).

Educational and Career Counseling

Kiselica and Murphy (1994) observed that educational and career counseling with teenage parents consists of two phases. During the prenatal phase, counseling is crisis oriented and focused on helping the teen parent to make immediate decisions regarding school and work. Because many teenage parents drop out of school subsequent to the pregnancy, the mental health counselor should instruct the client to carefully weigh all of the alternatives and consequences associated with such an action before dropping out. During the postnatal phase, the mental health counselor assists the client to develop long-term educational and career plans. The goal during this phase of counseling is to prevent the young adult from experiencing premature career foreclosure. Specifically, the mental health counselor helps the youth to clarify his or her career self-concept, to become aware of occupational options and their associated training requirements, and to develop long-term plans for fulfilling his or her career aspirations while meeting the demands of parenthood.

Conclusion

Facing an unplanned, out-of-wedlock pregnancy in conjunction with the demands of adolescent development, is an extremely stressful challenge for expectant teenage parents. By working with other professionals to develop full-service parenting programs, mental health counselors will be in a position to identify, recruit, and engage teenage parents in counseling to resolve the pregnancy, to address family issues, to prepare for parenthood, and to plan for fulfilling careers. Most importantly, these efforts will help young parents to enjoy one of life's most meaningful endeavors: responsibly and lovingly caring for a child.

References

Kiselica, M. S. (1995). *Multicultural counseling with teenage fathers: A practical guide.* Newbury Park, CA: Sage.

Kiselica, M. S., & Murphy, D. K. (1994). Developmental career counseling with teenage parents. *Career Development Quarterly, 42,*238 - 244.

Kiselica, M. S., & Pfaller, J. (1993). Helping teenage parents: The independent and collaborative roles of school counselors and counselor educators. *Journal of Counseling and Development, 72,* 42 - 48.

Kiselica, M. S., Stroud, J. C., Stroud, J. E., & Rotzien, A. (1992). Counseling the forgotten client: The teen father. *Journal of Mental Health Counseling, 14, 338* -350.

Kiselica, M. S., & Sturmer, P. (1993). Is society giving teenage fathers a mixed message? *Youth and Society, 24,* 487 - 501.

Moore, K. A., Snyder, N., & Halla, C. (1992). *Facts at a glance.* Washington, DC: Child Trends, Inc.

Vera Institute of Justice (1990). *The male role in teenage pregnancy and parenting: New directions of public policy.* New York: Author.

Mark S. Kiselica is an Associate Professor in the Department of Counseling and Personnel Services at Trenton State College, Trenton, New Jersey.

CHAPTER TWENTY–TWO

Sports Counseling: Helping Student Athletes

J. Scott Hinkle

During the past ten years there has been a dramatic increase in interest and participation in sports at the collegiate, as well as professional and leisure levels. The 1970s and 1980s have brought increased commercialization of sports. Despite the involvement of sanctioning bodies, countless student athletes are suffering from exploitation, personal excesses, and abuse including drugs and alcohol, as well as exhibiting various psychosocial problems. Approximately ten percent of American college athletes suffer from problems appropriate for counseling. At the collegiate level, many sports programs have become expensive preparatory programs for professional teams. Rarely a day passes without a news report of a student athlete in some type of psychosocio-behavioral difficulty directly or indirectly associated with sports performance. Student athletes are subject to emotional difficulties as a function of sports participation. Anxiety resulting from the threat of evaluation by others, lack of self-confidence, and unreasonable expectations from coaches and fans are but a few of the problems experienced by student athletes. Educational, developmental, and remedial programs are needed for student-athletes. Such programs are not available to all who need them, and programs which include any form of counseling are especially limited.

Counseling Athletes

Referral to sports counselors is becoming more common, resulting in a demand for counseling professionals sensitive to interventions for student athletes. Since sports psychologists focus on performance and coaches typically have physical education training, neither are qualified or prepared to work with individuals' psycho-emotional difficulties. Counseling professionals are needed to address the psycho-emotional needs of the student athletes.

Counselors are well prepared for the provision of educational and clinical services designed for student athletes, including lifestyle consultation, developmental programming, career development, and stress management. Direct performance enhancement per se may be out of the realm of most counselors' training. This area is typically best handled by sports psychologists or psychologists with motivational sports training. This is not to imply, however, that counselors' involvement with athletes does not enhance performance. Such enhancement is often indirect and as a result in improvements in areas associated with the counseling process. For example, a student athlete who overcomes a drug problem as a result of counseling will likely improve relative sport performance. The optimal sports counselor should be familiar with the sport. However, the counselor's interest in sport should not inhibit the helping process. The counselor should not neglect the individual for the sake of sports performance or the organization/team for which the student athlete performs.

In contrast to sports psychology, sports counseling's focus is on the athlete's development as an individual, including personal and clinical issues associated with sport performance. For example, sports counseling assists student athletes with reducing stress and anxiety, overcoming fear of failure and success, and burn-out. It also addresses interpersonal issues such as family and marital difficulty. In addition, counseling can assist with problem prevention, coping skills, relaxation training, decision-making, life management and career planning, therapeutic strategies, and crisis intervention. Ineffective attempts to deal with stress can result in the abuse of alcohol and other drugs. Timely assessments and treatment by sports counselors can provide student athletes with educational programs and information about drugs and substance abuse treatment.

Transitional periods are particularly stressful for student athletes. For example, many high school stars make limited progress on a college team while others have trouble adjusting when their college sports careers are over. Unfortunately, some examples of such phase-of-life problems are more extreme. Athletes experiencing difficulties with transitions have been known to become clinically depressed and even suicidal. Therefore, sports counseling services sensitive to the magnitude of the effects of sports on student athletes are crucial.

Student athletes not involved in revenue sports at the collegiate level may suffer from a lack of recognition and from the disparity of the college sports system. Crew members, swimmers, runners, gymnasts, wrestlers, triathletes, and others have their share of stress and difficulties that can be alleviated by counseling. As a result, sports counselors apply methods for becoming involved with and providing services for these "least known" athletes. Many of the difficulties experienced by student athletes will not require unique counseling techniques or therapeutic competencies. However, they do require the development of theoretical models that will increase the knowledge base of sports counseling and related proactive interventions.

In addition, athletes typically are not counseled in a vacuum. Coaches, parents, and significant others can learn effective communication skills from sports counselors and how to best serve as influential role models. Coaches can also learn relationship building skills from sports counselors. Similarly, the cultural aspects of student athletes are important components of the sports counseling process.

Counseling and Athletic Diversity

As with any endeavor, diversity abounds. Counselors involved professionally with student athletes must recognize the individual and group differences that characterize the athletic population. Women and minorities may differ in their needs to participate in sports and in the issues which arise as a result of their participation. Thus, the process of sports counseling needs to respect their individual needs. Women's sports, women's coaches, male coaches on female teams, and special athletes (e.g., wheelchair) also can benefit from sports counseling services.

Minority athletes also may differ in their motivations to take part in sports. Levels of preparation for sport may differ from one ethnic or other minority group to the next. The academic needs of minority athletes may also be different. For instance, Brown (1978) has referred to the "jock trap" in which athletes become caught at the collegiate level. This trap refers to the athlete who is left without an education after the institution has used the athlete's physical abilities and eligibility. Brown adds that although all types of athletes are affected, it appears that this happens to African-American athletes more often than to others.

Career Counseling and the Student Athlete

Collegiate athletes rarely make it to the pro ranks or to the Olympics. In fact, the majority do not make it to graduation. This reflects a need for career development and life planning with student athletes in the early stages of their careers. Student athletes' career decisions are often postponed due to the intense level of commitment required by their sport participation. Sports counselors have been successful using interventions which focus on development across the lifespan. In these classes, student athletes are informed and educated about the need for awareness of difficulties that may lie ahead and are taught skills necessary for effective personal problem management. Sports counselors working with student athletes are sensitive to the need for a wide range of career information. Moreover, sports counselors help student-athletes evaluate their academic performance and its important relationship to achieving athletic goals (Lee, 1983). Planning for athletic retirement can be a frustrating experience if prior considerations for this phase of life have not been addressed. Planning for a second career and *transferring* athletic skills to life skills are important issues for most student athletes.

Conclusion

Effective models and strategies for the implementation of sports counseling are needed. Such models should include career life planning, promoting collaboration between physical educators, coaches, and sports counselors, and adopting frequently used counseling formats to sports counseling. Reality therapy, for example, has been demonstrated to be an effective therapeutic modality in sports counseling. A few counselor education programs are currently offering sports counseling courses as an area of interest (e.g., Florida State University, University of North Carolina at Greensboro, University of South Carolina, Southern Illinois University, Syracuse University, and Springfield College).

Sports counselors working with student athletes assist this population with the various aspects of personal development affected by sports performance. Counselors also educate the public about the problems of living associated with athletic involvement. As our colleges and universities continue to utilize and make demands of student athletes and as the recognition of the work performed by sports counselors grows, the need for counselors to work effectively with the psychosocial concerns of the student athlete will continue to increase.

References

Brown, R. C., Jr. (1978). The "jock trap" – How the Black athlete gets caught. In W. F. Straub (Ed.). *Sport psychology: An analysis of athlete behavior* (pp. 195-198). Ithaca, NY: Mouvement.

Chartrand, J. M., & Lent, R. W. (1987). Sports counseling: Enhancing the development of the athlete. *Journal of Counseling and Development, 66*, 164-167.

Etzel, E. F., Farrante, A. P., & Pinkney, J. W. (1991). *Counseling college student athletes: Issues and interventions.* Morganton, WV: Fitness Information Technology.

Hinkle, J. S. (in press). Integrating sport psychology and sports counseling: Developmental programming, education, and research. *Journal of Sport Behavior.*

Kirk, W. D., & Kirk, S. V. (1993). *Student athletes: Shattering the myths and sharing the realities.* Alexandria, Va: American Counseling Association.

J. Scott Hinkle is Associate Professor of Counselor Education at the University of North Carolina at Greensboro, Greensboro, North Carolina.

III. Multiculturism in Mental Health Counseling

CHAPTER TWENTY–THREE

The Importance of the Multicultural Perspective in Mental Health Counseling

Paul Pedersen

The "multicultural perspective" has become very popular in the last decade or two, leading some to consider it a passing "fad" in mental health methods. This unit will attempt to demonstrate the essential and fundamental importance of the multicultural perspective as a continuing and permanent aspect of mental health counseling.

Overview

Culture defines reality for each of us with or without our permission and/or intentional awareness. Behavior occurs in a cultural context and that behavior is interpreted by others through culturally learned assumptions. Behaviors have no fixed meaning outside their cultural context. Not everyone who smiles at you is your friend and not everyone who shouts at you is your enemy. Multiculturalism is more than a method for understanding exotic groups, having gained the status of a generic and fundamental "fourth force" theory to supplement the psychodynamic, behavioral and humanistic interpretations of behavior (Sue, Ivey and Pedersen, in press).

The multicultural perspective has typically emphasized a "culture-specific" perspective, in which unique differences for each specific ethnic group are highlighted. A second approach has embraced a "culture-general" perspective where universal similarities across specific cultural groups are stressed. When differences have been overemphasized, groups become exclusionary and are typically viewed as competing for the same limited resources and are therefore, potentially hostile. When similarities have been overemphasized, the strongest group dominates all other groups, at the expense of individual or group identities. This unit will describe a third alternative that emphasizes both similarities and differences, recognizing that similar cultural values may be expressed by different behaviors.

Discussion

The multicultural perspective is based on the work of ethnic minority authors and researchers over the last several centuries who recognized the importance of cultural differences in a pluralist context. The historical perspective of multiculturalism evolved from the Civil Rights movement, Feminism, Ageism, and the powerful influence of special interest groups emphasizing the legitimacy of their unique cultural perspectives (Ponterotto, Casas, Suzuki and Alexander, 1995). The importance of ethnographic groups defined by nationality, ethnicity, and ethnological tradition constructed a foundation essential to the multicultural perspective.

The dominant, or "Euro-American" cultural values typically define the implicit but culturally-biased assumptions frequently apparent in counseling. Some of these dominant culture assumptions typically include: (a) the fixed definition of normal, (b) the universal importance of individualism, (c) the necessary encapsulation of professional boundaries, (d) the importance of abstract jargon, (e) the universal pathology of dependency, (f) the relative unimportance of support systems, (g) the primacy of linear thinking, (h) the necessity that individuals adjust to the status quo, (i) the irrelevance of historical tradition and (j) the absence of racism in ourselves (Pedersen, 1994). In subtle or sometimes not so subtle ways these underlying assumptions influenced and sometimes defined mental health counseling. The multicultural perspective suggests viable alternatives that challenge these dominant assumptions.

More recently, a broad definition of culture has become more important and includes demographic (age, gender, place of residence) status (social, economic, educational) and affiliations (formal and informal) categories. The broad definition of culture offers several advantages. First, it recognizes the importance of within-group differences. Second, it recognizes the complexity of each person's multiple interacting cultural identities. Third, it establishes the potential for common ground: the shared similarities of age, gender or affiliation among persons who would otherwise consider themselves different according to ethnicity or nationality. Fourth, it expands the application of culture to the generic practice of mental health counseling.

The presence of cultural bias has not facilitated good mental health counseling practice. Gilbert Wrenn (1985) described the destructive effects of cultural encapsulation which (a) defines reality according to the dominant culture assumptions, (b) minimizes the importance of cultural differences, (c) imposes a self-reference criterion in judging other's behavior, (d) ignores proof that disconfirms standard practice, (e) depends on techniques and quick or easy solutions to complicated problems, and (f) disregards the counselor's own cultural biases. The new interest in multiculturalism may be credited to demographic changes, increased visibility and pressure of minority groups, profit incentives for working with minorities, heightened group consciousness, legally mandated affirmative action in employment and education, affirmative action programs, bilingual educational programs, and a variety of other incentives (Ponterotto and Casas, 1991).

A Recommended Course of Action

The foundation of enhanced mental health counseling, which incorporates the multicultural perspective, is in need of good research. Ponterotto and Casas (1991) point out several weaknesses in the existing research.

1. There is no unified conceptual framework.
2. The counselor-client process variable is overemphasized and psychosocial variables are underemphasized.
3. Too much research is based on analogues outside the real world.
4. Intracultural within-group differences have been disregarded.
5. There is an overdependence on samples of convenience.
6. There is continued reliance on culturally biased measures.
7. The subject's cultural background is inadequately described.
8. The limits of generalizability are not defined.
9. There is inadequate minority input.
10. There is a failure of responsibility toward minority subject pools.

These weaknesses need to be addressed with more adequate research data as the first recommended course of action.

Sue, Arredondo and McDavis (1992) provide a three-stage developmental framework for multicultural competencies that outline a second recommended course of action. The first step is to audit counselors' own beliefs, attitudes, assumptions and awareness of culture. This involves their (a) being aware of their own cultural background, (b) knowing how culture influences psychological process, (c) recognizing the limits of their competency, and (d) becoming comfortable with cultural differences. The second step, based on awareness, is increased knowledge. This involves (a) knowing their own cultural heritage, (b) understanding how oppression, racism, discrimination and stereotyping affect them personally, (c) knowing their social impact on others, and (d) knowing the culture of the groups with whom they work. The third step, based on awareness and knowledge, is accurate and appropriate skill. This involves (a) seeking out training to expand their competencies, (b) developing a nonracist identity, (c) being involved meaningfully with culturally different clients. These competencies are expanded with examples and measures to help counselors incorporate the multicultural perspective in their own practice.

A third strategy for incorporating the multicultural perspective is through a Cultural Grid (Pedersen & Ivey, 1993) that separates culturally learned behaviors from expectations. We have already indicated that the same, shared, positive, common-ground expectations may be expressed by very different behaviors in different cultures. Interpreting behaviors outside their cultural context leads to inaccurate assessment, misunderstanding, and inappropriate change. The Cultural Grid matches same/congruent or different/incongruent behaviors on one dimension with same/positive of different/negative expectations on the other dimension, providing four combinations. The combination of same/positive expectation with different/incongruent behavior demonstrates how cross-cultural misunderstandings occur - if the behavior is interpreted out of context - but also allows two people to behave differently working toward the same positive expectation for respect, trust, safety, or friendship. If the apparently contrary behaviors are interpreted in the context of shared positive expectations the conflict can be constructive and positive for the relationships. Conflict between friends or within a family need not be destructive. The common ground of shared positive expectations becomes the focus rather than allowing the stronger person to force the weaker person to change and turning potential friends into enemies.

Conclusion

Multiculturalism has been presented too often as a necessary evil or inconvenience. This unit attempts to demonstrate the positive advantage and contribution that a multicultural perspective can make toward more effective mental health counseling through specific suggestions and guidelines.

The multicultural perspective is here to stay, along with our increasingly complicated life style, and is not a passing fad which will fade away. The competent mental health counselor will need to be knowledgeable about and comfortable with clients and colleagues from unfamiliar cultural backgrounds.

References

Pedersen, P. (1994). *A handbook for developing multicultural awareness. Alexandria,* VA: American Counseling Association.

Pedersen, P. B., & Ivey, A. E. (1993). *Culture-centered counseling and interviewing skills.* Westport, CT: Greenwood Press.

Ponterotto, J. G., & Casas, J. M. (1991). *Handbook of racial/ethnic minority counseling research.* Springfield, IL: Charles C. Thomas.

Ponterotto, J. G., Casas, J. M., Suzuki, L. A., & Alexander, C. M. (1995). *Handbook of multicultural counseling.* Thousand Oaks, CA: Sage.

Sue, D. W., Arredondo, P., & McDavis, R. J. (1992). Multicultural counseling competencies and standards: A call to the profession. *Journal of Counseling and Development, 70,* 477-486.

Sue, D. W., Ivey, A. E., & Pedersen, P. B. (in press). *Multicultural counseling theory.* Monterey, CA: Brooks Cole.

Wrenn, C. G. (1985). Afterward: The culturally encapsulated counselor revisited. In P. Pedersen (Ed.). *Handbook of cross-cultural counseling and therapy* (pp. 323-329). Westport, CT: Greenwood Press.

Paul B. Pedersen is Professor, Department of Human Studies, University of Alabama at Birmingham.

CHAPTER TWENTY–FOUR

Multicultural Counseling in Mental Health Settings

Brett N. Steenbarger

Overview

Multicultural counseling has been called a "fifth force" in the mental health professions. The term multicultural counseling covers a range of perspectives and helping approaches, embracing client populations of diverse racial, ethnic, religious, sexual, cultural, national, and socioeconomic backgrounds. While some limit the definition of multicultural counseling to helping processes between members of differing racial or national groups, others define culture in a sufficiently broad way so as to make all counseling essentially multicultural (Pedersen, 1994).

The realization that ethnic and racial minorities will constitute a statistical majority in the United States by the early 21st century has alerted mental health counselors to the importance of culture in the helping process (Sue & Sue, 1990). Nonetheless, developments within mental health counseling, particularly in regard to the increasing presence of managed care in the marketplace, may make it difficult for the profession to fully embrace multicultural ideals.

Multicultural Counseling: The Basics

While there are a large number of multicultural theories and counseling approaches in the professional literature, several common themes emerge (Steenbarger, 1993):

Social Systems Emphasis - Multicultural counseling does not view problems as wholly residing within individuals, but instead adopts a perspective in which problems result from interactions among persons and social environments. Specifically, the distress of individuals is traceable to clashes between the cultural norms of clients and the social norms of the dominant culture. Where such clashes result in expressions of violence, discrimination, prejudice, and devaluation toward members of the non-dominant culture, the result can be highly detrimental to development.

Awareness of Counselor Limitations - Multicultural counselors recognize that clients are likely to possess distinctive world views that differ from those of counselors. Accordingly, these counselors attempt to understand and work within the cultural frameworks of clients. By uncritically adopting the perspectives of the dominant culture, counselors can perpetuate the very patterns of misunderstanding and devaluation that generate client presenting problems.

Empowerment Focus - Multicultural counselors view their roles as developmental, emphasizing the creation of experiences of empowerment for clients. By affirming distinctive world views and raising clients' awareness of the often deleterious impact of the dominant culture, multicultural counselors facilitate identity development, enabling individuals to understand, accept, and value their own differences and those of others.

Skills Focus - Multicultural counselors recognize that clients may possess culturally-distinctive social norms and communication styles. Hence, multicultural counselors strive for "cultural competence" by learning how to recognize and work within the norms and styles presented by a diverse clientele.

Mental Health Counseling: Emerging Issues

While mental health counselors frequently espouse a sensitivity to the cultural backgrounds and issues of clients, it is not always easy to translate such sensitivity into practice. Staff and budget cuts at community agencies, college counseling centers, and hospitals have helped spur the trend toward problem-focused brief therapies. In some managed care settings, these therapies are prescribed as part of clinical protocols, eliminating counseling approaches that individualize helping processes along cultural dimensions. It is unclear how mental health counselors, seeing clients for five or fewer sessions, can adequately explore the cultural meanings and world views that may underlie a given presenting complaint (Steenbarger, 1993).

A second challenge to multicultural mental health counseling concerns assessment and diagnosis. In essentially all managed mental health care settings, therapists are required to render DSM-based diagnoses and deliver only "medically necessary" care and services. To the extent that mental health counselors seek state licensure and core provider status for inclusion in managed care networks, they may buy into a medical model of care that is inappropriate for culturally diverse clients. While mental health counselors have been very concerned with the trend toward clinical models of care, relatively little attention has been paid to the impacts of this trend upon multiculturalism. For example, a recent review of psychological assessment tools found that very few explicitly address the cultural background of the client (Quinn, 1993), implicitly assuming that traditional procedures are equally applicable to all clients and concerns.

Recent Trends

Several recent trends may help to facilitate a greater rapproachement between mental health and multicultural counseling. General disenfranchisement with DSM as a guide for the management of mental health care has led some service settings and managed care organizations to focus upon *functional impairments* as the basis for making treatment decisions. Instead of diagnosing problems in medical terms, therapists view presenting issues in the light of their *severity*: the degree to which the problems are interfering with the person's life. Such a framework bridges the gap between DSM-diagnosable and V-code conditions and allows clients to be seen for help even when their issues are best framed as developmental.

A second, intriguing trend is the movement toward greater flexibility in the allotment of sessions for clients, with case management rather than fixed session limits helping to ensure efficient utilization of resources. Recognition that not all clients can equally benefit from traditional brief therapy has led to a demand for processes that allot sessions based upon assessed need, instead of administrative fiat. Such flexibility would help mental health counselors work with clients requiring in-depth exploration of personal and cultural issues.

The trend toward managed healthcare is fueling efforts at outcomes assessment and greater standardization of care. Because of the relative youth of the approach, few if any controlled studies have been undertaken to document the populations and presenting problems uniquely benefiting from multicultural counseling. Such studies will no doubt help to effect a greater rapproachement with mental health counseling in the years ahead.

References

Pedersen, P. (1994). *A handbook for developing multicultural awareness* (2nd ed.). Alexandria, VA: American Counseling Association.

Quinn, J. R. (1993). Evaluation and assessment for transcultural counseling. In J. McFadden (Ed.), *Transcultural counseling: Bilateral and international perspectives* (pp. 287-304). Alexandria, VA: American Counseling Association.

Steenbarger, B. N. (1993). A multicontextual model of counseling: Bridging brevity and diversity. *Journal of Counseling and Development, 72,* 8-15.

Sue, D. W., & Sue, D. (1990). *Counseling the culturally different: Theory and practice* (2nd ed.). New York: Wiley.

Brett N. Steenbarger, Ph.D. is Assistant Professor, Department of Psychiatry and Behavioral Sciences, and Director of Student Counseling at the SUNY Health Science Center in Syracuse, N.Y. He has also served as the Director of PrimeCare of Central New York, Inc., a management services organization serving an 84 member multispecialty mental health group practice without walls.

CHAPTER TWENTY–FIVE

Multicultural Counseling Competency

Micah L. McCreary, Dawn K. Lewis & Tamara D. Walker

Overview

Multiculturalism has developed as an integral component of counseling practice and research. In part, multiculturalism as a field of investigation and practice, has increased in significance as American society has become more racially, ethnically, and culturally diverse.

In 1980, the Education and Training Committee of the Counseling Psychology Division of the American Psychological Association (APA) informed its membership of the need to develop minimal multicultural counseling competencies in their training programs. Hill and Strozier (1992) found three key facts in their research during the 1980s: (a) 87% of APA-approved counseling psychology training programs offered a multiculturally focused course, (b) 59% of these programs required a multicultural course for all graduate students, and (c) 45% of the counseling psychology programs allowed students to develop a multicultural subspecialty.

In the recent past, counselors who were culturally unaware often blamed their minority clients for unsuccessful counseling outcomes. Multicultural counseling research, however, has demonstrated that counseling ineffectiveness with ethnic and racial minority clients is linked critically to the multicultural competence of the counselor. Thus, multicultural counseling competency has become a very important aspect of the mental health profession.

This chapter will review the literature pertaining to multicultural counseling competency. First, key definitions and terms will be presented. Second, multicultural counseling guidelines will be summarized. Third, influences and implications of multicultural counseling training will be discussed. Fourth, promising instruments for assessing multicultural counseling competency will be presented.

Definitions of Key Concepts

Culture is important to multicultural counseling because an understanding of culture allows the multiculturally competent counselor to observe client behavior from within a cultural context. Culture is defined as the thoughts, beliefs, practices and behaviors of a people in the areas of history, religion, social organization, economic organization, political organization, and collective production. Culture provides a system in which people (a) set goals, make decisions, and solve problems; (b) explain and define social roles; (c) emphasize cooperation or competition; (d) view human nature, truth, time orientation, and property; and (e) define identity and individuality.

Racial and ethnic identity and worldview are additional concepts that are important to multicultural counseling competency. **Racial identity** is defined as a person's sense of identification based on physical characteristics and genetic origins. **Ethnic identity** refers to a person's identity based on a group's social and cultural heritage passed on to group members from one generation to the next. **Worldview** is defined as the perceptions, attitudes, beliefs, and assumptions that individuals and groups hold about the world. These terms are conceptualized as mediating variables between the individual's or group's cultural systems and resulting behaviors.

Multicultural counseling is defined as a counseling relationship between a counselor and client who adhere to different cultural systems. Multicultural counseling can be conducted in a competent or incompetent manner.

Multicultural counseling competency overlaps with essential attributes associated with basic counseling competency. A competent mental health counselor has the ability to establish rapport, display interest in the client's concerns, and comprehend the transactions between people and environments within a variety of social contexts. A multiculturally competent counselor is a competent counselor who applies psychological knowledge to the cultural concerns of the client. The counselor attends to his or her own worldview, racial- and ethnic-identity, as well as to the worldview, racial- and ethnic-identity of his or her client.

Thus, multicultural counseling competency is predicated on the general principles of counseling competency. Yet, multicultural counseling experts have developed specific guidelines for understanding culturally diverse and culturally different people.

Guidelines for Multicultural Counseling Competency

Most experts urge mental health counselors to consider interpersonal, intrapersonal, economic, cultural, and sociopolitical factors when assessing culturally diverse clients. Specific guidelines for conducting competent multicultural counseling were provided by the American Psychological Association in 1993. Briefly, these guidelines suggested that to be effective with clients who are culturally different, the counselor must be aware of and practice five competencies:

(1) acknowledge and recognize ethnic, racial, and cultural factors as significant to the counseling relationship;

(2) respect and be aware of the many ethnic, cultural, and racial factors that might contribute to the orientation and values of the client;

(3) consider the impact, importance, and potential support of community and social agencies that the client might be involved with;

(4) recognize and attend to the social, economic, and political acts of racism, sexism, discrimination, and prejudice; and

(5) consider within-group differences for clients of all ethnic, racial, cultural, gender, and class groups.

These guidelines are important, and one of the best ways to learn them is in formal training programs.

Training Programs To Provide Multicultural Counseling Competency

During the 1980s, many counseling training programs developed multicultural courses, requirements, and subspecialties (Hill & Strozier, 1992). Most multicultural training programs were based on the APA division 17 position paper on cross-cultural counseling competency (Sue et al., 1982). Sue et al. (1982) suggested that multicultural counseling competencies be developed in awareness, knowledge, and skills. To further aide training programs in developing aware, knowledgeable, and skilled multicultural counselors, Ponterotto, Alexander, and Grieger (1995) presented a checklist for multicultural competence training programs.

Recently, researchers determined that most counselor training programs are producing graduate students with competency in two of three domains, awareness and knowledge. However, few training programs are producing counselors who are skilled multicultural practitioners. All three aspects of multicultural counseling competency are important, and training programs are encouraged to measure how well their trainees develop these competencies.

Measurement Issues in Multicultural Counseling Competency

Instruments to assess counselor and client worldview, racial and ethnic identity, acculturation, and racist attitudes and beliefs have been developed (Sabnani & Ponterotto, 1992). However, until recently relatively little research and scholarship have been directed toward the development of psychometrically sound and conceptually anchored instruments that measure multicultural counseling competency (see Ponterotto, Rieger, Barrett, & Sparks, 1994 for a more exhaustive review). Currently, researchers have developed four promising instruments. These instruments with relatively sound psychometric properties are the Cross-Cultural Counseling Inventory-Revised (LaFromboise, Coleman, & Hernandez, 1991), the Multicultural Counseling Inventory (Sodowsky, Taffe, Gutkin, & Steven, 1994), the Multicultural Awareness Knowledge and Skills Survey (D'Andrea, Daniels, & Heck, 1991), and the Multicultural Counseling Awareness Scale-Form B (Ponterotto, Sanchez, & Magids, 1991).

Researchers (Ponterotto et al., 1994; Yutrzenka, 1995) have reviewed the formats, development, and psychometric properties of these instruments. They suggested that the instruments be used to evaluate the effectiveness of multicultural supervision, videotaped multicultural counseling sessions, and counseling students and trainees. Researchers also suggested that the instruments be used in multicultural counseling research.

Direction of Multicultural Counseling Competency

Two courses of action for multicultural counseling competency exist. First, researchers and practitioners must develop the multicultural counseling skills of practitioners. Programs must provide the counselor with clinical experiences that will allow him or her to apply cultural awareness and knowledge while working with diverse populations. These multicultural in-vivo experiences are to be designed for counselors to practice clinically appropriate techniques for multicultural counseling, and to apply the suggested multicultural guidelines with a variety of clients.

Second, researchers and practitioners must further develop assessment instruments for multicultural counseling competency. The instruments mentioned in this digest are at a promising stage of development, however, they still require additional testing and validation. Each instrument requires greater application with counselors and diverse clients. One obvious direction for researchers would be to conduct multi-trait/multi-method studies with the instruments to further test their psychometric properties.

Conclusion

Multicultural counseling competency is best developed by focusing on the three domains of awareness, knowledge, and skills. While most training programs for counselors are adequately developing trainees who are strong in multicultural awareness and knowledge, more work needs to be done to strengthen counselor skills. Moreover, assessment instruments for multicultural counseling competency have been developed but need further psychometric development to support and facilitate the continued development of multicultural counseling competency in counseling professionals and training programs.

References

Hill, H. L., & Strozier A. L. (1992). Multicultural training in APA-approved counseling psychology programs: A survey. *Professional Psychology: Research and Practice, 23,* 43-51.

LaFromboise, T. D., Coleman, H. L., & Hernandez, A. (1991). Development and factor structure of the Cross-Cultural Counseling Inventory-Revised. *Professional Psychology: Research and Practice, 22,* 380-388.

Ponterotto, J. G., Alexander, C. M., & Grieger, I. (1995). A multicultural competency checklist for counseling training programs. *Journal of Multicultural Counseling and Development, 23,* 11-20.

Ponterotto, J. G., Rieger, B. P., Barrett, A., & Sparks, R. (1994). Assessing multicultural counseling competencies: A review of instrumentation. *Journal of Counseling and Development, 72,* 316-322.

Ponterroto, J. G., Sanchez, C. M., & Magids, D. M. (1991, August). *Initial development and validation of the Multicultural Counseling Awareness Scale (MCAS).* Paper presented at the annual meeting of the American Psychological Association, San Francisco, CA.

Sabnani, H. B., & Ponterotto, J. G. (1992). Instrumentation in counseling research: A review, critique, and recommendations. *Measurement and Evaluation in Counseling and Development, 24,* 161-187.

Sue, D. W., Bernier, J. E., Durran, A., Feinberg, L., Pedersen, P., & Vasquez-Nuttall, E. (1982). Position paper: Cross-cultural counseling competencies. *The Counseling Psychologist, 10*(2), 45-52.

Yutrzenka, B. A. (1995). Making a case for training in ethnic and cultural diversity in increasing treatment efficacy. *Journal of Consulting and Clinical Psychology, 63*(2), 197-206.

Micah L. McCreary is an Assistant Professor of Psychology in the Department of Psychology at Virginia Commonwealth University.

Dawn K. Lewis is a clinical psychology graduate student in the Department of Psychology at Virginia Commonwealth University.

Tamara D. Walker is a counseling psychology graduate student in the Department of Psychology at Virginia Commonwealth University.

CHAPTER TWENTY–SIX

Preparing Mental Health Counselors for Multicultural Counseling

Mark S. Kiselica

Over the past two decades there has been a growing emphasis on training mental health counselors to be competent multicultural practitioners. As evidence of this trend, since 1976 the number of counselor education programs offering courses on multiculturalism as part of the core counseling curriculum has steadily increased (see Ponterotto & Casas, 1991).

According to Herr (1991) and Locke (1993), training in multicultural counseling for mental health counselors is important because cultural diversity is a national reality and a critical factor in counselor/client interactions. In order to effectively serve a culturally diverse range of clients, "all mental health counselors must be sensitive to and equipped with the skills necessary to engage in cross-cultural counseling as defined in ethnic, racial, and socioeconomic terms" (Herr, 1991, p. 18).

The multicultural movement in counseling has spawned several models of multicultural training (e.g., Pedersen, 1988; Sue, Akutsu, & Higashi, 1985; Sue & Sue, 1990). Collectively, these models were designed to promote the following: (a) self-knowledge, especially an awareness of one's own cultural biases; (b) knowledge about the status and cultures of different cultural groups; (c) skills to make culturally appropriate interventions, including a readiness to use alternative counseling strategies that better match the cultures of clients; and (d) actual experiences in counseling culturally different clients.

While it has been generally accepted that these components are essential to effective multicultural training, Kiselica (1991) has argued that additional measures may be necessary in order to enhance the preparation of mental health counselors for cross-cultural encounters. Specifically, Kiselica noted that the process of deciding whether or not to engage in multicultural counseling can be unsettling and anxiety provoking. Kiselica suggested that many mental health counselor trainees may need to address these powerful feelings in a highly supportive environment *before* they engage in more formal, multicultural training activities. The purpose of this paper is to extend Kiselica's (1991) recommendations by discussing four previously overlooked aspects of the multicultural training experiences of mental health counselors. Each aspect is presented as a task for counselor educators to achieve with mental health counselor trainees.

Task 1: Recognize that You Will Make Mistakes in Multicultural Encounters

Mental health counselor trainees often enter the arena of multicultural training and counseling with little prior contact with culturally diverse clients. As a result, trainees tend to be culturally encapsulated, that is, locked within their own ethnocentric perceptions of the world. According to Wrenn (1962), cultural encapsulation results in counselors disregarding the cultural variations of their clients. Culturally encapsulated counselors may not sensitively understand their clients' experiences and relate to their clients in a stereotypic manner.

While the training models highlighted above can help trainees to increase their cultural sensitivity by challenging their ethnocentric views, these models have failed to address the effects of cultural encapsulation on the self-efficacy of mental health counselors involved in the training process. Inevitably, ethnocentric trainees are bound to make mistakes as they attempt to transform rigid, unicultural modes of thinking and behavior with those that are more complex and multicultural in nature. Mental health counselors who err during the early stages of training need reassurance that making mistakes is a part of learning. They also need encouragement to persist with the training process. At the same time, they need to be gently pushed to positively alter their ethnocentric thoughts and behaviors. Balanced support of this kind can prevent many trainees from becoming discouraged during the early stages of multicultural training.

Task 2: Prepare to Be Challenged by Culturally Different Clients and Colleagues

Because trainees are likely to make mistakes during the early stages of training, they need to be supportively forewarned that cross-cultural encounters will likely result in challenges by culturally different clients and colleagues. For example, an Anglo trainee with a linear conception of time may fail to appreciate the American-Indian belief that time is flowing and circular. Consequently, an American-Indian client may avoid the counselor who adheres to a rigid appointment schedule and an American-Indian colleague might express anger toward the Anglo counselor for his or her cultural insensitivity. Situations such as these can be awkward for trainees and they require sensitive responses by the counselor educator. Trainees need to be encouraged not to shy away from multicultural counseling as a result of their discomfort with these situations. Instead, they should be urged to view these uncomfortable situations as opportunities to learn from their mistakes, how to make amends for culturally insensitive behavior, and how to develop culturally appropriate process and intervention skills with the culturally different.

Task 3: Don't Avoid Cross-Cultural Encounters Because of Preconceived Notions of the Culturally Different

In addition to the fears associated with making mistakes in cross-cultural contexts, mental health counselors sometimes avoid multicultural counseling because of preconceived notions of the culturally different. The literature on racial identity development suggests that cross-cultural interactions are side-stepped by many individuals because of their unquestioned acceptance of stereotypes about particular cultural groups. However, ongoing contact with the culturally different helps the culturally encapsulated person to question previously held stereotypes and develop a new-found appreciation for different cultures. To help trainees resist the urge to avoid cross-cultural contact, counselor educators are advised to empathically respond to the fears of trainees; forecasting that persistence in multicultural endeavors is likely to provide a new, multidimensional view of the culturally different.

Task 4: Discover the Joys Inherent in Multicultural Counseling

One of the most effective strategies for inspiring mental health counselors to embrace multicultural training is to emphasize the many joys that are inherent in cross-cultural encounters. The multicultural training literature has inadequately emphasized the potential for mental health counselors to experience the beauty of different cultures through multicultural counseling. Consequently, there is a need to widen the lens of multicultural training to focus on the opportunities for enrichment that await mental health counselors who enter the arena of multicultural counseling.

Conclusion

Multiculturalism is considered to be one of the major forces within mental health counseling (Pedersen, 1990). In order to sensitize and prepare the profession to work effectively in our multicultural society, counselor educators must help mental health counselor trainees to become aware of their own cultural backgrounds and those of the culturally different, develop a wide range of culturally sensitive counseling skills, and apply those skills in the context of cross-cultural counseling. By supportively teaching trainees to recognize that they might avoid such vital training due to unfounded stereotypic thinking and a fear of making mistakes with and being challenged by the culturally different, counselor educators will help mental health counselors to embrace the training as an enriching experience. The end result is that trainees will flourish as competent, multicultural counselors and, in the process, experience and celebrate the beauty and joy found in other cultures.

References

Herr, E. L. (1991). Challenges to mental health counselors in a dynamic society: Macrostrategies in the profession. *Journal of Mental Health Counseling, 13,* 6 - 20.

Kiselica, M. S. (1991). Reflections on a multicultural internship experience. *Journal of Counseling and Development, 70,* 126 - 130.

Locke, D. C. (1993). Diversity in the practice of mental health counseling. *Journal of Mental Health Counseling, 15,* 228 - 231.

Pedersen, P. (1988). *A handbook for developing multicultural awareness.* Alexandria, VA: American Association for Counseling and Development.

Pedersen, P. (1990). The multicultural perspective as a fourth force in counseling. *Journal of Mental Health Counseling, 12,* 93 - 95.

Ponterotto, J. G., & Casas, J. M. (1991). *Handbook of racial/ethnic minority counseling research.* Springfield, IL: Charles C. Thomas.

Sue, S., Akutsu, P. D., & Higashi, C. (1985). Training issues in conducting therapy with ethnic-minority-group clients. In P. Pedersen (Ed.), *Handbook of cross-cultural counseling and therapy* (pp. 275 - 280). Westport, CT: Greenwood Press.

Sue, D. W., & Sue, D. (1990). *Counseling the culturally different: Theory and practice* (2nd ed.). New York: John Wiley and Sons.

Wrenn, C. G. (1962). The culturally encapsulated counselor. Harvard *Educational Review, 32,* 444 - 449.

Mark S. Kiselica is an Associate Professor in the Department of Counseling and Personnel Services at Trenton State College, Trenton, New Jersey.

IV. Special Emphases in Mental Health Counseling

CHAPTER TWENTY-SEVEN

Pastors as Advocates in the Mental Health System

Steven Knight Rainey

Overview

The purpose of this chapter is to propose that parish-based pastors and local community mental health professionals could enhance the quality and validity of health care delivery to their citizens by being more aware of what each has to offer. A recent article by Weaver (1995) underscores the role of clergy as frontline workers in local mental health. Weaver cites research which suggests that approximately 40% of the American population turn to a clergyperson in times of personal distress.

However, 50-80% of Protestant, Catholic, and Jewish clergy who were the subjects of eleven different American and Canadian research studies between 1976 and 1989 reported that their seminary training was inadequate in preparing them to handle the mental health counseling demands in their parishes (Weaver, 1995). Nevertheless, Weaver notes that many people reported being helped by pastors. One study found that among those persons who sought counsel from the clergy, 58% reported being "helped or helped a lot" while only 11% indicated their experience with clergy "did not help." These figures compare favorably with those for psychologists and psychiatrists where 62% of the persons surveyed reported being "helped or helped a lot," whereby 20% claimed their experience "did not help."

Thus, while many clergy do not always feel well-trained to do therapy, research supports the fact that clergy continue to be sought out by people with personal problems. Our purpose is to suggest that parish-based pastors who do not have counseling training or skills can become *advocates* in the local mental health system.

Clergy as Advocates

The notion of pastors as advocates is an ancient theme. In fact, one Biblically based theological understanding of a pastor is as a model of the promise of Jesus in the Gospel of John to leave his followers a "helper," an Advocate, in the person of the Holy Spirit (John 14:15-17). Likewise, advocacy is not a new idea among clergy and mental health professions. In fact, the author is aware of several cooperative ventures in small North Carolina towns dating back to 1980 where clergy, mental health personnel, public school counselors, social workers, and representatives of the legal, medical, and nursing circles have rallied to offer workshops and civic club presentations on mental health topics such as child abuse and domestic violence. Additionally, there are parish-based pastors who are trained in counseling who donate their time or work part-time in their local mental health system offering various types of individual and marital counseling.

Pastoral advocacy in mental health counseling has four major themes:

1) Parish-based pastors who lack significant counseling skills as well as pastors who are trained to do brief, supportive pastoral counseling can *refer* people to mental health centers. The local mental health community can serve both as referral sources as well as offer continuing education in teaching clergy about the referral process. This is a difficult "art." A well-placed referral goes a long way toward affirming the confidence of the prospective client in the mental health community. Likewise, an inappropriate referral can be destructive at a time when a client is very vulnerable. In addition, the mental health disciplines can offer pastors mini-seminars on such important issues as recognizing the signs of potential suicide, clues for depression, and domestic violence.

2) Parish-based pastors can enhance their advocacy role by entering into supervision/consultation with a mental health professional. That is, since pastors are on the frontline of counseling and often handle crisis situations, a pastor can bring case studies or verbatim notes of conversations (with prior consent from the client of course) to supervision sessions with a mental health counselor in order for the pastor to be more effective in either referring or helping the client. (Also, this form of supervision is one of the ways pastors and other "helpers" have accrued hours leading to certification as pastoral counselors and marriage and family therapists).
3) Another option for being an advocate is for a pastor to intervene on behalf of people in the community who are receiving mental health services but who are virtually illiterate, or are intimidated by the various protocols, or who are not aware that a service exists. This role will become incredibly vital as mental health providers and other government agencies experience cutbacks in funding and personnel. Pastors can mutually advocate for the mental health worker as well as for the client who may get "lost in the shuffle."
4) Parish-based clergy need to be more open to how mental health professions can enhance their pastoral care and counseling ministries. We are all in this for the benefit of those who are hurting, helpless, and in need. *However, mental health professionals also need to be open to what services clergy offer.* Most seminary-trained, parish-based pastors are well skilled in grief counseling, in the existential issues regarding the meaning of life, freedom and responsibility, loneliness, and in conducting pre-marital interviews. In fact, mental health counselors should refer clients to competent pastors when religious and existential issues arise.

Conclusion

Advocacy is one of the highlighted roles of parish-based pastors who are on the frontline of community mental health. Four avenues of pastoral advocacy, in cooperation with local mental health professionals, have been suggested. Through seminars and continuing education events sponsored by mental health organizations and the clergy, pastors and mental health counselors may enhance their referral skills and learn to respect each other's gifts and graces for meeting needs in the community.

References

Clinebell, H. (1984). *Basic types of pastoral care and counseling: Resources for the ministry of healing and growth.* Nashville: Abingdon.

Hunter, R. (Ed.). (1990). *Dictionary of pastoral care and counseling.* Nashville: Abingdon.

Weaver, A. W. (1995). Has there been a failure to prepare and support parish-based clergy in their role as frontline community mental health workers: A review. *The Journal of Pastoral Care, 49,*129-147.

Steven Knight Rainey, D. Min., is pastor at the Black Mountain United Methodist Church in Black Mountain, North Carolina and is a member of the American Association of Pastoral Counselors as well as a licensed marriage and family therapist.

CHAPTER TWENTY–EIGHT

Religious Issues in Counseling

Taro A. Kurusu & Everett L. Worthington, Jr.

Overview

In recent years, the amount of research on religious issues carried out by psychologists has increased exponentially. Religious issues in counseling have become accepted as a legitimate area of study. Evidence of this lies in the works published in mainstream journals such as the *American Psychologist*, the *Journal of Consulting and Clinical Psychology*, and the *Journal of Counseling Psychology*, among others. This article will consider research on clients, counselors, and religious-counseling techniques. Each section highlights findings from Worthington, Kurusu, McCullough and Sandage's (1996) ten-year literature review (1984-1994) on religion and psychotherapeutic processes and outcomes.

To understand this area, definitions of descriptive terms must first be established. For the present article, **religious counselors** or clients are those people who hold to the primary beliefs associated with an organized religion and who highly value that religion. **Religious counseling** primarily involves content associated with religious issues. **Religious counseling techniques** are counseling interventions that take into account a religion's unique characteristics (e.g., a modified version of a cognitive-behavioral approach that incorporates Christian principles) (Propst, Ostrom, Watkins, Dean, & Mashburn, 1992) or interventions that utilize a religion's practices (e.g., prayer with or for a client). Although counselors may be religious, they may not necessarily do religious counseling; likewise, non-religious counselors may do religious counseling when they counsel about religious concerns. **Spirituality** is a belief in, and perhaps devotion to, transcendent powers or truths. Spirituality may be associated with organized religion, or not. Thus, people may be both spiritual and religious, neither spiritual nor religious, or either spiritual or religious (but not the other).

Religion and Clients

In 1981, Ellis suggested that religion was associated with irrationality, which would likely lead to negative mental health. Since then, research has found otherwise. Religion does not affect mental health negatively. In fact, there appears to be a small, positive relationship between religion and positive mental health. One way in which individuals can benefit positively from religion is by drawing on their religion to cope with stress (Pargament, 1990).

Religion affects the client's view of the world through religious frameworks (Worthington, 1988). This influences the types of counselors religious clients wish to see; religious clients tend to prefer meeting with counselors who highly value common religious beliefs. This also affects the way religious clients react to counselors (i.e., their appearance, actions, statements, etc.). Religious orientations of counselors may affect the client's willingness to disclose (e.g., religious clients may not disclose as much to non-religious counselors, and non-religious clients may not disclose as much to pastors, priests, or rabbis). Research on precounseling information is needed to know how to best prepare clients to maximally benefit from counseling.

Religion and Counselors

Many non-professionals counsel. Some of these are lay helpers, paraprofessional helpers, and clergy. Many lay and paraprofessional counselors have been found to be at least as effective as mental health professionals (Christensen & Jacobson, 1994), but only if clients are mildly or moderately disturbed and if counselors select, train, and supervise paraprofessionals. In some areas, clergy are more popular sources of counseling than are mental health professionals. Clergy generally see the same type of mental health problems with similar levels of severity as do mental health professionals. Clergy report that the issues with which they deal the most include marriage, divorce, depression, addictions, grief, guilt, and forgiveness. The client load that the clergy carry varies; however, clergy who have more education and positive attitudes toward community mental health, and who have attended mental health workshops, usually carry higher counseling loads and also are more willing to refer to mental health professionals. Most clergy desire more training in pastoral counseling, which should be provided considering the amount of counseling clergy perform.

Among mental health professionals, counselors are in substantial agreement about the values they wish to promote during therapy, (e.g., trust, openness, responsibility). They often disagree about whether counseling should deal with clients' religious values. Many counselors are spiritual (but not religious), when spirituality is broadly defined, and think that spirituality is appropriate for inclusion in therapy if the client and situation warrant it. However, highly religious clients may be unaccepting of counselors who are spiritual but not religious.

Some evidence suggests that counselors may be biased against highly religious clients. Counselors have rated individuals with extremely different ideologies as having more pathology, more internal and external stress, and being less mature than they rated those with less extreme ideologies. Whether highly religious counselors are biased against non-religious or anti-religious clients has not been investigated. Kelly and Strupp (1992) found that: (a) most value change in therapy by clients was away from the counselors' values; (b) value change is usually toward seeking more prosocial goals and becoming more personally competent, not toward adopting different morals; and (c) clients' religious values are especially impervious to change through psychotherapy.

Religious Counseling Techniques

Research on religious-counseling techniques is based mainly on Protestant counselors. Religious techniques typically used by Protestant counselors are prayer, teaching religious concepts, referring to Scripture, discussing faith, forgiveness, religious homework, and use of outside resources such as pastors or lay helpers. Similar results have recently been found for Mormon counselors (Richards & Potts, 1995). Lately, research on forgiveness has become popular, partly because it is not exclusive to the religious community. In general, research has found that promoting forgiveness tends to have positive health and mental-health outcomes.

Propst, et al. (1992) tested a religious version of a cognitive therapy approach against a non-religious cognitive approach. Both approaches were effective for religious clients. A pastoral counseling approach also was effective (though less so than the cognitive approaches). If religious and non-religious approaches are equally effective, the issue becomes one of customer service. If clients prefer religious interventions, why not give them what they prefer?

Conclusion

Religion is an important part of life for most people. Religious research has slowly become acceptable in the psychological community. The quality of much of the research has approached secular standards and the number of works published in mainstream journals has increased in the last decade; however, there is still much work to be done. More outcome research is needed to determine why and how religion is important for mental health, how it effects clients and counselors, and how service to religious clients can be improved.

References

Christensen, A., & Jacobson, N. S. (1994). Who (or what) can do psychotherapy: The status and challenge of nonprofessional therapies. *Psychological Science, 5,* 8-14.

Ellis, A. (1981). Science, religiosity, and rational emotive psychology. *Psychotherapy: Theory, Research and Practice, 18,* 80-99.

Kelly, T. A., & Strupp, H. H. (1992). Patient and therapist values in psychotherapy: Perceived changes, assimilation, similarity, and outcome. *Journal of Consulting and Clinical Psychology, 60,* 34-40.

Pargament, K. I. (1990). God help me: Toward a theoretical framework of coping for the psychology of religion. *Research in the Social Scientific Study of Religion, 2,* 195-224.

Propst, L. R., Ostrom, R., Watkins, P., Dean, T., & Mashburn, D. (1992). Comparative efficacy of religious and nonreligious cognitive-behavioral therapy for the treatment of clinical depression in religious individuals. *Journal of Consulting and Clinical Psychology, 60,* 94-103.

Richards, P. S., & Potts, R. W. (1995). Using spiritual interventions in psychotherapy: Practices, successes, failures, and ethical concerns of Mormon psychotherapists. *Professional Psychology: Research and Practice, 26, 163-170.*

Worthington, E. L., Jr. (1988). Understanding the values of religious clients: A model and its application to counseling. *Journal of Counseling Psychology, 35,* 166-174.

Worthington, E. L., Jr., Kurusu, T. A., McCullough, M. E., & Sandage, S. J. (1996). Empirical research on religion and psychotherapeutic processes and outcomes: A ten-year review and research prospectus. *Psychological Bulletin, 119,* 448-487.

Taro A. Kurusu is a doctoral student in Psychology at Virginia Commonwealth University in Richmond, Virginia. Everett L. Worthington, Jr. is a professor of Psychology, also at Virginia Commonwealth University.

CHAPTER TWENTY–NINE

Death and Loss Education for Mental Health Counselors

Ernest L. Cowger, Jr.

Myra is a 9-year-old girl whose Dad has just died. Myra's mother is wondering whether or not to allow Myra to attend her Dad's funeral. As a mental health counselor, how would you deal with her mother's concerns? Would you advise her to provide Myra with honest explanations of what is happening and to listen to Myra's reasons for going to the funeral or staying at home? Would dealing with this issue touch any emotions in yourself concerning death?

Robert is having problems dealing with his spouse's breast cancer that has spread to other parts of her body. They have two children: an 8-year-old son and a 14-year-old daughter. Robert and his wife Marsha are having difficulty sharing their feelings with each other and do not know what to say to their children about her illness. Robert telephones your office for a family appointment. What would you advise them about ventilating their own death-related feelings within earshot of their children? As you meet with them as a family, what feelings of your own might arise?

These are two of many death and loss related situations that may be presented to any mental health counselor. These and other grief/loss issues underline the importance of mental health counselors having sufficient knowledge in death education and specific training in grief or loss counseling. We all know that it is natural to eat when one is hungry, to sleep when one is tired, and to cry when one is hurt; grieving is as natural as each of these; "it is nature's way of healing a broken heart" (Manning, 1985, p. 60). Clearly, many mental health professionals increasingly acknowledge how death-related emotions affect daily life's quality and style (Kavanaugh, 1977). This support of the daily affect of death- or loss-related emotions has not always been the case.

Background Information

As recently as the early 1970s, it was common for persons in our society to perceive death as a taboo topic; and, as such, there was little research, writing, and educational opportunity available in this field of study (Corr, Nabe, & Corr, 1994; Kalish, 1985). As one of the earlier advocates of understanding the emotional needs of children in regard to death and loss, Grollman suggested that our "fear of death is not only a cultural phenomenon but a part of being human" (1967, p. 3) and that our mental health, our own meaning, understanding, genuineness, and dignity, is the acceptance of tragedy and not its denial. Kavanaugh (1977) stated that reflecting on death has taught him that actualization or fulfillment in life comes only from clearly defining what we want or hope to achieve before death so that we may live more joyfully and fully.

In her writings and workshop entitled *Life, Death, and Transition,* Kubler-Ross (1969) described stages that dying persons experience: denial, anger, bargaining, depression, and acceptance. Likewise, these stages have been applied to the grief process itself as a guide to understanding what caregivers might expect from those experiencing grief. Kubler-Ross also characterized participants' interest in death education in the following ways:

(a) the person coping with their own dying or bereavement,
(b) the helper involved in death-related work, and
(c) the helper dealing with his or her own mortality and losses.

This review presents ideas and techniques that mental health counselors might use themselves in coping with their own death or the death and corresponding grief for significant others, and with their clients who are experiencing difficulty in dealing with their own mortality or the death or loss of a significant other.

Methods for Dealing with Death/Loss Issues

The Helpers' Coping With Their Own Death or the Death/Grief of Another

Possibly one of the most important challenges confronting mental health counselors is coping with their own personal issues pertaining to their own death and loss issues. Dealing with their own death-related issues allows counselors to be more present with themselves and their clients and to be more forthcoming in helping others explore their own loss/grief issues. Often a mental health counselor may defer or even unconsciously avoid assisting a client in "working through" a loss or death issue because of the counselor's own unresolved issues. It is vitally important that counselors stay current with their own loss or grief issues in order to be more open to assisting others in doing so. Any unfinished grief/loss issues can most assuredly interfere with their own effectiveness in supporting others in their journey.

There are many techniques for "working through" loss or death issues. The most direct technique might be having another mental health counselor whom one can trust and see professionally for counseling. Having this person available will allow the counselor to have a safe and immediate outlet for loss and grief issues which are certain to arise in a variety of clients. Other methods for dealing with the counselor's own grief/loss issues include, but are not limited to, participating in workshops that are experientially oriented, attending seminars, bibliotherapy, participating in death education classes or workshops, writing letters to significant living and dead persons to complete unfinished business, and journaling.

Helping clients with their own death-related issues and those of others

Once mental health counselors are sensitized to their own grief/loss issues and how they may be more "present" in counseling with their clients, they are better prepared to support and guide their clients through the client's own pain and grief. Preventive techniques may be the first line of assistance. Designing and offering courses or seminars in death/loss education for clients and the general public provide a foundation of information from which individuals may work in preparing for their own death and the death of significant others. These courses or seminars can assist persons in discussing death-related issues and in preparing for their own death. Course/seminar projects may include: (a) keeping a journal in which participants enter their daily thoughts and feelings about the multitude of minor losses; (b) writing "letters," that may be kept, destroyed, or mailed to significant living persons in which expressions of appreciations and resentments are expressed; (c) writing "letters" expressing appreciations and resentments to significant deceased persons; (d) planning their own funeral/memorial service complete with readings, songs, speakers, and casket selection (if applicable); (e) arranging for their own disposition of their body through burial, cremation, or body donation; (f) writing their own wills and obituary; and (g) visiting a funeral home, crematorium, and cemetery.

These same techniques can be used successfully with individual clients through preventive and remedial work. Through individual sessions the mental health counselor can add the use of imagery and the Gestalt two-chair technique as a method for having an individual gain some kind of closure with the significant deceased person(s). The counselor may ask the client to perform the above educational techniques as a form of homework, bringing in the journal weekly and reporting on progress in completing the rest of the assignments. The letter-writing exercise can be a particularly powerful activity in helping clients gain closure with significant others or losses.

Conclusion

Death/loss education is a continual process. As mental health counselors gain more comfort and closure with their past losses and grief and their own death-related issues, they will find it necessary to stay current with their daily losses and grieving. Clients, much like Myra and her mother, and Robert, Marsha, and their two children, frequently present themselves to mental health counselors who are more comfortable in dealing with death and loss issues. Counselors cannot provide guidance to others if they are more concerned about running from their own fears. Our level of comfort and security as individuals will impact our ability to assist others effectively with their loss and grief.

References

Corr, C. A., Nabe, C. M., & Corr, D. M. (1994). *Death and dying: Life and living.* Monterey, CA: Brooks/Cole.

Grollman, E. A. (Ed.). (1967). *Explaining death to children.* Boston: Beacon.

Kalish, R. A. (1985). *Death, grief, and caring relationships* (2nd ed.). Monterey, CA: Brooks Cole.

Kavanaugh, R. E. (1977). *Facing death.* New York: Penguin.

Kubler-Ross, E. (1969). *On death and dying.* New York: Macmillan.

Manning, D. (1985). *Don't take my grief away from me.* Hereford, TX: In-Sight Books.

Ernest L. Cowger, Jr., is an associate professor in the Area of Behavioral Sciences at Louisiana Tech University who teaches primarily at their Barksdale AFB Program in Bossier City, LA.

CHAPTER THIRTY

Mental Health Counseling for Wellness

Jane E. Myers

The historical roots of mental health counseling lie in a developmental approach (Gladding, 1992). Ivey (1991) noted that development is concerned with positive human change and is the goal of all counseling interventions. Van Hesteren and Ivey (1990) emphasized that this concept is so integral to mental health counseling that it is impossible to do counseling without stating or implying a developmental approach. Furthermore, descriptions of developmental interventions are variously described as preventive or wellness-enhancing treatments (Myers, 1992).

Wellness approaches represent a different paradigm from the traditional medical model, which requires a diagnosis prior to treatment. Instead, mental health counselors believe that all people can benefit from counseling. Fully functioning people who experience everyday stress in their lives as well as those who are mentally ill can benefit from counseling interventions (Remley, 1991). At present, the medical model predominates among third-party payers, hence mental health counselors whose livelihoods depend on third-party payments cannot fully ignore the medical model. On the other hand, developmental interventions can, indeed, be used to treat pathology (Ivey, 1991). If we examine definitions and models of wellness, it becomes clear that the philosophical approach taken by mental health counselors can fully incorporate wellness into treatment and at the same time, use the medical model as a basis for diagnosis and reimbursement.

Definitions and Benefits of Wellness

Wellness may be defined as an holistic approach to facilitating optimum human functioning or human development. Archer, Probert, and Gage (1987), following an extensive review of the literature, defined wellness as "the process and state of a quest for maximum human functioning that involves body, mind, and spirit" (p. 311). This process is one in which the individual plays a vital and active role.

Wellness focuses on self-responsibility, on the need to be assertive in creating the life one wants rather than passive in just reacting to circumstances. Through an emphasis on freedom of choice, wellness increases the responsibility of individuals for their self-care. Wellness is essentially an empowering philosophy which has a goal of helping individuals identify areas of their lives over which they have control, and assisting them to make healthy lifestyle choices which enhance their physical and emotional well being, as well as their continued ability to make even more healthy choices.

The link between physical and mental health has been well established. Yet, mental health continues to receive less attention and less federal dollars than physical health, or more accurately, physical illness. More than 75% of federal health care dollars are spent caring for persons with a chronic illness, while less than one half of one percent is spent preventing these diseases, many of which are stress related, from occurring (United States Department of Health and Human Services, 1990). Through the provision of wellness interventions, mental health counselors have the potential to have a significant impact on physical as well as mental health across the lifespan.

Wellness Models

The provision of wellness interventions is made easier when mental health counselors use one or more of the existing models of wellness as a basis for assessment and treatment planning. Two such models are described briefly here.

Hettler (1984), is widely viewed as one of the major founders and proponents of the wellness movement. A public health physician, Hettler proposed a hexagonal model of wellness, which incorporates the following components: intellectual, emotional, physical, occupational, social, and spiritual. These components interact in such a way that change in any one area results in changes in other areas, both positive and negative.

A useful model of wellness for mental health counselors was developed recently by Witmer and Sweeney (1992). This model is based on cross-disciplinary research on characteristics of healthy individuals taken from a variety of disciplines, including anthropology, education, medicine, psychology, religion, and sociology, and has a strong theoretical foundation in Adlerian theory. A holistic view of wellness and prevention is symbolized in a circumplex model.

Spirituality, the core of the Wheel of Wellness, is one of five major life tasks. The other major life tasks are self-regulation, work, love, and friendship. The five life tasks exemplify the characteristics of a healthy person, and interact dynamically with several life forces: family, community, religion, education, government, media, and business/industry. The life forces and life tasks interact with and are affected by global events, both natural and human, positive as well as negative. In a healthy person, all life tasks are interconnected and interact for the well-being or detriment of the individual.

The life task of self-regulation is divided into 12 subareas of functioning. These include exercise, nutrition, and self-care, as do the other wellness models mentioned here. The Witmer and Sweeney model differs in that a variety of psychological constructs are included as self-regulatory processes. In addition to physical factors, these processes include a sense of worth, sense of control, realistic beliefs, emotional responsiveness and management; intellectual stimulation, problem solving and creativity, sense of humor, stress management, gender identity and culture identity.

Assessing Wellness as a Basis for Treatment Planning

To use wellness interventions in treatment, it is first necessary to choose a model of wellness, then assess the functioning of a client in each dimension of the model. Interventions can be planned to address one or more aspects of functioning. Since each model presupposes an interaction of wellness dimensions, positive change in one area may be expected to contribute to positive changes in other areas.

Hettler's model is the basis for Testwell (National Wellness Institute, 1988), a paper-and-pencil instrument which provides scores corresponding to the six dimensions of the Hettler model. A composite score for overall wellness also is provided.

The Wellness Evaluation of Lifestyle (WEL; Witmer, Myers, & Sweeney, 1994) is a paper-and-pencil instrument which assesses wellness in each dimension of the Witmer and Sweeney Wheel of Wellness. The WEL includes 17 subscale scores and two composite scores, one for overall self-regulation and one for total wellness. A workbook is available to assist individuals in developing personal wellness plans (Myers, Witmer, & Sweeney, 1995).

Wellness Interventions in Mental Health Counseling

Mental health counselors planning wellness interventions will benefit from conducting appropriate assessments which address holistic functioning in each area identified in one of the above models. Positive changes may be facilitated through creating a positive, healthy environment, in which counselors communicate a sincere belief in the capability of individuals to assume responsibility for their own total well-being. Such an environment is inherently empowering.

Virtually any aspect of wellness can form the basis for a treatment plan, or all aspects of wellness may be incorporated in the plan. Tackling one area at a time may be easiest for clients, as they are more likely to experience successes which are at once personally reinforcing and which contribute to positive changes in other aspects of their functioning.

Conclusion

Throughout the lifespan, the cumulative effect of lifestyle choices becomes increasingly significant. Although the negative impact of unhealthy choices becomes more evident, it is never too late to change. Positive, healthy lifestyle choices can enhance the quality of life across the lifespan, beginning whenever they are implemented. Mental health counselors can help to empower clients towards healthy lifestyles through assessment and treatment from a wellness perspective.

References

Archer, J., Probert, B. S., & Gage, L. (1987). College students' attitudes toward wellness. *Journal of College Student Personnel, 28* (4), 311-317.

Gladding, S. (1992). *Counseling: A comprehensive profession* (2nd edition). New York: Macmillan.

Hettler, B. (1984). Wellness: Encouraging a lifetime pursuit of excellence. *Health Values, 8*(4), 13-17.

Ivey, A. (1991). *Developmental strategies for helpers.* Pacific Grove, CA: Brooks/Cole.

Myers, J. E. (1992). Wellness, prevention, development: The cornerstone of the profession. *Journal of Counseling and Development, 68,* 136-140.

Myers, J. E., Witmer, J. M., & Sweeney, T. J. (1995). *The WEL workbook.* Greensboro, NC: Authors & Palo Alto, CA: MindGarden.

National Wellness Institute. *Testwell.* (1988). Stevens Point, WI: Author.

Remley, T. (1991, August). On being different. *Guidepost,* p. 2.

United States Department of Health and Human Services. (1990). *Health people 2000: National health promotion and disease prevention objectives.* Washington, DC: U.S. Government Printing Office.

Van Hesteren, F., & Ivey, A. E. (1990). Counseling and development: Toward a new identity for a profession in transition. *Journal of Counseling and Development, 68,* 524-528.

Witmer, J. M., & Sweeney, T. J. (1992). A holistic model for wellness and prevention over the lifespan. *Journal of Counseling and Development, 71,* 140-148.

Witmer, J. M., Myers, J. E., & Sweeney, T. J. (1994). *The wellness evaluation of lifestyle.* Greensboro, NC: Authors & Palo Alto, CA: MindGarden.

Jane E. Myers is Professor at the Department of Counseling and Educational Development, University of North Carolina at Greensboro, Greensboro, North Carolina.

CHAPTER THIRTY-ONE

Utilizing Outdoor Pursuits in Mental Health Counseling

J. Scott Hinkle

Outdoor pursuits and other experiential activities have steadily grown in this country since the inception of the Boy Scouts in 1910. What used to be mainly associated with summer camp is now a multifaceted industry offering personal growth, group development, and adventure travel (Ewert, 1989). From Outward Bound's establishment in 1941, to the foundation of the National Outdoor Leadership School (NOLS), to the development of the Association for Experiential Education (AEE), professionals interested in human development and growth have been utilizing the "outdoor classroom" as a therapy office. Such professionals have included teachers, youth leaders, social workers, therapeutic recreation and leisure professionals, psychologists, and more recently mental health counselors.

Although adventure activities have been defined in various ways, Ewert (1989) has defined outdoor adventure pursuits as:

> "A variety of self-initiated activities utilizing an interaction with the natural environment, that contains elements of real or apparent danger, in which the outcome, while uncertain, can be influenced by the participant and circumstance" (p. 6).

Associated terms with similar definitions may include adventure-based pursuits, nonstructured experiences, outdoor adventure education, as well as outdoor adventure, and environmental recreation (see Anderson-Hanley, 1997; Ewert, 1989; Schuett, 1993). Common outdoor pursuits include ropes and challenge courses, camping and backpacking, whitewater activities, sea kayaking, SCUBA, bicycling, spelunking, rock climbing and mountaineering, and various types of skiing.

It is important that adventure-based experiential programs be designed in a manner that provides for effective implementation to insure transference back to personal social life and the workplace. Fears of physical risk and misunderstanding of the activity's purpose are typical avenues of resistance from participants. The key to change for clients when utilizing adventure-based approaches are the same as when using more traditional treatment approaches; the counselor must get clients to risk trying something in which they are sure they cannot be successful (Gall, 1987).

Various types of outdoor programming have been implemented for a host of educational and therapeutic reasons: for example, Nicholson (1986) has described an outdoor adventure program (e.g., repelling) that utilized high-risk activities to promote personal potential among well-adjusted participants. Small-group discussions drew on implications from the repelling experience that made significant self-disclosures about personal growth possible. In a similar vein, Galagan (1987) has presented an adventure-based learning program. This "learning by doing" program's experiential base was positively associated with personal growth, accountability, support, trust, and personal energy. Likewise, Vester (1987) has presented a framework of leisure that focuses on adventure as a form of leisure. He has suggested that *routinization* is a critical dimension that contrasts with the romantic idealization of adventure and makes it impossible for people to perceive adventure as a sphere independent of society.

Mason (1987) has described an experiential process in which families engage in a wilderness experience (e.g., trekking, rafting). Outdoor activities were metaphorically translated into daily living patterns to deepen individual and family self-knowledge, self-esteem, and intimacy. Premises on which the wilderness therapy was founded include immediate feedback, trust, and "eustress". By weaving various threads into a family adventure tapestry, a family's unconscious can be unlocked, thus allowing family members to discover deeper parts of themselves and increase family congruency. Experiences of risk taken in a safe, supportive environment results in the family sharing mutual vulnerabilities, followed by increasing intimacy in their relationships.

Although risk is often a part of such activities, outdoor education and adventure-based counseling are legitimate educational and therapeutic pursuits that can benefit a variety of people (e.g., youth at risk, diverse groups, managers and supervisors, people with various impairments and disabilities, and individuals seeking personal growth and exploration). Personal psychoemotional dimensions enhanced by adventure-based experiences include self-esteem, self-concept, self-acceptance, self-actualization, and internal locus of control. Reduced racial strife, substance abuse, recidivism, and drop-out rates also have been reported (see Ewert, 1989). Intended outcomes may include enhancing the quality of learning experiences and assisting clients in finding direction and sources for creative, lasting, and generalized change (Gass, 1997). Adventure-based counseling goals also typically include challenge exercises, peak experiences, fun and humor, problem solving, and improving self-concept via trust building (Schoel, Prouty, & Radcliffe, 1990). Likewise, therapeutic wilderness programs have been found to address general and mental health, and school behavior problems (Davis-Berman & Berman, 1994). Outdoor activities allow for the opportunity to explore life and its meaning within a setting that is nontraditional.

In traditional counseling formats, clients may be able to "deny" issues and avoid intrapersonal confrontations. However, in the adventure-based counseling arena, group activities may "flush out" hidden issues and agendas (see Nassar-McMillan & Cashwell, 1997). Furthermore, typical educational classrooms and therapy offices are limited in comparison to the numerous outdoor experiences that can teach and heal. For example, rock climbers have reported that one of the attractions of the activity is the *degree of control* they have over the climb. This includes preparation for the climb, problem solving, and the personal satisfaction of doing something that may have been previously deemed impossible for the individual. Likewise, a raft floating down a whitewater river requires group planning, decision making, team work, and cooperation by its occupants. Although the use of spirituality in adventure programming is in its infancy, spiritual issues can be effectively explored via the outdoor experience. The integration of spirituality with other treatment goals can assist with perceptual shifts and new reflections on the meaning of symptoms and life (see Anderson-Hanley, 1997).

A Primer to Outdoor Education and Therapy Philosophy

Americans spend over 95% of their time indoors. This has resulted in a "closeted consciousness" which holds that living indoors is the best way to cope with life and the world. According to Cohen (1993), personal, interpersonal, and environmental problems exist because of the differences between *natural* and *indoor* programming. Nature works by interconnectedness, growth, and survival. Similarly, survival within man is not coincidental: existence, growth, meaning, direction, and purpose influence our survival as well as our connection to nature. Cohen suggests that it is not simply accidental that we refer to ourselves as human *being*. Furthermore, he indicates that "every being want(s) to continually form relationships with its surroundings" (p. 41). Moreover, a biological proof of this is our body's molecular replacement about every seven years, reflecting that our molecules are attracted to something outside ourselves (Cohen). Cohen (1993) has indicated that our "womb-like artificial tropical indoor world" is supported by our cultural story that reads: "For survival, people must respect, strengthen and obey reasoning and language" (p. 45). The natural world has been abandoned for trust in the labels and artifacts that language and reasoning represent. Reasoning and language are perceived as attractive to survival, whereas nature is perceived as unstable. As a result, various institutions and science are believed to be able to solve our problems. However, this may only hold to be reasonable from an indoors mentality.

In contrast, the outdoor adventure mentality focuses on *experience*. Cohen (1993) suggests that in addition to the five major senses, 53 connective senses are largely ignored by people with "indoor programming." Such sensitivities include thirst, compassion, place, space, sex, distance, camouflaging, spirit, bonds, intuition, and motion. For example, distance from others (and nature) can result from a *sense of camouflaging*, or a need to blend in. Cohen's (1993) *counseling with nature* concept suggests that backyards, parks, and wilderness become a partner for change and growth. His counseling approach argues that stress, mental disorders, and irresponsible behavior "arise from abandonment, real or remembered, caused by living closeted from nature" (p. 51).

One adventure-based approach has tested a model for predicting the personal, and activity, and setting attributes of a variety of adventure recreation skills and experiences. Findings support a model for identifying the types of social, psychological, and physical environments that are preferred by adventure recreationalists relative to their level of experience and engagement in the activity (Ewert & Hollenhorst, 1989). Attitudes toward intentional change and risk-taking in an outdoor development program have been investigated (Downs, 1989). Frequency of participation, perceived risk, and skill have been found to predict level of engagement in adventure-based activities (see Ewert & Hollenhorst, 1994; Schuett 1993). Philosophically, adventure-based counseling must match the client and the problem or issue with the appropriate outdoor activity.

Implications for Mental Health Counselors

Outdoor education leaders who are trained in counseling and psychotherapy are better prepared to utilize therapeutic communication skills (West-Smith, 1997). The outdoor education leader's use of basic therapeutic communication is one way to empower the client, establish interpersonal trust, and provide for an atmosphere of emotional and personal safety. For example, "doing" affirmations can contribute to enhancing the client's self-esteem (West-Smith, 1997). Such communication skills and other outdoor leadership skills and behaviors are consistent with mental health counseling. This includes human development, individual and group interaction skills, decision-making and problem-solving, human resource management, and program evaluation. Additional skills for mental health counselors (MHCs) engaging in outdoor experiential education necessarily include outdoor skills and techniques (e.g., rock climbing, rapelling, whitewater activities, backpacking, etc.), safety, first aid, risk management, and environmental ethics. Similarly, there are differences in job performance when MHCs leave the indoor office and assist people in the "outdoor office." Such differences include longer work days (sometimes 24-hour days), much less control over the environment, short-term interventions, and little to no direct supervision (see Ewert, 1989).

Many aspects of adventure therapy are based in the area of experiential education. Experiential exercises typically involve a non-competitive physical exercise that relies on group counseling dynamics and an extensive debriefing session (see Nassar-McMillan & Cashwell, 1997). Experiential learning focuses on direct experience in the process of growth. The teacher, or MHC, is responsible to the learner, not responsible for the learner. The learner is a participant and the learning process must be relevant in the present as well as in the future. The application of outdoor pursuits and adventure therapy is often adjunctive to other types of treatment (e.g., traditional counseling). Rather than replace other modes of therapy, experiential adventure therapy enhances and enriches other approaches by utilizing an "outdoor counseling environment" that is challenging and rewarding (see Gass, 1993). As one successful client put it, some of the principles of adventure therapy include challenge by choice and no minimizing of anyone's efforts (Eilers, 1997).

Conclusion

Adventure-based counseling is developing into a legitimate area of mental health intervention. Wilderness therapy typically occurs with small groups of clients in remote outdoor areas. Examples include Outward Bound (OB) and adapted OB programs. Long-term residential camping, also referred to as wilderness camping, primarily focuses on the placement of adolescent clients in outdoor camps (e.g., Eckerd Foundation Camps; see Gass, 1993). Adventure-based approaches generally occur close to the major therapeutic facility of the client, often on the grounds of the facility. Examples may include high and low rope challenge activities and indoor climbing walls. The efficacy of adventure-based counseling has been minimally supported. However, methodological flaws in research designs may actually minimize reported effectiveness rates (see Nassar-McMillan & Cashwell, 1997).

References

Anderson-Hanley, C. (1997). Adventure programming and spirituality: Integration models, methods, and research. *The Journal of Experiential Education, 20,* 102-108.

Cohen, M. J. (1993). Counselling with nature: Catalyzing sensory moments that let earth nurture. *Counselling Psychology Quarterly, 6,* 39-52.

Davis-Berman, J., & Berman, D. S. (1994). Research update: Two-year follow-up report for the Wilderness Therapy Program. *The Journal of Experiential Education, 17,* 48-50.

Downs, C. M. (1989). Self-esteem and attitudes toward intentional change and risk taking in an outdoor development program for managers. *Dissertation Abstracts International, 50* (6-A) 1526.

Eilers, G. M. (1997). My lessons for living from adventure therapy. *The Journal of Experiential Education, 20,* 61-65.

Ewert, A., & Hollenhorst, S. (1989). Testing the adventure model: Empirical support for a model of risk recreation participation. *Journal of Leisure Research, 21,* 124-139.

Ewert, A., & Hollenhorst, S. (1994). Individual and setting attributes of the adventure recreation experience. *Leisure Sciences, 16,* 177-191.

Ewert, A. W. (1989). *Outdoor adventure pursuits: Foundations, models, and theories.* Columbus, OH: Publishing Horizons.

Galagan, P. (1987). Between two trapezes. *Training & Development Journal, 41,* 40-48.

Gall, A. L. (1987). You can take the manager out of the woods, but . . . *Training & Development Journal, 41,* 54-58.

Gass, M. A. (1993). *Foundations of adventure therapy.* In M. A. Gass (Ed.), Adventure therapy: Therapeutic applications of adventure programming (pp. 3-10). Dubuque, IO: Kendall Hunt.

Gass, M. (1997). Facilitating experiential learning: Co-creating stories with better endings for clients. *The Journal of Experiential Education, 20,* 66-67.

Mason, M. J. (1987). Wilderness family therapy: Experiential dimensions. (Special Issue). *Contemporary Family Therapy, 9,* 90-105.

Nassar-McMillan, S. C., & Cashwell, C. S. (1997). Building self-esteem of children and adolescents through adventure-based counseling. *Journal of Humanistic Education and Development, 36,* 59-67.

Nicholson, J. A. (1986). Risk recreation: A context for developing client potential. *Journal of Counseling & Development, 64,* 528-530.

Schoel, J., Prouty, D., & Racliff, P. (1988). *Islands of healing: A guide to adventure-based counseling.* Hamilton, MA: Project Adventure.

Schuett, M. A. (1993). Refining measures of adventure recreation involvement. *Leisure Sciences, 15,* 205-216.

Vester, H. G. (1987). Adventure as a form of leisure. *Leisure Studies, 6,* 237-249.

West-Smith, L. (1997). Basic therapeutic communication: Theoretical and practical information for outdoor adventure professionals. *The Journal of Experiential Education, 20,* 68-74.

J. Scott Hinkle is a teacher at the University of North Carolina at Greensboro and an American Canoeing Association Certified Whitewater Kayaking Instructor.

CHAPTER THIRTY–TWO

Managed Behavioral Health Care and Mental Health Counseling: Overview and Implications

Brett N. Steenbarger

Overview

Rapid increases in the cost of health coverage have spurred the trend toward managed care. It is estimated that over 100 million Americans are currently enrolled in managed care plans, up from only 5 million in the 1970s. The rapid penetration of managed care has important implications for the delivery of services and the future of mental health counseling.

Mental health counselors, like providers in other helping professions, typically receive little education or training in managed care as part of their graduate studies. Hence, they are frequently unprepared for the appearance of managed care organizations (MCOs) in their communities. The present summary is designed to provide mental health counselors with an overview of *managed behavioral health care* and its potential impacts.

How Managed Care Organizations Attempt Cost Savings

In the United States, health benefits are typically offered and purchased by employers or the government. Traditionally, this insurance has been on an indemnity basis, such that patients see the qualified provider of their choice and insurers pay all legitimate expenses for services upon billing. This system led to considerable concern over costs, as expenses for specialty care, testing, and inpatient treatment skyrocketed.

In a managed care system, the insurer contracts with the purchaser of benefits, offering a range of healthcare services on a *capitated* basis. That is, the purchaser pays the MCO a fixed dollar amount per person per month to provide a defined menu of health care services. The appeal of such an arrangement to the purchaser is twofold. First, it allows healthcare costs to be known--and budgeted--in advance. Second, the capitation mechanism creates financial incentives to the MCO to contain costs. In a sense, managed care transfers the risk of high medical costs from the employer/purchaser to the MCO.

MCOs contain costs by managing the utilization of healthcare services. This is accomplished in several ways:

- Gatekeeping - Costly specialty and inpatient services may need to be approved by a primary care gatekeeper or utilization reviewer before they will be reimbursed.
- Benefit Exclusions - Managed care policies will typically exclude from coverage all services deemed not "medically necessary" (e.g., career counseling).
- Benefit Limits - MCOs may place caps upon the amount of services that can be accessed by enrolees in a given year (e.g., 20 outpatient therapy visits, 31 inpatient days, and 60 substance abuse visits).
- Case Management - MCOs will commonly review all ongoing cases at defined intervals to assure that continued services are medically necessary. Authorizations for continued care are dependent upon such reviews.
- Transfer of Insurance Risk - In markets typified by a high penetration of managed care, it is typical for MCOs to transfer insurance risk to provider groups by offering "case rates" (fixed lump sum reimbursements per client) or "subcapitation" arrangements (fixed monthly payments per member for a defined population).
- Provider Profiling - MCOs frequently monitor the quality and

cost-effectiveness of the services rendered by providers and provider groups. Over time, providers offering high quality, low cost care are given more referrals; providers failing to deliver effective, efficient care may lose their contracts.

Varieties of Managed Care Organizations

All managed care organizations are not alike. They differ both in their operational practices and in their levels of benefits. Most managed behavioral healthcare is delivered under one of the following structures:

- Health Maintenance Organizations (HMOs)–are insurers who deliver health and mental health care through a limited panel of providers. In the staff model, the panel consists of employees of the HMO. In an IPA model, members of one or more practitioner-owned group practices (Independent Practice Associations) contract with the HMO to provide care. Many HMOs offer health plans that allow their members to see providers "out-of-network" (e.g., outside the panel) at reduced levels of coverage. These point-of-service (POS) plans are attempts to combine the cost-savings features of HMOs with the freedom of choice of traditional, indemnity coverage.
- Preferred Provider Organizations (PPOs)–are insurers who contract with providers of care at a discounted fee structure in exchange for a flow of referrals. The most visible PPOs are large national organizations specializing in managed behavioral healthcare. As "carve-outs," they administer that portion of insurance dollars dedicated to mental health and substance abuse. The plans offered by carve-out organizations often feature richer benefits–and carry higher premiums–than those offered by HMOs.
- Provider-Hospital Organizations (PHOs)–are hybrid organizations consisting of a provider group and a hospital. PHOs may directly contract with employers/purchasers or may contract with HMOs as an insurance intermediary. PHOs are becoming increasingly common in academic health centers and large community hospitals.
- Management Services Organizations (MSOs)–do not provide care, but instead offer management services (e.g., billing, contracting, marketing) to provider groups. MSOs may contract with practitioner groups to assist in the management of care.

One common arrangement finds networks of individual providers, group practices without walls, forming their own MSOs to contract with HMOs and PPOs.

Implications

The expanding presence of managed care has a significant impact upon mental health services. Specifically, MCOs emphasize brief, problem focused approaches to counseling and divert inpatient care to intensive outpatient alternatives. Routine requests for assistance are frequently triaged to less expensive providers, limiting doctoral and medical providers to specialty care. A number of observers are predicting high unemployment in the mental health professions as an inevitable consequence. Mental health counseling finds itself uniquely impacted by managed care in two respects. First, many MCOs limit provider panels to licensed professionals, excluding mental health counselors in states without applicable licensure laws. This is an especially large threat in the public sector, where the trend toward managed Medicaid could exclude mental health counselors employed in community agencies. Second, because MCOs generally limit care to "medically necessary" conditions (e.g., DSM-diagnosable presenting problems), many preventive and developmental services may be excluded from coverage, pushing mental health counselors into a "clinical" mode. Interestingly, however, as provider care organizations assume insurance risk, preventive services that can document a decrease in the subsequent utilization of costly specialty and inpatient services will find considerable demand.

References

Feldman, J. L., & Fitzpatrick, R. I. (Eds.). (1992). *Managed mental health care: Administrative and clinical issues.* Washington, DC: American Psychiatric Press.

Kongstvedt, P. R. (1993). *The managed health care handbook* (2nd ed.). Gaithersburg, MD: Aspen.

Winegar, N. (1992). *The clinician's guide to managed mental health care.* New York: Haworth.

Brett N. Steenbarger, Ph.D. is Assistant Professor, Department of Psychiatry and Behavioral Sciences, and Director of Student Counseling at the SUNY Health Science Center in Syracuse. He also has served as the Director of PrimeCare of Central New York, Inc., a management services organization serving an 84 member multispecialty mental health group practice without walls.

CHAPTER THIRTY-THREE

Consultation in Mental Health Counseling Practice

DeWayne J. Kurpius & Felito Aldarondo

Overview

With recent changes in the delivery of mental health services due to reform in federal and state funding agencies, mental health consultation also has changed. Historically, much of the consultation that occurred in mental health agencies was composed of professionals consulting with other professionals regarding particular cases or types of cases. More recently, consultation in mental health settings has involved relatively few professionals consulting with large groups of para-professionals, with an expanded focus on case management. Although structural changes have occurred in the mental health system, consultation definitions, process, and models from the past remain a useful resource in providing a framework for understanding the professional's role as a mental health consultant.

Definition of Consultation

The definition of consultation has evolved profoundly since the term came into popular use in the early 1900s. Early definitions labeled the consultant as a one-on-one content expert helping to solve a problem.

Later, consultation began to focus on process helping and on working to improve whole systems. Recent definitions of consultation focus on content and process helping with an emphasis on collaborative efforts including every person in an entire system.

Fuqua and Kurpius (1993) concluded that consultants define consultation according to their work setting, educational background, goals, and conceptual models. Therefore, no unitary, encompassing, globally-accepted definition of consultation exists. However, consultation can be described generally as a process and conceptual framework for helping individuals in work settings to be more efficient, more effective, and to attain greater job satisfaction within their work environment. It also is important to remember that consultation tends to be issue focused and triadic in nature.

Definition of Mental Health Consultation

Mental health consultation is grounded in the notion of a community mental health system that utilizes consultants to help provide services to all members of the community who require assistance. Similar to the general definition of consultation, mental health consultation has been defined in various ways. One popular definition of mental health consultation is put forth by Caplan & Caplan (1993). They describe the process of consultation as one professional, who is seeing clients with problems outside her/his area of expertise, seeking help from another professional, who is considered an expert in the problem area. Throughout the consultation process, the expert consultant facilitates the treatment of the consultee's clients, either directly or by helping to develop a protocol to help clients of this nature. Like the evolution of consultation in general, mental health consultation is becoming more process focused with a more systems-oriented approach to intervention.

The Changing Face of Mental Health

The service provider delivery systems of many community mental health centers have been changing from a multi-discipline professional staff with perhaps one para-professional outreach worker to a few supervising professional staff with a cadre of case management staff. Within a mental health center organizational unit, one might now find a staffing consisting of a doctoral level coordinator, a doctoral-level supervisor, three master's-level therapists or social workers, and several case managers with a bachelor's degree or less. Case managers, for example, may work with families who have children that have been referred from the county Division of Family and Children's Services, court probation counselors, school systems, and other health and human service providers. The case managers stay involved with these families, providing intensive home based services two, three, or more times weekly until the family is functioning more effectively. The case managers have most of the direct contact with the family, while also significantly utilizing consultation and process interventions provided by the professional staff.

Case Example

A case example is provided to illustrate this emerging model of the therapist serving as the consultant to case managers. A child was referred to an elementary school counselor for assessment and counseling related to oppositional behavior and sometimes violent outbursts in the classroom. The counselor had talked with police and the local public child welfare office. The child and family were soon referred to the community mental health center. A doctoral-level therapist completed the child and family assessment protocol and then developed a family treatment plan which involved a case manager providing family intervention services in the home twice weekly. The case manager's responsibilities were to conduct continuous in vivo assessments of the family's functioning at home, to provide training in parenting skills as the needs were identified, link the child and family to other community support services, and to serve as an advocate for the child with the teachers, school psychologist, and principal at the elementary school. The case manager met weekly with the doctoral-level therapist to review the situation in a case consultation session. In the case consultation sessions, the case manager recounted the observed family problems and the process experienced while in the home with the family. The consulting therapist focused on both the process and conceptual framework employed by the case manager, and addressed specific skills required of the case manager while providing parent effectiveness training, clarifying parent roles and responsibilities, and intervening with the family-child process.

The need for consultation in cases similar to this one is the result of the direct service provider's lack of one or more of the following: knowledge, skill, objectivity, confidence, conceptual ability, or credentials. In the case management model as exemplified above, everyone can benefit because the client is in a less restrictive environment, is receiving several hours of contact each week, and is benefiting from the therapist both directly and indirectly. The mental health center is providing quality care to a low-income client while at same time remaining cost efficient.

Models of Consultation

Process versus Content

A distinction is often drawn between content and process consultation (Schein, 1989). Content consultation focuses on the actual problems that need to be solved. Process consultation focuses on the consultant and the consultee working together to implement some planned change. This planned change process is in turn internalized by the consultee as a learned ability (Fuqua & Kurpius, 1993).

In many ways, the above example exhibits the assumptions underlying content consultation following Schein's (1989) purchase of expertise model. Although the case manager usually does not hire the consultant, the case manager often gives a tentative diagnosis which (if necessary) is corrected by the consultant, acknowledges the consultant's capabilities to help solve the problem, communicates what the problem is to the consultant, and thinks through and accepts the consequences of the help from the consultant.

On the other hand, the case manager system also meets many of the assumptions of the process consultation model. The case manager often needs help in diagnosing the client and benefits from participating in the process. He or she has the best interests of the client in mind and has the problem-solving skills to help. Likewise, the case manager has the most direct contact with the client, may know what interventions will work best; and he or she learns new problem-solving skills through the process of diagnosis and intervention planning.

Caplans' Theory

Caplan & Caplan (1993) describe four important models of consultation: client-centered case consultation, consultee-centered consultation, program-centered administrative consultation, and consultee-centered administration consultation. In client-centered case consultation, the consultee asks the consultant for help with a difficult client case. The consultant personally diagnoses the client and makes recommendations for treatment to the consultee. In consultee-centered consultation, the focus is on the consultee's lacking professional performance in dealing with a particular client case. The client's improvement is not the main priority in this consultation mode; instead, it is the improved performance of the consultee. Program-centered administrative consultation focuses on the consultant helping with program administration or organizational problems. Consultee-centered administrative consultation focuses on the consultant helping the staff or administration function in their administrative duties (Caplan & Caplan).

Through the utilization of case managers in mental health agencies, Caplan & Caplan's (1993) notions of client-centered case and consultee-centered case consultation are combined. The goal of consultation within the case management system is to provide the best possible service in order to facilitate positive change in the client while at the same time enhancing the skills of the consultee (the case manager).

Conclusion

As a consequence of rapidly changing mental health organizations, the roles of mental health professionals are becoming more consultative in nature. Case management services are becoming one of the major forms of service delivery in mental health centers across the country. Mental health professionals may eventually spend less time engaged in therapy with clients and more time in consultation with case managers. Case managers utilize mental health professionals for consultation due to lack of knowledge, skill, objectivity, confidence, conceptual ability, or credentials. The consultation model employed by the mental health professional will vary depending on personal style and the relationship with the particular case manager, but will most likely have both a process and content focus. The consultant concentrates on helping the client while enhancing the skills of the consultee.

References

Caplan, G., & Caplan, R. B. (1993). *Mental health consultation and collaboration.* San Francisco: Jossey-Bass.

Fuqua, D. R., & Kurpius, D. J. (1993). Conceptual models in organizational consultation. *Journal of Counseling and Development, 71,* 607-618.

Schein, E. H. (1989). Process consultation as a general model of helping. *Consulting Psychology Bulletin, 41*, 3-15.

DeWayne J. Kurpius is a professor in the Department of Counseling and Educational Psychology at Indiana University.

Felito Aldarondo is a doctoral student in Counseling Psychology at Indiana University.

V. Psychodiagnosis in Mental Health Counseling

CHAPTER THIRTY–FOUR

Using the DSM-IV in Clinical Mental Health Counseling

J. Scott Hinkle

It is important for mental health counselors (MHCs) to be able to effectively and wisely use the *Diagnostic and Statistical Manual of Mental Disorders* (DSM). A DSM diagnosis is only the first step in evaluating a client, and it does not necessarily equal prognosis. Information regarding diagnosis is needed for effective treatment planning, clinical care, communication among practitioners, and systematic research to enhance the knowledge of mental disorders. Essentially, the diagnosis is the first step in the complicated process of treating the client (Ninan, 1990).

Ninan (1990) has indicated that on a basic level

> "a diagnostic system should serve a number of functions: to prevent confusion in communication about patients with the same constellation of symptoms within the framework of individual variations; to help define a homogenous group of patients for clinical research studies; to classify a group of patients for the definition of treatment issues in a clinical setting; and to have some predictive capacity" (p. 13).

Despite its limitations, the DSM system meets these criteria and is currently the best system we have (Ninan).The counseling profession has clearly recognized the importance of the DSM system by including it in counselor mental health education program instruction and licensure examinations. Although there are criticisms associated with the development and use of the DSM (e.g., Kutchins & Kirk, 1997), the manual has served an important role in mental health counseling for nearly twenty years..

Even under the best of circumstances, using diagnostic labels remains a troubling issue for many counselors. It is their contention that labels cause the dehumanization of clients which may lead counselors to devalue clients, to discredit their concerns, and to disengage from authentic interaction (Benson, Long, & Sporakowski, 1992). Moreover, Carlson, Hinkle, and Sperry (1993) have indicated that, "counselors have expressed the concern that they will be losing some of their hearts or possibly selling their souls by incorporating diagnosis into their practice" (p. 308). Despite this, diagnosis is required for third party reimbursement (Cowger, Hinkle, DeRidder, & Erk, 1991).

Although criticisms regarding the use of the DSM have been made, in reality counselors have been working with people experiencing disorders described in the DSM for decades. For example, depression and anxiety are the most common clinical symptoms associated with personal problems. More specifically, alcohol and drug issues among adults, adolescents, and children are treated everyday by counselors in mental health clinics, colleges, universities, and public schools.

In the early 1980s the DSM-III achieved unexpected recognition (Spitzer, 1985). This success was unanticipated by its supporters because DSM-I and DSM-II (APA, 1952, 1968) had been criticized by clinicians who maintained that these earlier versions were unscientific and encouraged negative labeling. In contrast, the developers of DSM-III claimed that their edition was unbiased and much more scientific (Spitzer, 1980). Even though many of the earlier problems persisted, reservations about the manual were offset by the increasing demand that psychotherapists report a DSM diagnosis for clients who qualify for reimbursement for treatment from private insurers or from governmental programs (Kutchins & Kirk, 1989).

Utilization of the DSM within the counseling profession is not without controversy. Although literature concerning the use of the DSM in mental health counselor education programs is limited, assigning a psychodiagnosis to a client is uncomfortable for many counselors. The disadvantages associated with using the DSM have included the promotion of a mechanistic or "cookbook" approach to mental disorder assessment, a false impression that the understanding of mental disorders is more advanced than is actually the case; and an excessive focus on the signs and symptoms of mental disorders to the exclusion of a more comprehensive understanding of the client's problems (Hinkle, 1994; Williams, Spitzer, &

Skodol, 1985, 1986). It also has been said that the DSM focuses too much attention on surface phenomena at the expense of clinical manifestations and human development (Vaillant, 1984).

At the same time, advantages to implementing the DSM have included the development of a common language for discussing diagnoses, an increase in the utilization of behavioral definitions, the advancement of prescriptive treatments, and the facilitation of the overall learning of psychopathology. The DSM undergoes periodic revisions, which add to the arguments concerning advantages and disadvantages.

Conclusion

MHCs have used the DSM in the past, use it today, and will use it in the future. An understanding of this diagnostic system and its vast implications in counseling, both positive and negative, will be imperative to the effective and ethical delivery of professional community mental health counseling services (Hinkle, 1994).

References

American Psychiatric Association (1952). *Diagnostic and statistical manual of mental disorders.* Washington, DC: Author.

American Psychiatric Association (1968). *Diagnostic and statistical manual of mental disorders.* (2nd ed.). Washington, DC: Author.

Benson, M. J., Long, J. K., & Sporakowski, M. J. (1992). Teaching psychopathology and the DSM-III-R from a family systems perspective. *Family Relations, 41,* 135-140.

Carlson, J., Hinkle, J. S., & Sperry, L. (1993). Using diagnosis and DSM-III-R and IV in marriage and family counseling and therapy: Increasing treatment outcomes without losing heart and soul. *The Family Journal: Counseling and Therapy for Couples and Families, 1,* 308-312.

Cowger, E. L., Hinkle, J. S., DeRidder, L. M., & Erk, R. R. (1991). CACREP community counseling programs: Present status and implications for the future. *Journal of Mental Health Counseling, 13,* 172-186.

Hinkle, J. S. (1994). The DSM-IV: Progress and implications for mental health counselors. *Journal of Mental Health Counseling, 16,* 174-183.

Kutchins, H., & Kirk, S. A. (1989). DSM-III-R: The conflict over new psychiatric diagnoses. *Social Work, 14,* 91-101.

Kutchins, H., & Kirk, S. A. (1997). *Making us crazy.* New York: Free Press.

Ninan, P. T. (1990). *Diagnostic issues.* In S. T. Levy & P. T. Ninan (Eds.), Schizophrenia: Treatment of acute psychotic episodes (pp. 1-15). Washington, DC: American Psychiatric Association.

Spitzer, R. (1980). Introduction. In American Psychiatric Association, *Diagnostic and statistical manual of mental disorders,* (3rd ed.). Washington, DC: American Psychiatric Association.

Spitzer, R. (1985). Introduction. In Work group to revise DSM-III, *DSM-III-R in development,* (p. 5). Washington, DC: American Psychiatric Association.

Vaillant, G. E. (1984). A debate on DSM-III: The disadvantages of DSM-III outweigh its advantages. *American Journal of Psychiatry, 141,* 542-545.

Williams, J. B. W., Spitzer, R. L., & Skodol, A. E. (1985). DSM-III in residency training: Results of a national survey. *American Journal of Psychiatry, 142,* 755-758.

Williams, J. B. W., Spitzer, R. L., & Skodol, A. E. (1986). DSM-III in the training of psychiatric residents and medical students: A national survey. *Journal of Psychiatric Education, 10,* 75-86.

Zimmerman, M. (1988). Why are we rushing to publish DSM-IV? *Archives of General Psychiatry, 45,* 1135-1138.

J. Scott Hinkle, Ph.D., NCC, CCMHC teaches at the University of North Carolina at Greensboro.

CHAPTER THIRTY–FIVE

Psychodiagnosis for Counselors: The DSM-IV

J. Scott Hinkle

The profession of counseling is growing rapidly as reflected by the proliferation of professional community mental health counseling graduate programs. Graduates of these programs are providing counseling services in mental health centers, psychiatric hospitals, employee assistance programs, and various other community settings. At the foundation of effective mental health care is problem conceptualization and treatment planning which rely on the establishment of a valid diagnosis. This has caused an increase in the number of graduate community mental health counseling programs requiring course work in abnormal behavior, psychopathology, and psychodiagnosis. As a result, utilization of the *Diagnostic and Statistical Manual of Mental Disorders, Fourth Edition* (DSM-IV) American Psychiatric Association (APA,1994) also has been dramatically increased in counselor education training. Skill in its use is undoubtedly necessary when assessing clients who seek services in community mental health settings.

Utilization of the DSM-IV within the counseling profession is not, however, without controversy. Assigning a diagnosis to a client is uncomfortable for many counselors. The disadvantages associated with using the DSM have included the promotion of a mechanistic approach to mental disorder assessment, the false impression that the understanding of mental disorders is more advanced than is actually the case, and an excessive focus on the signs and symptoms of mental disorders to the exclusion of a more in-depth understanding of the client's problems including human development. Wakefield (1992) has recently argued that the DSM concept of *mental disorder* would better serve people if it were referred to as a *harmful dysfunction*. He has based this on numerous citations that have suggested psychodiagnosis is used to control or stigmatize behavior that is actually more socially undesirable than disordered.

Conversely, advantages to implementing the DSM have included the development of a common language for discussing diagnoses, an increase in attention to behaviors, and facilitation of the overall learning of psychopathology. Seligman (1990) has indicated that knowledge of diagnosis is important for counselors so that they may provide a diagnosis for clients with insurance coverage and inform clients if their counseling will be covered by medical insurance. In addition, a DSM diagnosis assists with accountability and record keeping, treatment planning, communication with other helping professionals, and identification of clients with issues beyond areas of expertise.

Major Psychodiagnostic Features of the DSM-IV

According to the DSM-IV, mental disorders are conceptualized as clinically significant behavioral or psychological syndromes or patterns that occur in a *person* and are associated with *distress* (a painful symptom) or *disability* (impairment in one or more important areas of functioning) or with increased risk of suffering death, pain, disability, or an important loss of freedom. In addition, the syndrome or pattern must not be an expectable response to a particular event (APA, 1994).

Although the DSM system can be difficult to interpret for those with limited clinical experience or personal familiarity with mental disorders, it is relatively easy for experienced counselors to learn. Each DSM-IV contains specific diagnostic criteria, the essential features and clinical information associated with the disorder, as well as differential diagnostic considerations. Information concerning diagnostic and associated features, culture, age, and gender characteristics, prevalence, incidence, course and complications of the disorder, familial pattern, and differential diagnosis are included. Many diagnoses require symptom severity ratings (mild, moderate, or severe) and information about the current state of the problem (e.g., partial or full remission).

The DSM-IV contains fifteen categories of mental disorders. *Disorders Usually First Diagnosed in Infancy, Childhood or Adolescence* focuses on developmental disorders and other childhood difficulties. *Delirium, Dementia, Amnestic and Other Cognitive Disorders* include Alzheimer's conditions and Vascular Dementia. *Mental Disorders Due to a General Medical Condition* include anxiety and mood difficulties as well as personality change due to physical complications. *Substance Related Disorders* consist of drug and alcohol abuse and dependence. *Schizophrenia and Other Psychotic Disorders* are a continuum of difficulties that include lack of contact with reality as well as Delusional Disorders. *Mood Disorders* and *Anxiety Disorders*, including Major Depression and Posttraumatic Stress Disorder are featured diagnoses often used by counselors. *Somatoform Disorders, Factitious Disorders, Dissociative Disorders, Sexual and Gender Identity Disorders, Eating Disorders, Sleep Disorders, Impulse Control Disorders, Adjustment Disorders*, and *Personality Disorders* are among the other diagnostic categories in the DSM-IV. In addition, several lesser disorders referred to as V Codes are included (e.g., Parent-Child Relational Problem, Partner Relational Problem, Bereavement, and Occupational Problem). Due to the V Codes' "minor status," they are typically not covered by third party payers.

The Multiaxial System

Diagnoses in the DSM-IV are coded by the *multiaxial system* which incorporates five axes. All diagnoses except for Personality Disorders are coded on Axis I. Only Personality Disorders and Mental Retardation are coded on Axis II. Axis III is for physical disorders and conditions. Axes IV and V represent Severity of Psychosocial and Environmental Problems and Global Assessment of Functioning (GAF), respectively, and are used for treatment planning and prognosticating. For example, a full multiaxial diagnosis would be presented as:

AXIS I: 309.00 Adjustment Disorder with Depressed Mood
V61.12 Partner Relational Problem
AXIS II: 799.90 Diagnosis deferred on Axis II
AXIS III: None
AXIS IV: Change of jobs
AXIS V: GAF=66

In DSM-IV, the multi-axial diagnosis is optional. When considering a DSM-IV diagnosis, the frequency, intensity, and duration of symptoms as well as premorbid functioning must be addressed.

Sociocultural Implications

Professional counselors utilizing DSM-IV diagnoses wield sizeable power that can be interpreted as oppressive to some groups of people. Third party interests (i.e., insurance carriers) also may bring nonscientific values into the diagnostic process.

An accurate psychodiagnosis depends on ethnocultural and linguistic sensitivity (Malgady, Rogler & Constantino, 1987). Clients of lower socioeconomic class may experience, define, and manifest mental disorders differently from middle- and upper-class clients. Moreover, the DSM's lack of focus on the problematic features of a social context may be perpetuating the oppression of certain groups of people (e.g., women). Gender and race of clinician also have been found to impact an accurate psychodiagnosis (Loring & Powell, 1988). Counselors using the DSM-IV will need to be keenly aware of the implications associated with its use as well as the impact a diagnosis may have on a client's treatment –within and outside of the counseling process.

In conclusion, the DSM-IV is not the only psychodiagnostic nomenclature in existence, but it is the most popular and is here to stay. Counselors have utilized it in a professional manner in the past, use the DSM-IV today, and will use the DSM-V in the future. An up-to-date under standing of this diagnostic system and its vast implications in counseling will be imperative to the effective and ethical delivery of professional community mental health counseling services.

References

American Psychiatric Association. (1994). *Diagnostic and statistical manual of mental disorders* (4th ed.). Washington, DC: Author.

Hinkle, J. S. (in press). The DSM-IV is coming: Prognosis and implications for mental health counselors. *Journal of Mental Health Counseling.*

Loring, M. & Powell, B. (1988). Gender, race, and DSM-III: A study of the objectivity of psychiatric diagnostic behavior. *Journal of Health and Social Behavior, 29,* 1-22.

Malgady, R. G., Rogler, L. H., & Constantino, G. (1987). Ethnocultural and linguistic bias in mental health evaluation of Hispanics. *American Psychologist, 42,* 228-234.

Pavkov, T. W., Lewis, D. A., & Lyons, J. S. (1989). Psychiatric diagnoses and racial bias: An empirical investigation. *Professional Psychology: Research and Practice, 20,* 364-38.

Perry, S., Frances, A., & Clarkin, J. (1990). *A DSM-III-R casebook of treatment selection.* New York Brunner/Mazel.

Seligman, L. (1990). *Selecting effective treatments: A comprehensive systematic guide to treating adult mental disorders.* San Francisco: Jossey-Bass.

Wakefield, J. C. (1992). The concept of mental disorder: On the boundary between biological facts and social values. *American Psychologist, 47,* 373-388.

J. Scott Hinkle is Associate Professor of Counselor Education at the University of North Carolina at Greensboro.

CHAPTER THIRTY–SIX

Diagnosing Children's Mental Disorders Using the DSM-IV

Thomas H. Hohenshil

Diagnosis of children's mental disorders is a process which often involves several mental health professionals, as well as parents, teachers, and others who have significant knowledge of the child involved. The process may take place in a mental health agency, private practice setting, hospital, school, or some combination of these settings. Although some clinicians use the terms testing, assessment, and diagnosis interchangeably, there are some significant differences which are important to note. Assessment is the process of collecting information for use in the diagnostic process and can involve such sources as standardized tests, interviews, questionnaires, checklists, behavioral observations, projective tests, and reports (medical, etc.) by significant others. Tests, then, are only one of several ways to collect assessment information to use in the diagnostic process. Diagnosis, on the other hand, is the meaning that is derived from assessment information using some type of mental health classification system. The *Diagnostic and Statistical Manual of Mental Disorders* (DSM-IV; American Psychiatric Association, 1994) is the classification system used in mental health settings. Diagnosis involves a comparison, or matching, of the child's symptoms with lists of DSM-IV diagnostic criteria. If the symptoms meet or exceed the criteria, then a diagnosis is made (Hohenshil, 1995).

The Diagnostic and Treatment Process

In practice, the diagnostic and treatment processes are interdependent and interact through the following six steps:

Step 1.

Referral: Since children normally do not self refer, someone else usually refers the child. This may be the parent(s), medical personnel, social services, school personnel, or the court system. Although some elementary school children refer themselves through elementary school counseling programs, it is a general rule that the younger the child the lower the probability of self referral. Preschool children are almost always referred by parents, social services, or medical personnel. As noted later in this digest, this can be a problem in both diagnosis and treatment processes.

Step 2.

Symptom Identification: Identification of the child's symptoms is a critical part of the diagnostic process since the DSM-IV is highly dependent upon behavioral symptoms. Information about number, type, duration, and severity of symptoms is developed from a variety of sources. The most frequently used techniques are semi-structured child diagnostic interviews, mental status examinations, interviews with significant others (parents, teachers, siblings, peers, etc.), behavioral observation, medical and social reports, psychological testing, and educational records.

Step 3.

Diagnosis: Diagnosis is a comparison of the symptoms the child exhibits with the diagnostic criteria for the mental disorders included in the DSM-IV. A DSM-IV diagnosis also requires that the symptoms be considerably in excess of those expected from other children of a similar developmental age. The degree of symptom severity is important because most children have at least some of the symptoms listed in the DSM-IV in various degrees. The DSM-IV requires that one or more of the following "severity" criteria must be met in order to diagnose a mental disorder: significant distress must be present in the child; or there must be significant impairment of educational, occupational, or social functioning; or the symptoms must cause significantly increased risk or loss of freedom. In practice, children with diagnosable mental disorders usually meet more than one of the severity criteria.

Step 4.

Treatment Planning: Effective treatment planning is highly dependent upon accurate diagnoses because the therapeutic techniques selected are determined by the type of mental disorder diagnosed. Research on differential therapies is relatively new; however, we are at a point where it is possible to determine the specific therapeutic techniques that are effective with most of the children's mental disorders. The treatment plan normally includes a description of the disorder, both short-and long-term treatment objectives, interventions to be used, and the prognosis.

Step 5.

Treatment: The treatment techniques should follow the course outlined in the treatment plan. The techniques, frequency of treatment, and the type or orientation of the clinician are obviously important factors. After the conclusion of successful treatment, it may be necessary to change the diagnosis, for the child's symptoms may be in remission. Or, other disorders might become more evident as treatment progresses, and additional diagnoses may need to be made. In any event, there is often a fluid nature to the diagnostic and treatment processes where neither can be considered independent of the other.

Step 6.

Follow-up: This step is important in determining whether the treatment is effective and if other counseling techniques may be helpful. Follow-up to successful treatment also is important to determine if the symptoms remain in remission (Hohenshil, 1995).

Special Problems Diagnosing Children

The DSM-IV has a section which includes mental disorders that are usually first diagnosed in infancy, childhood, or adolescence. Some of the most frequently diagnosed children's disorders are Mental Retardation, Learning Disorders, Attention Deficit Hyperactivity Disorder, Conduct Disorder, Autism, Elimination Disorders, and Separation Anxiety. It is important to note that most of the disorders included in other sections of the DSM-IV can also be diagnosed in children and adolescents, including Mood Disorders, Anxiety Disorders, Substance-Related Disorders, Psychotic Disorders, Adjustment Disorders, Sexual and Gender Identity Disorders, and Sleep Disorders (American Psychiatric Association, 1994; Hohenshil, 1994; Popper & Steingard, 1994). In fact, adolescents can be diagnosed with practically any of the disorders included in the DSM-IV.

Due to a number of factors, it is frequently more difficult to diagnose children than adults, and the younger the child the more tenuous the diagnosis. The fact that children do not normally self-refer can cause a problem of motivation. Persons who self-refer are more cooperative in the diagnostic process and more likely to make progress in treatment. Also, children who are referred by others are frequently not well-prepared by the referring party, and thus do not understand why they are being seen by a mental health counselor although they are sure that it is not because things are going well for them. A second problem is that young children have limited language facility which requires more inferences by the clinician; and the younger the child, the more language is a problem. Even if a young child uses many of the same words as adults, the meaning ascribed to them may be quite different. A third problem in diagnosing children is that significant others (e.g., parents, teachers, etc.) often provide a major part of the information about the child's behavior. The clinician then has to determine the validity of the adults observations of the child's behavior; in other words, is the parent or teacher a reliable observer of the child's behavior? Most experienced clinicians have seen children where it is strongly suspected that the problem resides more with the parent than with the child. Due to the problems noted here, the diagnoses of children are simply less reliable because clinicians have to make more inferences about the child's behavior and emotional status while arriving at a diagnosis (Hohenshil, 1995; Sattler, 1988).

Conclusion

Diagnosing children's mental disorders presents an interesting challenge to most clinicians. Psychopathology research clearly suggests that children should not be considered as just "little adults" in the diagnostic and treatment process. Over the last 40 years, testing instruments, semi-structured interview procedures, and observational techniques have been developed to reflect the unique nature of children's language and psychological development. The DSM series also has focused significant attention on the disorders of children, and each revision has resulted in a refinement of the diagnostic criteria. The current DSM-IV probably reflects more changes in the section for children than in any other section. The result is more clearly defined behavioral criteria and more accurate diagnoses. However, due to the nature of young children's language and cognitive development, the reliability of child diagnoses should be viewed with caution.

References

American Psychiatric Association. (1994). *Diagnostic and statistical manual of mental disorders* (4th ed.). Washington, DC: Author.

Hohenshil, T. H. (1994). *DSM-IV: What's new. Journal of Counseling and Development, 73,* 105-107.

Hohenshil, T. H. (September, 1995). *Using the DSM-IV with children and adolescents.* Blacksburg, VA: Donaldson Brown Hotel and Conference Center.

Popper, C. W., & Steingard, R. J. (1994). Disorders usually first diagnosed in infancy, childhood, or adolescence. In R. H. Hales, S. C. Yudofsky, & J. A.

Talbott, (Eds.), *Textbook of psychiatry.* Washington, DC: American Psychiatric Press.

Sattler, J. M. (1988). *Assessment of children.* San Diego: Jerome M. Sattler, Publisher.

Thomas H. Hohenshil, Ph.D., is Professor of Counseling and Psychology at Virginia Tech, Blacksburg.

References

CHAPTER THIRTY-SEVEN

Disorders Usually First Diagnosed in Infancy, Childhood, or Adolescence: the DSM-IV

Shirley Delva

Overview

The DSM-IV (American Psychiatric Association, 1994) contains a myriad of disorders that are usually first diagnosed in infancy, childhood, or adolescence. Although the provision is made for this category, it is often difficult to make a clear distinction between adult and childhood disorders. When diagnosing children or adolescents, it is imperative that counselors not limit the diagnosis to a specific category. If the client meets the full criteria for a disorder, then a diagnosis should be considered. Because of the brevity of this paper, each disorder will not be extensively elaborated. However, the essential features of each disorder and a summarization will be presented. The following disorders are included in this section of the DSM-IV:

Mental Retardation

Mental Retardation refers to substantial limitations in cognitive functioning. It is characterized by significantly subaverage general intellectual functioning, existing concurrently with related limitations in two or more of the following adaptive skills areas: communication, self-care, home living, social/interpersonal skills, use of community resources, self-direction, functional academic skills, work, leisure, health, and safety. In addition, the onset of Mental Retardation must occur before age 18.

Persons with Mental Retardation have typically been classified according to the degree of severity of their problems. Mild, moderate, severe, and profound retardation are used to specify the degree of severity. The following are the approximate IQ levels used to specify the severity of Mental Retardation: mild retardation, IQ level 50-55 to approximately 70; moderate retardation, IQ level 35-40 to 50-55; severe mental retardation, IQ level 20-25 to 35-40; and profound mental retardation, IQ level below 20-25.

Learning Disorders

Learning Disorders, formerly known as Academic Skills Disorders, are diagnosed when there is a discrepancy of more than 2 standard deviations between academic achievement and IQ. Usually, the client's achievement on mathematics, reading, or written expression is below what is expected for age, schooling, and level of intelligence. Also, learning problems should adversely affect academic achievement or daily living that require reading, writing, or mathematic skills.

Motor Skills Disorder

Developmental Coordination Disorder is associated with significant impairment in the development of motor coordination. Children may display clumsiness when performing daily living tasks. For example, buttoning shirts, tying shoelaces, walking, or crawling. Diagnosis is made if developmental coordination is not a result of a medical condition, and significantly interferes with daily living activities and academic achievement. If Mental Retardation is present, developmental coordination must be in excess of what is usually associated with the degree of Mental Retardation.

Communication Disorders

The following communication disorders are included in the DSM-IV: Expressive Language Disorder, which can occur in individuals who have a family history of Communication or Learning Disorders and is usually recognized by age 3. Expressive Learning Disorder is diagnosed when the scores obtained from standardized measures of expressive language development are below those obtained from standardized measures of both nonverbal intellectual capacity and receptive language development. Difficulties with expressive language interfere with academic, social communication, and occupational achievement.

If the person suffers from a Mixed Receptive/Expressive Language Disorder, the individual will have difficulty understanding words, sentences or specific types of words. The client will score low on the standardized measure of nonverbal capacity. Problems with expressive language significantly interfere with academic or occupational achievement, and with social communication.

Phonological Disorder, formerly Developmental Articulation Disorder, is a failure to use developmentally expected speech sounds that are appropriate for age and dialect. The difficulties in speech sound production may interfere with academic or occupational achievement or with social communication.

The onset of Stuttering, a fluency disorder, is usually between the ages of two and seven years. Stuttering entails a disturbance in the normal fluency and time patterning of speech that is inappropriate for the individual's age. The disturbance in fluency interferes with academic or occupational achievement, or with social communication.

Pervasive Developmental Disorders

The characteristics of many developmental disorders are not entirely distinct. In young children, differentiating among these conditions is often difficult. All of the disorders in this category are characterized by severe and pervasive impairment in several areas of development: communication skills, interests and activities, the presence of stereotyped behavior, and reciprocal social interaction. The Pervasive Developmental Disorders are usually associated with a myriad of other medical conditions. Autistic Disorder, Rett's Disorder, Childhood Disintegrative Disorder, and Asperger's Disorder are included in this category.

Attention-Deficit and Disruptive Behavior Disorders

Individuals with attention problems display persistent patterns of distractibility and or hyperactivity-impulsivity. The onset is usually before age seven. Impairment from the symptoms must be present in at least two settings. For example, the symptoms must be present at home and at school or work. The majority of individuals with Attention-Deficit Disorder have symptoms of both inattention and hyperactivity-impulsivity. However, there are some individuals in whom one or the other pattern is predominate. The following are the subtypes of Attention-Deficit/Hyperactive Disorder (AD/HD): AD/HD, combined type; ADHD, predominantly inattentive type; and ADHD, hyperactive-impulsive type.

Feeding and Eating Disorders of Infancy or Early Childhood may be due to a general medical condition. For example, an infant's eating habits may change if he or she suffers from a gastrointestinal or endocrinological condition. However, a diagnosis of Feeding Disorder of Infancy or Early childhood should be made if there is a persistent failure to eat adequately with significant failure to gain weight or significant loss of weight over at least one month. Additionally, the onset of the disorder must be before age six.

Tic Disorders

A tic is characterized by rapid, recurrent vocalization or stereotyped motor movement. Tourette's Disorder, Chronic Motor or Vocal Tic Disorder, and Transient Tic Disorder are three disorders included in this section. Tourette's Disorder is characterized by recurrent motor or phonic tics that usually appear by age seven and have a waxing-and-waning course (Pauls, Leckerman, & Cohen, 1993). This disorder causes significant impairment in occupational, social, or related areas of functioning and the onset is before age 18.

Chronic Motor or Vocal Tic Disorder is characterized by recurrent vocal or motor tics, but not both. Tic Disorder differs from Tourette's Disorder in which there must be both multiple motor and one or more vocal tics. Like Tourette's Disorder, the diagnosis should be made if the disturbance is not due to physiological effects of a substance or a general medical condition, there is significant distress in social or occupational functioning, and the onset is before age 18. The essential features of Transient Tic Disorder are the same as for Tourette's Disorder, except that the tics are single or multiple motor and or vocal tics, may occur several times a day, and may occur daily for at least four weeks but for no longer than twelve consecutive months.

Elimination Disorders

Encopresis, repeated passage of feces into inappropriate places and Enuresis, repeated voiding of urine on to bed or clothes are included in Elimination Disorders. These diagnoses should be made whether the behavior is intentional or involuntary, but when the disorder is not due to a general medical condition or the physiological effect of a substance. Also, Encopresis should be diagnosed if the person is at least four years old and the behavior occurs at least once a month for at least three months. However, the diagnosis of Enuresis should be made if the child is at least five years and behavior occurs twice per week for at least three months.

Conclusion

The DSM-IV is a useful guide in diagnosing psychological disorders. However, the DSM-IV should not be the sole criteria for diagnosis. The counselor's clinical judgement as well as cultural and ethnic considerations are important in the diagnostic process. Proficiency in the DSM-IV is critical for professional counselors, and its use will assist counselors with accountability and record keeping. Finally, an essential benefit of the DSM-IV is the improvement of treatment planning, particularly with infants, young children, and adolescents.

References

American Psychiatric Association (1994). *Diagnostic and Statistical Manual of Mental Disorders,* (4th ed.). Washington, DC: Author.

Pauls, D. L., Leckerman, J. F., & Cohen, D. J. (1993). Familial relationship between Gilles de la Tourette's Syndrome, attention deficit disorder, learning disabilities, speech disorders and stuttering. *Journal of the American Academy Child and Adolescent Psychiatry, 32,* 1044-1050.

Pauls, D. L., Raymond, C. L., Leckman, J. F., & Stevenson, J. M. (1991). A family study of Tourette's syndrome. *American Journal of humanistic Genetics, 48,* 154-163.

Shirley Delva is a school counselor in Greensboro, North Carolina.

CHAPTER THIRTY–EIGHT

Attention Deficit/Hyperactivity Disorder (AD/HD)

Robert R. Erk

Counselors in schools, agencies or counseling centers, and private practice are increasingly viewed by many in our society as the contact person for information on the prevalence, probable causes, and treatment for individuals diagnosed with AD/HD. Research has given counselors useful information concerning AD/HD. Although estimates for the prevalence rate of AD/HD can vary, the disorder seems to occur in 5 to 10% of school-age children, adolescents, or adults. A few researchers have reported a prevalence rate as high as 20% of children who are school-age. AD/HD is diagnosed in boys three to five times more frequently than in girls.

There are sufficient lines of research evidence to support the claim that AD/HD is a genetically based disorder, resulting in an irregular metabolism of brain chemicals which are thought to fuel the AD/HD symptoms and problematic behaviors. These factors are presumed to significantly contribute to multiple problems with organization, attention, impulsivity, and hyperactivity at school and in the home. AD/HD is not a disease or illness, instead it needs to be viewed by counselors as a reflection of the physiology and biochemistry of the person. AD/HD should be regarded as a neurobiological or neurobehavioral condition that can be reliably diagnosed.

The DSM-IV and AD/HD

Counselors should be skilled in the use of the *Diagnostic and Statistical Manual of Mental Disorders* (American Psychiatric Association, 1994) because it is the primary diagnostic tool for diagnosing AD/HD. The DSM-IV (1994) codes AD/HD based on subtypes with different predominating symptom patterns that have persisted in the individual for at least six months. AD/HD is divided into three subtypes: AD/HD, Predominantly Inattentive Type which includes individuals who present six or more symptoms of inattention but not hyperactivity or impulsiveness; AD/HD, Predominantly Hyperactive-Impulsive Type which includes individuals with six or more symptoms of hyperactivity and impulsivity but who are not significantly inattentive; and AD/HD, Combined Type which includes individuals with six or more symptoms of inattention and six or more symptoms of hyperactivity-impulsivity. Subtypes of AD/HD help counselors recognize that a unique pattern of symptoms or problems exist and these individuals deserve special attention which focuses on the prominent features connected to their subtype.

The Diagnosis of AD/HD: A Multimethod, Multisource, Multisetting Approach

The diagnosis of AD/HD can present particularly difficult diagnostic decisions. AD/HD is often mishandled with many individuals being undiagnosed or incorrectly diagnosed. When such occurs, these persons are denied the benefits of correct treatment. In cases of individuals suspected to have AD/HD, the designing of a multi-method (medical examination, direct observations, AD/HD behavior rating scales or checklists, psychoeducational evaluation, academic records or report cards, sociometric devices); multi-source (child, adolescent, or adult, parents, siblings, physician, school psychologist, school counselor, speech, hearing, or learning disabilities specialist, mental health, agency, or private practice counselor, peergroup); and a multi-setting (home or family, school or classroom, play activities, community) approach can produce the necessary collection of quality information or data. Importantly, this approach allows the counselor to verify that the diagnosis of AD/HD stands the test of time and assessment across methods, sources, and settings.

Multidimensional Treatment of AD/HD

Counselors are moving to the view that AD/HD is a condition that requires a long-term and broad-based treatment approach. Researchers have concluded that co-occurring or coexisting conditions such as academic underachievement, peer group or personal-social problems, learning disorders, communication disorders, oppositional defiant disorder, conduct disorders, anxiety disorders, attachment difficulties, mood swings, and depression may often be connected to individuals diagnosed with AD/HD.

The weight of research evidence supports the multidimensional treatment approach as enhancing or optimizing the potential of individuals diagnosed with AD/HD and any comorbid or co-occurring conditions. Multidimensional treatment usually includes the following interventions: medication, individual or group counseling sessions, parent and teacher education and training on the disorder, behavioral management techniques, social skills training, self-esteem training, and family counseling. Counselors have become increasingly aware that the multi-skill deficits and multiple problems that these individuals can present necessitate an ongoing multiple treatment plan. Furthermore, treatment or interventions for AD/HD are more effective when they are tailored by counselors to accommodate the individual's specific needs, address individual deficits, the antecedents and the consequences of the problematic behaviors, and embrace the interventions or resources needed to facilitate healthy development or growth.

Conclusions for Counseling Individuals with AD/HD

Counselors are encouraged to participate in the following ways: (a) serve as the coordinator or manager for the assessment and delivery of services or interventions for individuals diagnosed with AD/HD; (b) serve as a consultant for the problematic behaviors that are exhibited; (c) design or modify counseling programs or services to fit the needs of these individuals across settings (Counselors who hesitate to modify or adjust their therapeutic orientation or techniques to match the cognitive and behavioral deficits or problems of clients with AD/HD may experience far less success); (d) provide feedback on personal-social functioning or development; (e) organize and provide seminars or workshops on AD/HD for parents and teachers; and (f) serve as community advocates for individuals with the disorder.

An important component in the counseling of individuals with AD/HD can be the personal style of the counselor. The personal style of the counselor must be one of humane service, diplomacy, sensitivity, and compassion. It should be pointed out that moralizing, overly judgmental attitudes, and a condescending style assure poor rapport with AD/HD clients and their families and reduces or diminishes motivation for individuals with AD/HD and their families to invest in counseling.

Individuals with AD/HD view many of their problems as "not their own", routinely blaming and distrusting teachers, parents, siblings, and peers. These individuals have often been traumatized by years of frustration, failure, and rejection. Many have used denial as their main defense mechanism and may have retreated into a make-believe world where their problems cannot hurt them. The counselor that can display accurate empathy, unconditional positive regard, genuineness, and maintain a here-and-now orientation in counseling may be able to develop a positive relationship with these clients.

Counselors should remember that in many instances counselees with AD/HD often are concrete in their thinking, operate largely on a here-and-now orientation; are often disinterested in delaying gratification or rewards, can be argumentative or inattentive; may not be especially verbal, have difficulty with internal speech and find verbalizing or articulation to be a tenuous task; and typically find that counseling lacks novelty or uniqueness after a session or two. Counselors who can build a positive relationship, identify areas of achievement and good functioning, promote pride and pleasure, and salvage self-esteem may have the greatest chance to facilitate long-term change. Improving the self-esteem of these individuals should often be a core concern of counselors. Counselors who can thrive on the challenge that many individuals with AD/HD present and who can remain remarkably patient and understanding in counseling seem to have a distinct advantage.

References

American Psychiatric Association (1994). *Diagnostic and statistical manual of mental disorders* (4th ed.). Washington, DC: Author.

Barkley, R. A. (1990). *Attention-deficit hyperactivity disorder: A handbook for diagnosis and treatment.* New York: Guilford.

Erk, R. R. (1995). The conundrum of attention deficit disorder. *The Journal of Mental Health Counseling, 17,* 131-145.

Friedman, R. J., & Doyal, G. T. (1992). *Management of children and adolescents with attention-deficit hyperactivity disorder.* Austin, TX: Pro-Ed.

Goldstein, S., & Goldstein, M. (1990). *Managing attention disorders in children: A guide for practitioners.* New York: John Wiley.

Merrill, K. W. (1994). *Assessment of behavioral, social, and emotional problems: Direct and objective methods for use with children and adolescents.* New York: Longman.

Robert R. Erk is an associate professor in the Department of Educational Studies at the University of Tennessee at Martin, TN.

CHAPTER THIRTY–NINE

DSM-IV: Delirium, Dementia, and Amnestic and Other Cognitive Disorders

Carol D. Verhulst

One of the unique abilities of the human brain is the capacity to experience a sense of self. Memory is a critical component of this sense of self because it is constructed from personal experiences that are catalogued in the memory. The loss of memory becomes one of life's cruelest tragedies, robbing the person of a sense of self. When a person has ongoing problems with their memory and cognitive functions, the counseling professional's clients are not the only affected person, families also suffer. An understanding of cognitive disorders, as classified by the *Diagnostic and Statistical Manual of Mental Disorders,* Fourth Edition (DSM-IV) (American Psychiatric Association, 1994), will help the mental health counselor to correctly diagnose individuals affected by a loss of memory and cognitive functioning. Cognitive functions include memory, learning, and attention, and these functions control the acquiring, storing, and usage of information.

Delirium, Dementia, and Amnestic and other Cognitive Disorders comprise the second category of mental disorders in the DSM-IV. Losses in cognitive functions or memory, or both, with the losses representing a significant change from previous levels of functioning characterize this category of disorders. The sections included in this category are delirium, dementia, amnestic disorders, and cognitive disorders not otherwise specified. The specified causes of each disorder are a general medical condition, the use of a substance (e.g., abusable substance or medication), or a combination of the two. While cognitive disorders are generally associated with older adults, some of these disorders can affect all ages, including children.

Delirium

Delirium is a disorder of attention. The term comes from the Latin *de lira,* meaning "off the path." The primary feature is a disturbance of consciousness accompanied by a change in cognition. This disturbance develops over a short period of time, usually hours to days, and has a tendency to fluctuate during the day. The delirious person is less aware of the surrounding environment, becomes easily distracted, and has difficulty with concentrating and following commands. Changes in cognition can include memory impairment, disorientation, language disturbance, or a perceptual disturbance such as hallucinations, illusions, or misinterpretations (e.g., misinterpreting the sound of a door banging as a gunshot). Changes in the sleep-wake cycle are often associated with delirium, including nighttime sleeping difficulties, daytime sleepiness, or a complete reversal of the normal night-day sleep-wake cycle. This disorder is more prevalent in older adults, but also can occur in children and younger adults. Possible causes include a general medical condition, substance use, multiple medical conditions, or a combination of the two etiologies.

Examples of general medical conditions that may cause delirium include: fluid or electrolyte imbalances, systemic infections, metabolic disorders such as hypoglycemia, postoperative states, head trauma, and thiamine deficiency. Children and older adults are more susceptible to these medical conditions and to delirium caused by these conditions. The counselor may have difficulties in correctly diagnosing delirium, since it is considered relatively normal for both age groups to have difficulties in concentrating, to be easily distracted, and to seem disoriented. The counselor can interview family members to verify the sudden and unusual nature of the symptoms. Confirmation of the diagnosis of Delirium Due to a General Medical Condition requires evidence that the cognitive disturbance is the direct physiological consequence of a general medical problem. The diagnosis must specify that medical condition as part of the diagnosis (e.g., Delirium Due to Thiamine Deficiency).

The symptoms for Substance-Induced Delirium are the same as for other deliriums, but the etiology must include a history of substance intoxication, substance withdrawal, exposure to toxin(s), or medication use that is etiologically related to the symptoms. The mental health counselor must name the specific substance as a part of the diagnosis. Delirium Due to Multiple Etiologies is indicated if the delirium has the following causes: multiple general medical conditions, a general medical condition plus substance or medication or toxin use, or a combination of any of these etiologies. The counselor actually codes each diagnosis separately; there is no coded diagnosis for Delirium Due to Multiple Etiologies. If the person displays the symptoms required for a diagnosis of delirium, but the etiology is different from the above etiologies, then the diagnosis is Delirium Not Otherwise Specified. An example of such an etiology is sensory deprivation.

Dementia

Dementia is a disorder that occurs almost exclusively in older adults and it is characterized by memory impairment and the development of multiple cognitive deficits. The term comes from the Latin *de mens*, meaning "from the mind." Cognitive deficits include: aphasia (impaired language function), apraxia (impaired ability to perform motor activities despite intact motor abilities, sensory function, and understanding of the required task), agnosia (impaired ability to recognize or name objects despite intact sensory function), or a disturbance in executive functioning (e.g., performing new tasks). Memory and cognitive impairments must be severe enough to cause significant impairment in social or occupational functioning, and the impairments must represent a decline from a previous level of functioning. Other symptoms commonly found among dementia patients include: spatial disorientation, poor judgment and insight, disinhibited behavior such as neglecting personal hygiene or disregarding social rules of conduct, over-estimation of abilities, and personality changes.

The estimated prevalence rates for dementia are 5% of adults aged 65 and over, and 20% of adults aged 85 and over (Ineichen, 1987). The most common cause of dementia is Alzheimer's disease, estimated to cause more than 50% of all dementias. The next most common cause is vascular disease. Other causes documented in the DSM-IV are: HIV disease, head trauma, Parkinson's disease, Huntington's disease, Pick's disease, Creutzfeldt-Jakob's disease, other general medical conditions, substance-induced dementia, multiple etiologies, and causes not otherwise specified.

The onset of Dementia of the Alzheimer's Type is insidious, usually beginning with slight deficits in short-term memory, and the course of the dementia is progressive and irreversible. Persons with dementia of the Alzheimer's type gradually lose control over most cognitive functions. They may not be able to recognize family members, know how to eat or dress themselves, or remember where they are and how they came there. Patients with advanced dementia must be monitored 24 hours a day, since they may wander or attempt to perform activities that may become dangerous to themselves (e.g. leaving the stove on). Caretaking of the Alzheimer's patient becomes a major strain on family members. Persons with dementia of the Alzheimer's Type live, on average, from 8 to 10 years from the onset of the disease.

The diagnosis of this dementia is made only when other etiologies are ruled out, since the only definitive diagnosis can occur with a brain autopsy. The DSM-IV distinguishes between early onset, defined as occurring before the age of 65, and late onset, defined as occurring after age 65. Subtypes identify prominent features of the patient's dementia: with delirium, with delusions, with depressed mood, and uncomplicated type.

Persons with Vascular Dementia typically exhibit an abrupt onset that is followed by rapid changes in functioning, but the course also may be highly variable and could be gradual in nature. Exhibited memory and cognitive deficits are usually "patchy" in nature, since specific areas of the brain are being affected by the vascular disease process. As a result of this patchiness, certain cognitive functions may remain relatively unimpaired. For instance, the person may not remember the names of family members but remain capable of balancing the checkbook and taking care of personal hygiene activities. Early treatment of the underlying vascular problems may prevent further progression of this dementia. Subtypes of this dementia are the same subtypes used for Dementia of the Alzheimer's Type: with delirium, with depressed mood, and uncomplicated.

The other causes of dementia occur much less frequently than Alzheimer's and vascular disease. The following causes of dementia may occur before the age of 65: HIV disease, head trauma, Huntington's disease, Pick's disease, Creutzfeldt-Jakob's disease, other general medical conditions, and Substance-Induced Persisting Dementia. Of the above causes, Pick's disease, Creutzfeldt-Jakob's disease, and Substance-Induced Persisting Dementia have dementia as a prominent and expected outcome of that condition. Pick's disease is a rare degenerative disease of the brain and Creutzfeldt-Jakob's disease is a rare central nervous system disease. Huntington's disease is an inherited degenerative disease involving cognition, emotion, and movement deficiencies, and rarely causes dementia.

Other causes of dementia more typically found in older adults are: Parkinson's disease, which is a neurological condition, Dementia Due to Multiple Etiologies, and Dementia Not Otherwise Specified (NOS). Dementia NOS is the coding used for dementias that do not meet the criteria for any of the other dementias listed above.

Amnestic Disorders

Persons with amnestic disorders experience disturbances in memory that impair the ability to learn new information or recall previously learned information or past events. The memory disturbance is sufficiently severe to cause impairment in social or occupational functioning and represents a significant decline from previous levels of functioning. Unlike the television soap opera sufferer of amnesia, the person with an amnestic disorder has difficulty recalling new information as well as the recall of past events, and the person rarely forgets his or her own identity and sense of self. The person with an amnestic disorder usually lacks insight into the memory impairments and may deny having memory impairments despite evidence to the contrary.

Amnestic disorders are classified as transient, with the duration lasting from hours to days and for no more than one month, or as chronic for disturbances lasting longer than one month. Causes of amnestic disorders are: general medical condition, substance use, including medications; and causes not otherwise specified, when the specific etiology is unknown. General medical conditions causing amnestic disorders are usually conditions that cause damage to the brain. Examples include head traumas, penetrating missile wounds, surgical intervention, and hypoxia. When evidence exists that the cause of the disorder is related to the persisting effects of substance use, the diagnosis is Substance-Induced Persisting Amnestic Disorder. Substance use includes drugs of abuse, medications, or toxins. This disturbance persists after the other effects of the substance use dissipate. Amnestic Disorder Not Otherwise Specified is the diagnosis for amnestic disorders with causes that do not match any of the above causes.

Cognitive Disorder Not Otherwise Specified

This category includes disorders caused by a general medical condition with cognitive dysfunctions that do not meet the criteria for any of the specific deliriums, dementias, or amnestic disorders previously listed in this DSM-IV category. Examples include: postconcussional disorder characterized by continuing cognitive impairments following a concussion caused by a closed head injury; and a mild neurocognitive disorder characterized by mild deficits in at least two areas of cognitive functioning; with each disorder not meeting the criteria for other cognitive disorders or for other mental disorders.

Mental Health Counseling Implications

The cognitive disorders belonging to this DSM-IV category dramatically affect the social and occupational functioning of the person suffering from their effects. Such individuals may experience depression and anxiety, particularly during the early stages following diagnosis. These disorders dramatically affect family members, who also may experience depression and anxiety. Mental health counselors must be prepared to not only treat the direct effects of the disease, such as the loss of cognitive abilities and memory, but also the indirect effects arising from awareness of the increasing loss of the sense of self.

References

American Psychiatric Association. (1994). *Diagnosis and statistical manual of mental disorders* (4th ed.). Washington, DC: Author.

Birren, J. E., Sloane, R. B., & Cohen, G. D. (Eds.). (1992). *Handbook of mental health and aging* (2nd ed.). San Diego: Academic Press.

Hinkle, J. S. (1990). An overview of dementia in older persons: Identification, diagnosis, assessment, and treatment. *Journal of Mental Health Counseling, 12*, 368-383.

Ineichen, B. (1987). Measuring the rising tide: How many dementia cases will there be by 2001? *British Journal of Psychiatry, 150*, 193-200.

Carol D. Verhulst, Ed.S., NCC is a doctoral student in Gerontological Counseling in the Department of Counseling and Specialized Educational Development at the University of North Carolina at Greensboro.

CHAPTER FORTY

DSM-IV and the Substance-Related Disorders

Guttorm Toverud

The fourth edition of the *Diagnostic and Statistical Manual of Mental Disorders* (American Psychiatric Association, 1994) was published in 1994. In DSM-I (1952) alcoholism and drug dependence were a subset of sociopathic personality disturbance. The DSM-II (1968) did not improve the diagnosis of chemically dependent persons, still considering them a threat to societal order.

In 1980, the DSM-III took a giant step away from implied moralizing and contained separate categories for substance use disorders including abuse and dependence. The DSM-III-R (1987) emphasized the alcohol dependence syndrome of Edwards and Gross (1976). This included compulsive use, characterized by cognitive, behavioral, and psychological factors. These less restrictive criteria allowed for the identification of the substance dependence symptoms of tolerance or withdrawal.

The DSM-IV Substance-Related Disorders encompass 13 different disorders: Alcohol-Related Disorders, Amphetamine (or Amphetamine-Like)-Related Disorders, Caffeine-Related Disorders, Cannabis-Related Disorders, Cocaine-Related Disorders, Hallucinogen-Related Disorders, Inhalant-Related Disorders;, Nicotine-Related Disorders, Opioid-Related Disorders, Phencyclidine (or Phencyclidine-Like)-Related Disorders,

Sedative, Hypnotic-, or Anxiolytic-Related Disorders; Polysubstance-Related Disorder; and Other (or Unknown) Substance-Related Disorders. These Substance-Related Disorders are divided into two groups; Substance Use Disorders (dependence and abuse) and the Substance-Induced Disorders which include: Substance Intoxication, Substance Withdrawal, Substance-Induced Delirium, Substance-Induced Persisting Dementia, Substance-Induced Persisting Amnestic Disorder, Substance-Induced Psychotic Disorder, Substance-Induced Mood Disorder; Substance-Induced Anxiety Disorder, Substance-Induced Sexual Dysfunction and Substance-Induced Sleep Disorder. The Substance-Induced Disorders are located in the sections of the DSM-IV that have disorders of similar phenomenology. Adding Substance-Induced Disorders is a significant change from the DSM-III-R and aids in differential diagnosis (1994).

Comorbidity, or co-occurrence, plays an important role in the diagnosis and treatment of individuals with psychiatric disorders. Major Depression, Dysthymia, Anxiety Disorders (including phobia), Antisocial Personality Disorder and Sexual Disorders are the most conspicuous psychiatric disorders associated with the Substance-Related Disorders. Studies show that up to 50% of substance abusers have diagnosable psychiatric disorders (Miller, Leukefeld, & Jefferson, 1994). It may be difficult to make accurate diagnostic distinctions because symptoms can mimic each other.

It is interesting to note that the seeking of treatment for substance abuse is associated with psychopathology. The literature is sparse and often not in agreement as to the relationship between substance use and psychopathology. This also is evident in terms of self-medication and the etiology of the different disorders, time of onset, clinical course, and what type of treatment is appropriate. Nathan (1991) argues that individuals need to be "clean and sober" for 4-6 weeks before one can reliably diagnose a psychiatric disorder that is not a Substance-Induced Disorder.

The DSM-IV (1994) defines substance dependence as:

> "A cluster of cognitive, behavioral, and physiological symptoms showing that the individual continues use of the substance despite significant substance-related problems. There is a pattern of repeated self-administration that usually results in tolerance, withdrawal, and compulsive drug-taking behavior. A diagnosis of substance dependence can be applied to every class of substance except caffeine" (p. 176).

Substance dependence entails a maladaptive pattern of substance use across all substance categories, leading to clinically significant impairment or distress, as manifested by three (or more) of the following, occurring any time in the same 12-month period:

1) tolerance, as defined by either of the following:
   a) a need for markedly increased amounts of the substance to achieve intoxication or desired effect
   b) markedly diminished effect with continued use of the same amount of the substance;
2) withdrawal, as manifested by either of the following:
   a) the characteristic withdrawal syndrome for the substance
   b) the same (or a closely related) substance is taken to relieve or avoid withdrawal symptoms;
3) the substance is often taken in larger amounts or over a longer period than was intended;
4) there is a persistent desire or unsuccessful efforts to cut down or control substance use;
5) a great deal of time is spent in activities necessary to obtain the substance, using the substance, or recover from its effects
6) important social, occupational, or recreational activities are given up or reduced because of substance use;
7) the substance use is continued despite knowledge of having a persistent or recurrent physical or psychological problem that is likely to have been caused or exacerbated by the substance (1994, p. 181).

Likewise, substance abuse is defined as: "a maladaptive pattern of substance use manifested by recurrent and significant adverse consequences related to the repeated use of substances" (p. 182). This definition is in contrast to the DSM-III-R where substance abuse became a residual category when the criteria for substance dependence was not met. Criteria for substance abuse entail a maladaptive pattern of substance use leading to clinically significant impairment or distress, as manifested by one (or more) of the following, occurring within a 12-month period:

1) recurrent substance use resulting in a failure to fulfill major role obligations at work, school, or home;
2) recurrent substance use in situations in which it is physically hazardous;
3) recurrent substance-related legal problems;
4) continued substance use despite having persistent or recurrent social or interpersonal problems caused or exacerbated by the effects of the substance. The symptoms must not have ever

met the criteria for Substance Dependence for the specific substance (1994, P. 182-183).

It is now believed that the distinction between substance abuse and substance dependence is central to the diagnosis of the Substance-Related Disorders. In the DSM-IV, substance abuse is no longer a residual category. Substance abuse can now be diagnosed according to specific behaviors associated with the social consequences of substance use.

Substance dependence maintains the emphasis on compulsive use and social and occupational impairment from both the DSM-III and DSM-III-R. Recent studies have been conducted to respond to criticism from previous editions of the DSM regarding generalization of the dependence syndromes across substances. Morgenstern, Langenbucher, and Labouvie (1994) found that there was strong support for the employment of a single set of criteria for alcohol, cannabis, cocaine, stimulants, sedatives, and opiates. They did not find the same results for hallucinogens regarding dependence as hallucinogens do not appear to result in tolerance or withdrawal.

Langenbucher, Morgenstern, and Miller (1995) found that most drugs correlated with the test variables in the nosological comparison between DSM-III, DSM-IV, and the ICD-10. Even lifetime DSM-IV diagnosis of alcohol, cannabis, cocaine and opiate dependence was deemed excellent in terms of reliability.

In conclusion, the DSM-IV is the latest in a series of The Diagnostic and Statistical Manual of Mental Disorders attempting to unify the nomenclature. The Substance-Related Disorders section enables a clinician to diagnose substance dependence without evidence of tolerance or withdrawal. This strengthens the validity of the criteria across all substance classes.

References

American Psychiatric Association. (1952). *Diagnostic and statistical manual of mental disorders.* Washington, DC: Author.

American Psychiatric Association. (1968). *Diagnostic and statistical manual of mental disorders* (2nd. ed.). Washington, DC: Author.

American Psychiatric Association. (1980). *Diagnostic and statistical manual of mental disorders* (3rd. ed.). Washington, DC: Author.

American Psychiatric Association. (1987). *Diagnostic and statistical manual of mental disorders* (3rd. ed. Revised). Washington, DC: Author.

American Psychiatric Association. (1994). *Diagnostic and statistical manual of mental disorders* (4th ed.). Washington, DC: Author.

Carroll, K. M., Rounsaville, B. J., & Bryant, K. J. (1994). Should tolerance and withdrawal be required for substance dependence disorders? *Drug and Alcohol Dependence, 36,* 15-22.

Edwards, G., & Gross, M. M. (1976). Alcohol dependence: Provisional description of a clinical syndrome. *British Medical Journal, 1,* 1058-1061.

Langenbucher, J. W., Morgenstern, J., & Miller, K. (1995). DSM-III, DSM-IV, and ICD-10 as severity scales for drug dependence. *Drug and Alcohol Dependence, 39,* 139-150.

Miller, T. W., Leukefeld, D. S. W., & Jefferson, B. (1994). Dual diagnosis: Clinical issues in substance abuse treatment. *Journal of Contemporary Psychotherapy, 24,* 169-177.

Morgenstern, J., Langenbucher, J., & Labouvie, E. W. (1994). The generalizability of the dependence syndrome across substances: An examination of some properties of the proposed DSM-IV dependence criteria. *Addiction, 89,* 1105-1113.

Nathan, P. (1991). Substance use disorders in the DSM-IV. *Journal of Abnormal Psychology, 100,* 356-361.

Guttorm Toverud MA, is a doctoral student at the University of North Carolina at Greensboro, Department of Counseling and Educational Development.

CHAPTER FORTY–ONE

Schizophrenia and Other Psychotic Disorders

Wendy B. Charkow

Many definitions of the term *psychotic* currently exist. Generally, they relate to three separate characteristics: the presence of active symptomology such as delusions and/or hallucinations; impairment of functioning so that the individual is unable to meet ordinary life demands; and the loss of ego boundaries or reality testing. Psychotic Disorders share a common set of symptomology, and are categorized as disorders of thought, speech, affect, orientation, and psychomotor activity. For example, many individuals suffering from a Psychotic Disorder may experience grammatical incoherence, inappropriate affect, and thought broadcasting (the individual believes that everyone can hear his or her thoughts). In addition, Psychotic Disorders are associated with delusional activity, such as delusions of persecution or of grandeur, and may feature hallucinations or perceptions that are not reality-based.

Psychotic Disorders may be the result of an abnormality in the brain, defective genes, chemical imbalances, or an unsupportive family environment. Some assert that Psychotic Disorders result from living in an uncaring society that too strongly emphasizes the importance of conformity among all members. It is most probable that Psychotic Disorders result from a myriad of factors. Whatever the etiology, it is generally accepted that those afflicted suffer greatly and can benefit from a combination of psychotropic treatments, "talking" therapy, and the support of significant others.

Schizophrenia

Schizophrenia is the most commonly given diagnosis for individuals with Psychotic Disorders. The lifetime prevalence of Schizophrenia is usually found to be between 0.5% and 1%, with incidence rates at approximately 1 per 10,000 persons per year. An individual with Schizophrenia can best be described as one who engages in bizarre ways of thinking, behaving, and feeling that interfere with his or her ability to function in everyday life. Whitaker and Puente (1992) described the three primary characteristics of Schizophrenia as lack of communication with others, inability to distinguish fantasy from reality, and extreme fear. Schizophrenic symptoms are often categorized as either positive or negative. Positive symptoms are usually acute, and include phenomena such as delusions or hallucinations. Negative symptoms tend to present themselves as chronic and include social isolation, ahedonia, and blunted affect. In order for an individual to be accurately diagnosed with Schizophrenia, the characteristic signs and symptoms must have been present for a significant amount of time in a one-month period, with signs of Schizophrenia persisting for at least six months (APA, 1994).

Five subtypes of Schizophrenia have been established by the DSM-IV. The "Paranoid Type" is specified if the prominent symptoms include a preoccupation with frequent delusions or hallucinations. A second subtype, "Disorganized Type" is specified when the individual displays prominent disorganization of speech, behavior, and affect. "Catatonic Type" is indicated when the person experiences two or more of the following: motor immobility, excessive motor activity, extreme negativism, mutism, peculiarities of voluntary movement, echolalia, and echopraxia. The fourth subtype, "Undifferentiated Type" is accurately applied when the person displays characteristic symptoms of Schizophrenia but cannot be classified as under the first three subtypes. Finally, the fifth subtype, "Residual Type" is used when there has been at least one episode of Schizophrenia, but the individual no longer displays positive psychotic symptoms. There is still evidence in this subtype of negative symptoms or less severe positive symptoms. This subtype may represent a transition between active episodes and remission, or may be present for years.

The average age of onset of Schizophrenia is between the mid to late twenties. According to McGlashan (1994), approximately 10% of cases occur after the age of 40. The majority of individuals display gradual characteristics of this disorder before active-phase symptoms appear. The course and outcome of this disorder vary widely among individuals: some display exacerbations and remissions, whereas others display chronic symptoms indefinitely. Complete remission is rare, and interventions are generally aimed at helping the individual develop coping skills and improving his or her quality of life.

Schizophreniform Disorder

Unlike persons with Schizophrenia who display symptoms for at least 6 months, individuals with Schizophreniform Disorder display symptoms of Schizophrenia from one to six months. In addition, individuals diagnosed with Schizophreniform Disorder do not necessarily experience impaired social or occupational functioning as do those with Schizophrenia (APA, 1994).

The DSM-IV established two specifiers for Schizophreniform Disorder. The first specifier, "With Good Prognostic Features" is applied when at least two of the following characteristics are evident: the individual displayed symptoms within four weeks after the first noticeable change in behavior, experienced confusion or perplexity at the apex of the psychotic episode, displayed good premorbid functioning,or experienced no blunted or flat effect. If these features are not evident, "Without Good Prognostic Features" is then applied. Generally, one-third of those diagnosed with Schizophreniform Disorder recover within six months, whereas the following two-thirds progress to a diagnosis of Schizophrenia or Schizoaffective Disorder.

Schizoaffective Disorder

The major characteristics of Schizoaffective Disorder entail concurrent symptoms of both Schizophrenia and either a Depressive, Manic, or mixed Episode for a substantial duration of the Psychotic Disorder. In addition, delusions or hallucinations must be present for at least a two-week period with no signs of mood disturbance. The average individual with Schizoaffective Disorder first experiences delusions and hallucinations for a two-month period, followed by a major depressive episode. These conditions normally occur together for about three months, after which the individual recovers from the major depressive episode. The psychotic symptoms usually persist for about one month before disappearing (1994).

The DSM-IV established two subtypes for this disorder. The first subtype, "Bipolar Type" is specified when the mood disturbance is either a Manic or mixed Episode. The second subtype, "Depressive Type" is specified if the mood disturbance includes only a Major Depressive Episode (APA, 1994).

The typical age of onset is early adulthood, although it can occur anytime between adolescence and later life. The prognosis for this disorder is generally more positive than that for Schizophrenia, although it is worse than the outcome for Mood Disorders. It is possible that those diagnosed as "Bipolar Type" can expect a better prognosis.

Delusional Disorder

Individuals with Delusional Disorder experience bizarre delusions (beliefs not based in reality), but none of the symptoms that characterize the other psychotic disorders. If the individual's functioning is impaired, it is due to the impact of the delusions. These delusions must last for at least one month.

The DSM-IV has established seven subtypes of Delusional Disorder. The first subtype, "Erotomanic Type" involves delusions that another person is in love with the individual. The second subtype "Grandiose Type" is noted when the individual experiences delusions of inflated power, worth, knowledge, or special relationships. "Jealous Type" is specified if the individual has delusions that his or her sexual partner is unfaithful. The fourth subtype "Persecutory Type" involves delusions that the individual is being treated in a malevolent manner. "Somatic Type" is specified when the delusions involve a physical defect or medical condition. The sixth subtype "Mixed Type" is noted when there are delusions that are characteristic of more than one of the type mentioned above. Finally, "Unspecified Type" is used when the dominant delusional belief cannot be classified into the suggested typology.

Unlike Schizophrenia, the average age of onset for Delusional Disorder is generally in middle to late adulthood. The course is quite variable, with some individuals experiencing intermittent delusions with periods of remission, some experiencing chronic delusions, and some experiencing a full remission.

Brief Psychotic Disorder

The main characteristic of Brief Psychotic Disorder is a sudden onset of psychotic symptoms, including delusions, hallucinations, disorganized speech, or grossly disorganized or catatonic behavior. The duration of these symptoms is one day to one month, with eventual full return to premorbid functioning. The DSM-IV has established specifiers for this diagnosis dealing with the presence of marked stressors or a postpartum state prior to the psychotic episode (1994).

This disorder is uncommon. The average age of onset is in the late twenties or early thirties. It should be noted that if the symptoms last longer than a month, a diagnosis of Schizophreniform Disorder can then be applied.

Shared Psychotic Disorder

Shared Psychotic Disorder occurs when an individual who is closely involved with someone who already has a Psychotic Disorder with prominent delusions, also experiences the same or similar delusions. This most often occurs in close two-person relationships, where the person who is diagnosed with Shared Psychotic Disorder was initially healthy. This is a rare disorder that has not been widely researched. When intervention occurs and the individual is separated from the person with the primary Psychotic Disorder, the delusions disappear.

Psychotic Disorder Due to a General Medical Condition

An individual diagnosed with Psychotic Disorder due to a General Medical Condition experiences prominent delusions or hallucinations that are a direct physiological consequence of a medical condition. The delusions or hallucinations cannot be accounted for by another mental disorder, or they occur solely in the course of a delirium. Medical conditions that may cause psychotic symptoms include neurological conditions, endocrine conditions, metabolic conditions, fluid or electrolyte imbalances, hepatic or renal diseases, and autoimmune disorders associated with the central nervous system. The onset and course of this disorder reflect the etiological medical condition (1994).

Substance-Induced Psychotic Disorder

An individual who receives the diagnosis of Substance-Induced Psychotic Disorder can best be described as experiencing delusions or hallucinations that develop during Substance Intoxication or Withdrawal, or are related to medication use. The clinician must show that the disturbance is not better accounted for by a Psychotic Disorder that is not substance induced; therefore, symptoms must not precede substance use or persist for a significant amount of time following the cessation of substance use. Further, the psychotic symptoms must not occur exclusively during a delirium. When coding this disorder, the subtypes, "With Delusions" or "With Hallucinations" and the specifiers, "With Onset During Intoxication" and "With Onset During Withdrawal" should be applied to the diagnosis, as well as the specific substance that induces the disorder (APA, 1994).

Associated Disorders

Research has shown that Psychotic Disorders are often associated with other psychological problems such as various Substance-Related Disorders, Mood Disorders, Personality Disorders, Obsessive Compulsive Disorder, Dementia of the Alzheimer's Type, Vascular Dementia, and Body Dysmorphic Disorder. The DSM-IV notes that Schizophrenia shares characteristics with and may be preceded by Schizotypal, Schizoid, or Paranoid Personality Disorder. The DSM-IV also points out that many individuals with psychotic disorders also experience mood disturbances. It is important for clinicians to take these secondary problems into account and incorporate them into the evaluation and treatment of clients (APA, 1994).

Atypical Psychotic Disorders

It is often a difficult task to apply a DSM-IV diagnosis when evaluating persons with psychotic disorders; many of the symptoms for the different disorders are associated. In addition, it is sometimes confusing when a mood disorder or personality disorder is superimposed on a psychotic disorder. Finally, not all of the clients with presenting psychotic symptoms can be easily classified into specific disorders. Therefore, the DSM-IV contains a Not Otherwise Specified (NOS) category in each diagnostic class to be used when the clinical features of a disorder suggest the class of disorders but do not meet all of the criteria for any of the specific disorders in that class (APA, 1994).

Psychotic Disorder NOS may include, but is not limited to, the following examples:

(1) postpartum psychosis that does not meet the specific criteria for any of the specific Psychotic Disorders or Mood Disorders with Psychotic Features;

(2) psychotic symptoms that have lasted for less than one month without remission;

(3) persistent auditory hallucinations without any other features;

(4) persistent non-bizarre delusions with periods of overlapping mood episodes that are present for a substantial portion of the delusional disturbance; and

(5) situations when psychotic symptoms are present but cannot be determined if caused by the psychotic disorder, medical condition, or substance use.

Continuum of Prognosis

Research shows that complete recovery for individuals with psychotic disorder is rare, although there may be long periods of remission. Therefore, individuals presenting with psychotic disorders generally require long-term services and interventions. Clients will benefit from a constellation of different treatments including neuroleptic medication, vocational rehabilitation, and counseling. In addition, many individuals with psychotic disorders require assistance both in coordinating interventions and in functioning in everyday life. Therefore, it is important for counselors to act as supportive advocates and coordinators for these clients.

References

American Psychiatric Association. (1994). *Diagnostic and statistical manual of mental disorders* (4th ed.). Washington, DC: Author.

Cooperrider, C. (1988). Psychoses and schizophrenia. In G. W. Clawson & C. Cooperrider (Eds.), *Clinical psychopharmacology: A practical reference for nonmedical psychotherapists.* (33 - 40). Maryland: Aspen.

Liberman, R., Marshall, B., Marder, S., Dawson, M., Nuechterlein, K., & Doane, J. (1984). The nature and problem of schizophrenia. In A. S. Bellack (Ed.), *Schizophrenia: Treatments, management, and rehabilitation.* (pp.1 - 34). Florida: Grune and Stratton.

McGlashan, T. H. (1994). Late onset schizophrenia. In T. A. Widiger, A. J. Frances, H. A. Pincus, M. B. First, R. Ross, & W. Davis (Eds.), *DSM-IV sourcebook (Volume I).* (pp. 441-446). Washington, DC: American Psychiatric Association.

Mendel, W. M. (1989). *Treating schizophrenia.* California: Jossey-Bass.

Whitaker, L. C. & Puente, A. E. (1992). *Schizophrenic disorders: Sense and nonsense in conceptualization, assessment, and treatment.* New York: Plenum.

Wendy B. Charkow is a graduate student at The University of North Carolina at Greensboro.

CHAPTER FORTY–TWO

Dual Diagnosis and Co-Dependency

J. Scott Hinkle

Dual diagnosis, a common problem, is the combination of a DSM-IV Axis I disorder and a Substance-Related disorder (Jonas & Gold, 1992). The percentage of individuals in treatment for drug and alcohol difficulties, who also have at least one mental disorder, ranges from 30% to 70%. A significant number of the nearly one million people with chronic mental disorders in the United States have problems with substance dependence. Of the approximate three million homeless people in this country, it is estimated that somewhere between 33% and 75% have this comorbidity (Wilens, O'Keefe, O'Connell, Springer, & Renner, 1993). For example, over half of cocaine abusers have a mood disorder (Sederer, 1990). Similarly, the prevalence of depression in the alcohol dependent population has been estimated to range from 20% to 90%. A lifetime history of substance-related problems was found in 47% of individuals with schizophrenia, 56% of those with bipolar disorder, and 86% of these with antisocial personality disorder (Reiger, Narrow, & Rae, 1990). Unfortunately, dual diagnosis is often related to crime, domestic violence, suicide, fatal accidents, job loss, family dysfunction, and poor treatment outcome (Goodwin & Lotterhos, 1991; McKelvy, Kane, & Kellign, 1987; Wilens, et al., 1993).

Dixon, Haas, Weiden, Sweeney, & Francis, 1990, among others, have argued that substance-dependent individuals use substances to self-medicate distressful affective states and other psychological symptoms. Allen and Frances (1986) have described four possibilities that may contribute to the co-occurrence of a substance-related disorder with another mental disorder. First, the coexisting mental disorder could be a direct result of the pharmacologic and behavioral consequences of the substance abuse. This position also has been posited by Schuckit (1983, 1988) for mental disorders that begin during or after the onset of a substance-related disorder. Secondly, the substance-related disorder may be the direct result of another preexisting mental disorder, such as depression or panic disorder, which can lead to self-medication. Thirdly, the presence of a substance-related disorder in the presence of a mental disorder could simply be coincidental. This option, however, is becoming unacceptable since studies are revealing that the risk of almost all of the mental disorders is elevated among individuals with any history of substance or alcohol abuse. Lastly, both the substance-related and the co-occurring mental disorder could be the result of a third, unidentified, common etiological factor that may be biological, familial, or social in nature.

Making the Dual Diagnosis

Dual *or multiple* diagnoses are easy for professionals to overlook. The term "dual diagnosis" is not restricted to psychoses and mood disorders alone, but includes anxiety disorders, eating disorders, and other disorders that interfere with full well-being (Zweben, 1992). Dual diagnoses can result in diagnostic confusion since they may have a different course and prognosis because of the interaction between the disorders (Sederer, 1990).

Substance abuse affects all aspects of life. For instance, employment difficulties include absenteeism, poor work performance, stressed work relationships, being out of step with peers, and secondary difficulties associated with the rigors of the workplace (Fahnestock, 1993). Thus, data from all life areas needs to be obtained in order to make an accurate dual diagnosis.

There exists a need for specific diagnostic criteria for identifying clients with diagnoses encompassing mental and substance abuse disorders. Furthermore, dual diagnoses clients are not a homogeneous group. For example, what may work for chronically depressed alcohol-dependent individuals may not work for anxious individuals who abuse prescription drugs (see Ford, Hillary, Giesler, Lassen, & Thomas, 1989).

Treatment of Dual Diagnosis

The presence of a dual diagnosis influences the timetable of recovery and plays an underestimated role in relapse (Zweben, 1992). For instance, substance abuse clients with a co-existing personality disorder have a poorer response to intensive treatment (Nace & Davis, 1993). Furthermore, many alcohol-dependent individuals will not require medication (e.g., an antidepressant) once they are sober. However, a subgroup of clients who continue to be depressed when sober may have a co-existing major depressive disorder which requires intensive treatment (Sederer, 1990).

Individuals with a dual diagnosis have historically been difficult to counsel. They frequently use emergency services, are often misdiagnosed, and are at risk for violence and suicide. Specialized services are needed for this group because of their poor fit in either the mental health or substance abuse treatment systems. Individuals with a dual diagnosis are often treated by mental health counselors who have little formal training or experience with substance abuse, or such patients are seen in the substance abuse arena by individuals with little training in mental health counseling. Many detoxification facilities cannot accept clients who require psychotropic medications, while many psychiatric units are hesitant to admit a patient prior to detoxification (Wilens et al., 1993). When these individuals are seen jointly, it is likely that information is not shared. Moreover, dual diagnosis clients may not be eligible for services because their mental disorder is not clearly evident. Therefore, counselors should be cross-trained in comorbid substance abuse and mental disorder diagnosis and treatment (Wolfe & Sorensen, 1989).

Dually diagnosed clients typically are not good candidates for medication therapy and are often shuttled back and forth between psychiatric hospitals and alcohol abuse programs. In either event, therapists typically treat one disorder rather than integrate treatment strategies (Rahav et al., 1993). Moreover, dual diagnosis subgroups may require different treatment plans. For instance, higher functioning individuals may be referred to Alcoholics Anonymous and counseling. Moderate functioning individuals with family and social support may receive similar treatment, but may require more intensive counseling or inpatient treatment. Low functioning individuals may require professionally staffed medical treatment and long-term follow-up care (Morris & Wise, 1992). Interestingly, McLellan (1986) has found that individuals with substance dependency and a mental disorder, who are counseled by peers (i.e., "recovering counselors"), decreased in functioning and had lower follow-up recovery rates than those treated by professionals. In addition, there appears to be a significant positive relationship between degree of progress and duration of treatment. Highly structured environments that incorporate small and large counseling groups have been found to be effective in the treatment of dual diagnosis. This includes aspects of psychoeducational recovery-directed self-help groups that focus on self-awareness (Wilens et al., 1993). In addition, family and relationship counseling is often beneficial, particularly when co-dependency is an issue.

Co-Dependency

There is currently a plethora of information on the concept of *co-dependency.* However, it is not recognized in the DSM-IV. Harper (1988) has noted that billions of dollars in health insurance is spent on alcoholism treatment and that many professionals in the chemical dependency field would like to fit co-dependency into a diagnostic and health insurance reimbursable category. Greenleaf (1981) used the term *co-alcoholic* to describe an adult who "assists in maintaining the social and economic equilibrium of the alcoholic person" (p. 3). The term co-alcoholic was transformed to co-dependency in order to be a more inclusive term for people involved in a relationship with a substance dependent individual (Cermak, 1986). The concept of co-dependency has its roots in the theory of alcoholism as a family issue (see Shorkey & Rosen, 1993; Woititz, 1983).

Subby and Freil (1984) have defined co-dependency as a

> "dysfunctional pattern of living and problem solving which is nurtured by a set of rules within the family system...these rules make healthy growth and change very difficult" (p. 3).

Co-dependency has been further defined as the product of dysfunctional families in which children cannot develop a clear identity. Yet, another perspective focuses on real or perceived abuse and neglect as the cause of co-dependency (Subby, & Friel, 1984). Moreover, without empirical documentation, co-dependency has been expanded to include enabling relationships with disturbed individuals who are not necessarily substance dependent (Shorkey & Rosen, 1993).

Co-dependent individuals often share in the denial of the problem with the addicted person. They believe the problem will magically discontinue, that life circumstances will mitigate against the problem, or that the dependent person will suddenly recognize the problem and change his or her behavior (Whitfield, 1984). The non-abusing co-dependent person may lose his or her sense of identity over time and may habitually focus on protecting and meeting the needs of others. They also may be unprepared for the major changes in their social and emotional environment and may experience devastating fear, anxiety, resentment, and depression as the familiar is replaced by the unknown and unpredictable (Shorkey & Rosen, 1993). Co-dependency can be described within a family of origin framework in which people reared in dysfunctional families fail to develop a clear and coherent sense of personal identity (Shorkey & Rosen, 1993). A family systems, problem-solving framework is useful not only for conceptualizing how co-dependency develops, but also is helpful as a guide to assessment and treatment with families having a chemically dependent member (D'Zurilla & Goldfried, 1971; Nezu & D'Zurilla, 1981a, 1981b).

When problem-solving efforts fail, the co-dependent individual may suffer heightened emotional disturbances as a result of repeated frustrations. This process often continues until one or more family members develops an emotional disorder that requires treatment, the family system deteriorates, someone dies, or the chemically dependent family member begins to take steps toward recovery (Woititz, 1983). Shorkey and Rosen (1993) have asked: Why do so many individuals choose ineffective problem-solving strategies to attain personal or family goals? The answer may be a lack of knowledge about the dynamics of an addicted family system. Fortunately, knowledgeable mental health counselors can be of great service to such families.

References

Allen, M. H., & Francis, R. J. (1986). Varieties of psychopathology in patients with addictive disorders: A review. In R. E. Meyer (Ed.), *Psychopathology and addictive disorders* (pp. 17-38). New York: Guilford.

Cermak, T. L. (1986). Diagnostic criteria for codependency. *Journal of Psychoactive Drugs, 18,* 15-20.

Dixon, L., Haas, G., Weiden, P., Sweeney, J., & Francis, A. (1990). Acute effects of drug abuse in schizophrenic patients: Clinical observations and patients' self-reports. *Schizophrenic Bulletin, 16,* 69-79.

D'Zurilla, T. J., & Goldfried, M. R. (1971). Problem solving and behavior modification. *Journal of Abnormal Psychology, 78,* 107-126.

Fahnestock, R. (1993). The impact of substance abuse and post-traumatic stress disorder. In E. M. Freeman (Ed.), *Substance abuse treatment: A family systems perspective* (pp. 157-188).

Ford, J., Hillary, J. R., Giesler, L. J. Lassen, K. L., & Thomas, H. (1989). Substance abuse/mental illness: Diagnostic issues. *American Journal of Drug and Alcohol Abuse, 15,* 297-307.

Goodwin, L. R., & Lotterhos, J. F. (1991). Substance abuse counselor education program. *Rehabilitation Education, 5,* 43-51.

Greenleaf, J. (1981). *Co-alcoholic: Para-alcoholic.* Los Angeles: The 360 Foundation.

Harper, F. D. (1988). Alcohol and black youth: An overview. *Journal of Drug Issues, 18,* 7-14.

Jonas, J. M., & Gold, M. S. (1992), The pharmacologic treatment of alcohol and cocaine abuse: Integration of recent findings into clinical practice. *Pediatric Psychopharmacology, 15,* 179-190.

McKelvy, M. J., Kane, J. S., & Kellign, K. (1987). Substance abuse and mental illness double trouble. *Journal of Psychosocial Nursing, 25,* 20-25.

McLellan, A. T. (1986). Psychiatric severity as a predictor of outcome from substance abuse treatments. In R. E. Meyer (Ed.), *Psychopathology and addictive disorders* (pp. 97-139). New York: Guilford.

Morris, J. A., & Wise, R. P. (1992). The identification and treatment of the dual diagnosis patient. *Alcoholism Treatment Quarterly, 9,* 55-64.

Nace, E. P., & Davis, C. W. (1993). Treatment outcome in substance-abusing patients with a personality disorder. *American Journal on Addictions, 2,* 26-33.

Nezu, A., & D'Zurilla, T. J. (1981a). Effects of problem definition and formulation on decision making in the social problem-solving process. *Behavior Therapy, 12,* 100-106.

Nezu, A., & D'Zurilla, T. J. (1981b). Effects of problem definition and formulation on the generation of alternatives in the social problem-solving process. *Cognitive Therapy and Research, 5,* 265-271.

Rahav, M., Guagenti-Tax, E., Rivera, J., Raskin, R., Gross, B., Sturz, E. L., Struening, E. L., Pepper, B., & Link, B. G. (1993). Dually diagnosed men in different community treatment programs: A longitudinal evaluation study. In J. A. Inciardi, F. M. Tims, & B. W. Fletcher (Eds.), *Innovative Approaches in the Treatment of Drug Abuse* (pp. 71-84). Westport, CT: Greenwood Press.

Regier, D. A., Narrow, W. E., & Rae, D. S. (1990). The epidemiology of anxiety disorders: The epidemiologic catchment area experience. *Journal of Psychiatric Research, 24,* 3-14.

Schuckit, M. (1983). Alcoholic patients with secondary depression. *American Journal of Psychiatry, 140,* 711-714.

Schuckit, M. (1988). Evaluating the dual diagnosis patient. *Drug Abuse and Alcoholism Newsletter, 17,* 1-4.

Schuckit, M. A., & Gold, E. O. (1988). A simultaneous evaluation of multiple markers of ethanol/placebo challenges in sons of alcoholics and controls. *Archives of General Psychiatry, 45,* 211-216.

Sederer. L. I. (1990). Mental disorders and substance abuse. In H. B. Milkman & L. I. Sederer (Eds.), *Treatment choices for alcoholism and substance abuse* (pp. 163-181). Westport, CT: Greenwood Press.

Shorkey, C. T., & Rosen, W. (1993). Alcohol addiction and codependency. In E. M. Freeman (Ed.), *Substance abuse treatment: A family systems perspective* (pp. 100-121). London: Sage.

Subby, R., & Friel, J. (1984). Co-dependency–A paradoxical dependency. In *Co-dependency: An emerging issue.* Pompano Beach, FL: Health Communications.

Treffert, D. A. (1978). Marijuana use in schizophrenia: A clear hazard. *American Journal of Psychiatry, 135,* 1213-1215.

Whitfield, C. L. (1984). Co-alcoholism: Recognizing a treatable illness. *Family and Community Health, 7,* 16-27.

Wilens, T. E., O'Keefe, J., O'Connell, J. J., Springer, R., & Renner, J. A. (1993). A public dual diagnosis detoxification unit. *American Journal on Addictions, 2,* 91-98.

Woititz, J. G. (1983). *Adult Children of Alcoholics.* Deerfield Beach, FL: Health Communications.

Wolfe, H. L., & Sorensen, J. L. (1989). Dual diagnosis patients in the urban psychiatric emergency room. *Journal of Psychoactive Drugs, 21,* 169-175.

Zweben, J. E. (1992). Issues in the treatment of the dual-diagnosis patient. In B. C. Wallace (Ed.), *The chemically dependent: Phases of treatment and recovery* (pp. 298-309). New York: Brunner/Mazel.

J. Scott Hinkle, Ph.D., NCC, CCMHC teaches at the University of North Carolina at Greensboro.

CHAPTER FORTY–THREE

Cannabis-Related Disorders

Liliana R. Sznaidman

As with most other substances of abuse, Cannabis-Related Disorders should be assessed in the light of the diagnostic guidelines for all Substance-Related Disorders. The generic diagnosis criteria apply to Cannabis Dependence, Cannabis Abuse, and Cannabis Intoxication, however, additional information specific to cannabis, is worth noting.

The percentage of delta-9-tetrahydrocannabinol (THC), the compound responsible for the psychoactive effects of cannabis, has considerably increased in the past three decades, although its content in marijuana tends to vary. This needs to be taken into account in diagnosing and in attempting to evaluate possible physiological effects.

Other Cannabis-Induced Disorders (not discussed in this paper) which are included in the *Diagnostic and Statistical Manual of Mental Disorders, Fourth Edition* (1994) are: Cannabis Intoxication Delirium, included in the Delirium, Dementia, and Amnestic and other Cognitive Disorders; Cannabis Induced Psychotic Disorders, found in the Schizophrenia and Other Psychotic Disorders section, and Cannabis-Induced Anxiety Disorder, discussed under Anxiety Disorders. The rationale for this separate grouping lies in their shared phenomenology with each specific cluster of disorders. However, these diagnoses are actually made under the Substance-Related Disorders category.

Cannabis Dependence

The Cannabis Dependence diagnosis is given to individuals who display compulsive use and who have developed tolerance due to chronic use. Individuals with this diagnosis spend a great deal of their time obtaining the drug, and use high doses of it throughout the day, for months or years (1994).

As stated in the DSM-IV, physiological dependence is not generally present, and psychological dependence, while not common, is more likely to occur. Some studies, however, have shown that physical dependence can take place if the drug is administered in very high doses at short intervals, leading to some short duration withdrawal symptoms such as sweating, nausea, diarrhea, and mood changes. Jones (1992) points out that the reason why tolerance and dependence may not be prevalent is that

> "...most controlled research studies..... give experimental doses only during waking hours, thus allowing significant intoxication-free periods each day" (p.112).

When doses are comparable to those needed for opiates or alcohol intoxication, abstinence symptoms become apparent.

Cannabis Abuse

Cannabis Abuse is associated with interference with work or school performance as well as legal and family problems, provided that tolerance stays at moderate levels and that these problems are not the result of compulsive use. The latter would warrant a Dependence diagnosis.

Because cannabis has been a very popular drug for years among adolescents, it is useful to recognize the experimental nature without further consequences of its use, among young individuals. Keeping this perspective in mind will aid the clinician in avoiding a premature diagnosis. Conversely, frequent monitoring of these types of users is advisable in order to ascertain the risk of later multiple drug use (Millman & Beeder, 1994).

Cannabis Intoxication

Individuals would be considered intoxicated by cannabis if, *shortly* after recent use of the drug, they were to display significant maladaptive behaviors and psychological changes, along with two additional signs such as dry mouth, tachycardia, increased appetite, and/or conjunctival injection.

It is important for the clinician to note that these symptoms occur when it is clear that other physical or mental disorders which could account for the cause, are not part of the diagnosis.

Inconclusive Findings

There seems to be some contradiction surrounding the existence of withdrawal symptoms, as well as in the long term physiological and psychological effects of cannabis use. The *DSM-IV* has not included a section on withdrawal symptoms for Cannabis Related Disorders, due to the lack of clinical significance associated with research findings.

The incidence of cannabis in the development of schizophrenia and other psychoses remains to be proven, in spite of some study results pointing in that direction. Other long term effects, such as organic brain damage are mentioned in the literature, although not everyone espouses that concept.

A motivational syndrome as a result of heavy cannabis use, has been described as an overall absence of motivation and goal directed activity, as well as lack of ambition and a deterioration of self-caring habits and social skills. Studies conducted in relation to this syndrome, however, have been flawed due to the absence of control groups or other factors compromising their validity, thus limiting its diagnostic feasibility (Millman & Beeder, 1994).

Treatment

Due in part to its popularity during the 1960s, and to the significance of this date among adolescents and young adults, individuals do not tend to seek treatment or acknowledge heavy use, as they do with other substances. According to the DSM-IV, knowledge of physical or psychological consequences may not deter cannabis dependent individuals from continuous use. Contrary to this criteria, Erickson's (1989) study found that "a concern with health effects might restrain (though clearly not eliminate) the frequency of use in a group of committed users" (p. 181). This would suggest that psychoeducational programs would be a beneficial treatment. But it is important to keep in mind that effective treatment needs to be encompassing and should address the needs of a population that may have complex lifestyles (e.g., multiple drug use). The inclusion of alternative rewards, as well as a focus on what should be done instead of focusing only on what should not be done, is critical during treatment (Millman & Beeder, 1994)

Some of the modalities used in the treatment of cannabis abuse, resemble that of other substance disorders. Group counseling has proven to be beneficial in most cases, whereas 12-Step programs have not been highly regarded among cannabis users, mainly due to a reported lack of commonality. Other treatment modalities may include: family counseling, psychotherapy, behavioral therapy, and inpatient programs.

Cannabis-Related Disorders have been studied for a number of years, however, the presence of contradictory findings concerning numerous diagnostic and treatment issues warrants further intensive research.

References

American Psychiatric Association. (1994). *Diagnostic and statistical manual of mental disorders* (4th ed.). Washington, DC: Author.

Erickson, P. G. (1989) Living with prohibition: Regular cannabis users, legal sanctions, and informal controls. *The International Journal of the Addictions,* 24(3), 175-188.

Hammer, T., & Vaglum, P. (1990) Initiation, continuation or discontinuation of cannabis use in the general population. *British Journal of Addiction, 85,* 899-909.

Jones, R. T. (1987) Drug of abuse profile: Cannabis. *Clinical Chemistry, 33/11B,* 72B-81B.

Jones, R. T. (1992) What have we learned from nicotine, cocaine, and marijuana about addiction? In C. P. O'Brien & J. H. Jaffe (Eds.), *Addictive states (*pp. 109-122). New York, NY: Raven Press.

Millman, R. B., & Beeder, A. B. (1994) Cannabis. In M. Galanter & H. D. Kebler (Eds.), *The American psychiatric press textbook of substance abuse treatment* (pp. 91-109). Washington, DC: American Psychiatric Press.

Wells, F. (1982). Cannabis and dependency. In M. M. Glatt & J. Marks (Eds.), *The dependence phenomenon* (pp.103-117). Ridgewood, NJ: George A. Bodgen & Son, Inc.

Liliana R. Sznaidman is a graduate student in the Department of Counseling and Educational Development at the University of North Carolina at Greensboro.

CHAPTER FORTY–FOUR

Mood Disorders in the DSM-IV

Daniel L. Sander

Overview

Of the mental disorders described in the DSM-IV (American Psychiatric Association [APA], 1994), the Mood Disorders are perhaps the most commonly found in the general public. Mental health counselors in many different settings are likely to work with individuals presenting with a mood disorder. In addition, symptoms mimicking those of the mood disorders are likely to be associated with other presenting problems. For these reasons, it is important for counselors to have a good working knowledge of the mood disorders described in the DSM-IV. Familiarity with the disorders will assist mental health counselors in reaching accurate diagnostic impressions and in setting meaningful treatment goals for clients. Subsequent treatment strategies are then more likely to contribute to a successful and timely resolution of client distress.

An Overview of the Mood Disorders in DSM-IV

The DSM-IV divides the mood disorders into three broad categories, the Depressive Disorders, Bipolar Disorders, and Other Mood Disorders.

Within each category, specific disorders are described in terms of their diagnostic features; specifiers related to the characteristic patterns of symptoms normally found in the disorder; associated features; and specific culture, age, and gender features. Further information related to prevalence in the population, typical course or progression of symptomatology, and characteristic familial patterns is presented. In addition, considerable discussion of differential diagnosis is provided for each disorder. Finally, very specific diagnostic criteria are presented for each of the specific mood disorders.

The information on the specific disorders is preceded by an extensive discussion of mood episodes. These episodes are described in a similar fashion to the disorders, but do not themselves receive categorization as separate diagnoses. Rather, they are presented as the building blocks of the disorders which follow.

The mood disorders section in the *DSM-IV* concludes with a section presenting specifiers intended for use with these episodes. This information is presented in two subsections. The first discusses specifiers intended for use in describing the most recent episode. The second presents specifiers describing the course of recurrent episodes.

Mood Episodes

The mood episodes are closely related to the disorders themselves. Four distinct episodes are identified. These are major depressive episode, manic episode, mixed episode, and hypomanic episode.

A major depressive episode is presented as " a period of at least two weeks during which there is either depressed mood or the loss of interest or pleasure in nearly all activities" (APA, 1994, p. 320). A list of seven additional specific symptoms includes disturbance in eating patterns or weight, disturbance in patterns of sleep, observable changes in psychomotor behaviors, fatigue or energy loss, feelings of worthlessness or guilt not founded in reality, disturbance in thought or concentration, and recurrent thoughts of death or suicide. At least four of the seven symptoms, in addition to one of those noted above, must be present. As with all the mood disorders, symptoms must be associated with impairment in social, occupational, or other important areas of functioning, must not be due to a medical condition or the effect of a drug or medication. Also, the symptoms must not be better accounted for by a mixed episode or by the condition of bereavement.

A manic episode is presented as "a distinct period during which there is an abnormally and persistently elevated, expansive, or irritable mood"

(APA, 1994, p. 328). Abnormal mood must last for at least one week or require hospitalization prior to that time frame and must include at least three further symptoms taken from a list including inflated self-esteem, diminished need for sleep, pressured speech, racing thoughts, distractibility, increased activity directed towards some goal, or excessive pursuit of pleasurable activities potentially leading to undesirable consequences. The symptoms must not be better accounted for by a mixed episode.

A mixed episode is described as a period of time in which the criteria both for a Manic Episode and for a Major Depressive Episode are met nearly every day (1994). The episode must last at least one week and be characterized by moods that alternate rapidly. Symptoms are again expected to interfere with social or occupational functioning or, in this case, to require hospitalization or be accompanied by psychotic features.

A hypomanic episode is described as "a distinct period during which there is an abnormally and persistently elevated, expansive, or irritable mood" (1994, p. 335). At least three of the additional symptoms described for a manic episode must be present and there must be an unarguable change, noticeable to others, in normal functioning of the individual. Unlike the other episodes, however, impairment in social or occupational functioning need not be present.

Depressive Disorders

Perhaps the most commonly recognized mood disorder is Major Depressive Disorder. The primary identifying feature of a Major Depressive Disorder is the presence of one or more Major Depressive Episodes and the absence of a history of any Manic, Mixed, or Hypomanic Episodes. Additionally, the episodes in question must not be better accounted for by another mental disorder. Specifiers that may be applied to the current episode of a Major Depressive Disorder include mild, moderate, severe with or without psychotic features, in partial or full remission, chronic, with catatonic, melancholic, or atypical features, and with postpartum onset. Specifiers that may be applied to the course of the disorder include with or without full interepisode recovery and with seasonal pattern. Further, a diagnostic distinction is made between a Major Depressive Disorder, Single Episode and a Major Depressive Disorder, Recurrent, where two or more major depressive episodes distinguish the recurrent diagnosis.

Dysthymic Disorder features "a chronically depressed mood that occurs most of the day more days than not for at least two years" (APA,

1994, p. 345). In addition, at least two of the remaining symptoms characterizing a major depressive episode must be present, except that thoughts of death or suicide, disturbance in psychomotor behaviors, and loss of interest or pleasure are not included in the list of relevant symptoms for Dysthymic Disorder. Specifiers applying to Dysthymic Disorder include *early onset, late onset,* or *with atypical features.* Finally, Depressive Disorder Not Otherwise Specified is the diagnosis used for a disorder with clinical symptoms of depression that do not meet the criteria for other depressive disorders, nor are they better accounted for by other mental disorders.

Bipolar Disorders

Bipolar I Disorder features a course including one or more manic episodes or mixed episodes. It is often, though not necessarily, characterized as well by one or more major depressive episodes. Bipolar I Disorder may be distinguished as Bipolar I Disorder, *Single Manic Episode, Most Recent Episode Hypomanic, Most Recent Episode Manic, Most Recent Episode Mixed, Most Recent Episode Depressed,* or *Most Recent Episode Unspecified.* Further, the specifiers noted for Major Depressive Disorder, as well as *With Seasonal Pattern* and *With Rapid Cycling,* also may be applied to either the current or most recent episode. Symptoms and/or episodes should not be attributable to another mental disorder.

Bipolar II Disorder features a course including one or more major depressive episodes accompanied by at least one hypomanic episode. In addition, the symptoms may result in distress or impairment of social or occupational functioning and must not be attributed to another mental disorder. The disorder may be further distinguished as Bipolar II Disorder, *Hypomanic* or *Depressed,* as appropriate to the current or most recent episode. The specifiers noted for other Mood Disorders should also be included in the diagnosis, as appropriate.

Cyclothymic Disorder is characterized by a chronic, fluctuating mood disturbance involving numerous periods of hypomanic symptoms and numerous periods of depressive symptoms. Symptoms are not of the severity or duration to meet the criteria for a Manic Episode or a Major Depressive Episode, but they must not disappear for longer than two months in a two year period for an adult and must cause significant impairment in social or occupational function.

Bipolar Disorder Not Otherwise Specified is the diagnosis reserved for disorders characterized by symptoms found in the bipolar disorders but not meeting the strict criteria for a specific disorder.

Other Mood Disorders

Mood Disorder Due to a General Medical Condition is the diagnosis set out for those disorders which feature "prominent and persistent disturbance in mood that is judged to be due to the direct physiological effects of a general medical condition" (APA, 1994, p. 366). Symptoms may resemble those of any of the mood episodes, and may lead to a distinction in subtype. These include *With Depressive Features, With Major Depressive-Like Episode, With Manic Features,* or *With Mixed Features.*

Substance-Induced Mood Disorder is reserved for those disorders that exhibit similar disturbance in mood directly linked to the physiological effects of a substance. There must be evidence that the symptoms developed in direct association with substance intoxication, or within a month of withdrawal from a substance. The disturbance may not be better accounted for by a mood disorder not related to ingestion of a substance. Specifiers include *With Depressive Features, With Manic Features, With Mixed Features, With Onset During Intoxication,* and *With Onset During Withdrawal.*

Mood Disorder Not Otherwise Specified is the diagnosis reserved for those disorders whose symptoms reflect disturbance of mood, but fail to meet the criteria for any other specific mood disorder (APA, 1994).

In conclusion, it is likely the mental health counselor will encounter a client presenting with symptoms resembling those used to delineate mood episodes and subsequently the mood disorders. A working knowledge of the DSM-IV diagnostic criteria will assist the counselor to employ effective treatment services.

References

American Psychiatric Association. (1994). *Diagnostic and statistical manual of mental disorders* (4th ed.). Washington, DC: Author.

Daniel L. Sander, M.S., M.Ed., is a doctoral student in the Department of Counseling and Educational Development at the University of North Carolina at Greensboro.

CHAPTER FORTY–FIVE

Bipolar Disorders in DSM-IV: Diagnosis and Treatment Matching

Gary G. Gintner

Overview

Bipolar Disorders have undergone major modifications in the fourth edition of the *Diagnostic and Statistical Manual of Mental Disorders* (DSM-IV; American Psychiatric Association , 1994). Many of these changes were driven by accumulating research evidence that suggested particular features of a mood episode could predict course and potential treatment response (APA, 1994). For example, a pattern of rapid cycling (i.e., four or more mood episodes in the past year) is associated with a chronic course and a poor response to lithium (Jefferson, 1995). As a result, the diagnosis of bipolar disorders in DSM-IV has become more descriptive with the addition of new types (Bipolar I or II) and mood specifiers (e.g., With Rapid Cycling). The purpose of this digest is to present on overview of Bipolar I and II Disorders in DSM-IV and to discuss treatment implications in relation to diagnostic features.

Diagnosis of Bipolar Disorders

Types of Mood Episodes

The diagnosis of Bipolar Disorders entails assessing both current and past mood episodes. The DSM-IV (APA,1994) describes four basic types of mood: Manic, Hypomanic, Major Depressive, and Mixed. A Manic Episode is characterized by at least a week of elevated, expansive or irritable mood plus three other manic symptoms (four if only irritable mood is present). These symptoms must be so severe that they necessitate hospitalization, occur with psychotic features or cause marked impairment in social or occupational functioning. A Hypomanic Episode has the same symptoms as a Manic Episode except that the mood episode can be briefer (i.e., four days) and the symptoms are not so severe that they markedly impair functioning (e.g., no need for hospitalization). A Major Depressive Episode requires five depressive symptoms that persist for at least two weeks.

Finally, a Mixed Episode entails a week or more of both Manic and Major Depressive symptoms nearly every day. For example, a typical symptom picture might include racing thoughts, grandiosity, increased energy, irritability, hopelessness, and depressed mood (Swann, 1995). Once a careful history of these mood episodes has been taken, the mental health counselor can then determine whether the client's symptoms meet criteria for either Bipolar I or II Disorder.

Bipolar I Disorder

Bipolar I Disorder is characterized by a history of at least one Manic or Mixed Episode. The mental health counselor should be sure that the symptoms were not simply the result of a medical condition e.g., stroke , epilepsy, HIV or a substance; e.g., AZT, thyroid medications, anti-depressant medication, (Jefferson, 1995). Diagnostic coding of Bipolar I is determined by noting the type of current mood episode from the following categories:

Single manic episode. This code name is used when the individual presents with a Manic or Mixed Episode but has no previous history of any type of mood episode.

Most recent episode manic. These individuals are currently in a Manic Episode but also have a history of some kind of mood episode.

Most recent episode hypomanic. Instead of grandiosity and pressured speech which is more characteristic of mania, these individuals present with toned-down manic symptoms such as uncritical self-confidence and a loud tone of voice (APA, 1994).

Most recent episode mixed. About 30% of manic-like episodes are of the Mixed type. In comparison to a Manic Episode, those who present in a Mixed Episode may have more hostility and cognitive impairment. Incidence is higher in those who abuse substances, have neurological problems, or are female (Swan, 1995).

Most recent episode depressed. Depressive Episodes either follow or precede Manic Episodes about 60% to 70% of the time (APA, 1994). In comparison to pure Major Depressive Disorder, depression in Bipolar Disorders is more likely to present with increases in sleeping and eating, psychomotor retardation, and delusions (Coryell, et.al., 1995).

Most recent episode unspecified. This is used if the current mood episode has not yet met duration criteria. For example, mixed symptoms are being assessed on the third day of the episode.

Specifiers. The current episode can be further delineated by the addition of specifiers indicating severity of the mood episode e.g., mild, moderate, etc., as well as other specifiers if present: *With Catatonic Features* e.g., excessive motor activity, posturing, and *With Postpartum Onset* (within four weeks of giving birth). If the current mood episode is depressed, then any of the major depressive disorder specifiers can be used (e.g., Melancholic, Chronic, Atypical).

Specifiers also have been added to note the course or pattern of mood episodes over time. These include: *With Rapid Cycling, With Seasonal Pattern* (seasonality of depression only), and *With or Without Full Interepisode Recovery* (presence or absence of symptoms between the last two mood episodes).

The following is an example of how a diagnosis might appear:

296.62 Bipolar I Disorder, Most recent Episode Mixed, Moderate, With Postpartum Onset, With Full Interepisode Recovery.

Bipolar II Disorder

In Bipolar II Disorder there is one or more Major Depressive Episodes along with a history of at least one Hypomanic Episode. A major distinction from Bipolar I Disorder is the absence of any history of manic or mixed episodes. Because this means that episodes of elevated mood are not as extreme, clients may not recall episodes as accurately as those with Manic Episodes. Furthermore, they typically seek treatment during their depressive phase which further obfuscates the presence of a Bipolar Disorder. Misdiagnosis can be particularly problematic because, like Bipolar I Disorder, the use of antidepressants can precipitate mania or rapid cycling (Jefferson, 1995). As a result, it is particularly important for the mental health counselor to collect collateral data from medical records and family members.

Bipolar II Disorder can be further specified by adding the current mood episode (i.e., Hypomanic or Depressed). If the current mood is depressed, the same specifiers listed above for Bipolar I can be used (e.g., With Postpartum Onset). Likewise, the same course specifiers for previous episodes can be added; e.g., With Rapid Cycling. A sample diagnosis might be:

> 296.89 Bipolar II Disorder, Depressed, Moderate, With Rapid Cycling, With Full Interepisode Recovery.

Treatment Implications

Lithium was once considered the miracle drug for Bipolar Disorders. However, more recent longitudinal studies indicate that only 35% of those who regularly take lithium are considered to have a favorable outcome (Goldberg, Harrow, & Grossman, 1995; Jefferson, 1995). Findings like these have had clinical researchers reexamine alternative medications as well as the role of psychosocial treatments.

Recent reviews of lithium efficacy have begun to delineate bipolar features that predict good outcome. Lithium is most effective in young and middle-aged adults who present with acute mania or acute bipolar depression (Jefferson, 1995). However, lithium is only minimally effective in those who are either adolescent or elderly, or who have any of these features: currently in a mixed episode, presence of rapid cycling, mania that is secondary to a medical condition, or comorbid substance use. The drug of choice if any of the above features are present is an anti-convulsant such as divalproex (Depakote)(Goldberg, et al., 1995; Swan, 1995).

Psychosocial Treatments

A number of psychosocial factors have been associated with mood episode onset and severity. These include moderate to severe stress, introversion, low social support, and obsessiveness (Solomon, Keitner, Miller, Shea, & Keller, 1995; Swendsen, Hammen, Heller, & Gitlin, 1995). In line with these findings, a number of counseling interventions have been found to enhance long-term outcome when combined with medications. For example, family, couple, and group therapy are each associated with decreased hospitalizations and increased rates of recovery (Solomon, et al., 1995). Cognitive-behavior therapy for medication compliance also has been associated with fewer hospitalizations (Solomon, et al., 1995).

Conclusion

The diagnosis of bipolar disorders in DSM-IV (APA,1994) requires careful specification of mood features. While the diagnostic process can be complex, one major advantage is that treatments can be more systematically matched to the client's particular symptoms. Likewise, research findings are indicating that counseling interventions have a critical role in the overall treatment of Bipolar Disorders.

References

American Psychiatric Association. (1994). *Diagnostic and statistical manual of mental disorders* (4th ed.). Washington, D.C.: Author.

Coryell, W., Endicott, J., Maser, J. D., Keller, M. B., Leon, A. C., & Akiskal, H. S. (1995). Long-term stability of polarity distinctions in the affective disorders. *American Journal of Psychiatry, 152*(3), 385-390.

Goldberg, J. F., Harrow, M., & Grossman, L. S. (1995). Course and outcome in bipolar affective disorder: A longitudinal follow-up study. *American Journal of Psychiatry, 152*(3), 379-384.

Jefferson, J. W. (1995). Lithium: The present and the future. *Journal of Clinical Psychiatry, 56*(1), 41-48.

Soloman, D. A., Keitner, G. I., Miller, I. W., Shea, M. T., & Keller, M. B. (1995). Course of illness and maintenance treatments for patients with bipolar disorder. *Journal of Clinical Psychiatry, 56*(1), 5-11.

Swann, A. C. (1995). Mixed or dysphoric manic states: Psychopathology and treatment. *Journal of Clinical Psychiatry, 56*(3), 6-10.

Swendsen, J., Hammen, C., Heller, T., & Gitlin, M. (1995). Correlates of stress reactivity in patients with bipolar disorder. *American Journal of Psychiatry 152* (5), 795-797.

Gary G. Gintner, Ph.D. is an Associate Professor in Counselor Education at Louisiana State University, Baton Rouge, Louisiana.

CHAPTER FORTY–SIX

The DSM-IV Anxiety Disorders

Patricia Polanski

The category Anxiety Disorders in the DSM-IV (APA, 1994) contains the following disorders: Panic Disorder Without Agoraphobia, Panic Disorder With Agoraphobia, Agoraphobia Without History of Panic Disorder, Specific Phobia, Social Phobia, Obsessive-Compulsive Disorder, Posttraumatic Stress Disorder, Acute Stress Disorder, Generalized Anxiety Disorder, Anxiety Disorder Due to a General Medical Condition, Substance-Induced Anxiety Disorder, and Anxiety Disorder Not Otherwise Specified.

Since Panic Attacks and Agoraphobia occur within the context of several of these disorders, the beginning of this chapter offers descriptive information about panic attacks and agoraphobia. This information is useful in helping the mental health counselor begin to discern whether or not the symptoms described by the client match the characteristics for these two central features.

Panic attacks can appear as part of the presentation of a variety of anxiety disorders. A panic attack is a discrete period in which there is the sudden onset of intense apprehension, fearfulness or terror, feelings of impending doom, and fear of "going crazy" or losing control. Also present are physiological symptoms such as shortness of breath, palpitations, chest pain or discomfort, and choking or smothering. Panic attacks are further differentiated into three types according to the relationships between the onset of the attack and the presence or absence of situational triggers. These types are: unexpected (uncued) panic attacks, situationally bound (cued) panic attacks, and situationally predisposed panic attacks. Agoraphobia refers to anxiety about being in places or situations where escape might be difficult or embarrassing or where help may not be available in the event of a panic attack or the onset of panic-like symptoms. This anxiety typically leads to the pervasive avoidance of characteristic clusters of situations that may include being alone at home or outside the home, being in a crowd of people or standing in line, being on a bridge or in an elevator, and traveling in a bus, train, or automobile. Further differentiation is made with regard to whether or not the situations are completely avoided, endured with marked distress about having a panic attack or panic-like symptoms, or require the presence of a companion (APA, 1994).

Panic Disorder involves the presence of recurrent unexpected panic attacks about which there is persistent concern. Agoraphobia may or may not occur along with Panic Disorder. Specific Phobia is a marked and persistant fear of clearly discernible objects or situations. Social Phobia is a marked and persistant fear of social or performance situations. In both of these disorders, the exposure to the feared object or situation invariably provokes an immediate anxiety response, that may take the form of a panic attack.

Obsessive-Compulsive Disorder is characterized by recurrent obsessions i.e., persistent ideas, thoughts, impulses or images which cause one or more of the following: marked anxiety or distress or compulsions, or repetitive behaviors which serve to neutralize anxiety. In addition to causing marked distress, the obsessions or compulsions must be time consuming i.e., take more than 1 hour per day, or significantly interfere with one's normal routine, occupational functioning, or usual social activities and relationships with others. In adults with this disorder, there is some level of recognition that the obsessions or compulsions are excessive or unreasonable. This requirement does not apply with children who may lack sufficient cognitive ability to make this judgment.

Posttraumatic Stress Disorder involves the development of characteristic symptoms following exposure to an extremely traumatic event. The diagnostic criteria includes specific information regarding the event, the reexperiencing of the event, avoidance of stimuli associated with the trauma, numbing of general responsiveness, and symptoms of increased arousal. Other qualifying features include duration (more than 1 month) of the disturbance and the extent of distress or impairment caused by the disturbance. The symptoms of Acute Stress Disorder are similar to those of Posttraumatic Stress Disorder. However, with Acute Stress Disorder the disturbance lasts for at least two days and does not persist beyond four weeks after the traumatic event.

Generalized Anxiety Disorder is characterized by excessive anxiety and worry about a number of events or activities, occurring more days than not, over a period of at least six months. This excessive anxiety and worry results in the individual having difficulty controlling worrisome thoughts and keeping those thoughts from interfering with attention to everyday tasks.

The main feature of Anxiety Disorder Due to a General Medical Condition is clinically significant anxiety that is the direct physiological consequence of a general medical condition as evidenced by client history, physical examination, or laboratory findings. Substance-Induced Anxiety Disorder involves the presence of prominent anxiety symptoms that are due to the direct physiological effects of a substance: i.e., a drug of abuse, a medication, or toxin exposure.

Finally, the category, Anxiety Disorder Not Otherwise Specified, includes disorders with prominent anxiety or phobic avoidance that do not meet criteria for any specific anxiety disorder. For those counselors familiar with the DSM-III-R, it may be useful to consult Appendix D of the DSM-IV for an annotated listing of changes that were made in the revision process; for example, Avoidant Disorder of Childhood and Overanxious Disorder of Childhood have been subsumed by Social Phobia and Generalized Anxiety Disorder, respectively. There are other changes noted in this appendix.

Medical/Physical Considerations

Barlow (1988) points out that the study of anxiety and its disorders needs to proceed with a full consideration and integration of biological and psychological factors. Two concepts related to this idea are worth noting here. The first concept has to do with the use of medications in treatment and the second is related to the physiological symptoms associated with panic attacks.

In the short-term treatment of Panic Disorder, three drug classes have been found to be effective–the tricyclic antidepressants, the monoamine oxidase inhibitors, and the benzodiazepines (Schatzberg & Ballenger, 1991). Cases of severe Panic Disorder may be associated with particularly high morbidity as evidenced by increased rates of alcohol abuse, suicidal behavior, depression and financial dependence. According to

Schatzberg & Ballenger, the decision to use pharmacological therapies should be based on whether or not the individual meets the criteria for acute treatment. These criteria include recent severe or frequent panic attacks or generalized anxiety, clear morbidity, secondary comorbid disorders and significant family history of suicide or alcohol abuse.

While the literature is clear in delineating the efficacy of behavioral treatments, particularly *in vivo* exposure in the alleviation of phobic avoidance behaviors, the effectiveness of behavioral treatments in the alleviation of panic attacks remains uncertain (Laraia, Stuart, & Best, 1989). There also is research indicating that cognitive-behavioral approaches are more effective than medication alone in maintaining treatment gains over time (Meichenbaum, 1995). Given the complexity and multifaceted nature of the panic/agoraphobia syndrome, it is likely that a combination of pharmacological and psychological approaches may provide the most effective treatment; for example, psychological treatments that encourage the individual to confront fear-provoking cues serve as an appropriate adjunct to medication in cases where persons continue to exhibit some avoidance behavior despite having their panic attacks blocked.

Research data compiled over the last decade have indicated that Obsessive-Compulsive Disorder (OCD) is relatively common and frequently co-exists with other psychiatric disorders (Zetin & Kramer, 1992). As with Panic Disorder, psychological and biological approaches have been applied to understanding OCD, and it appears that a combination of psychological and pharmacological treatments are useful. Long-term treatment with medication seems to be required for most individuals with OCD. *In vivo* exposure with response prevention is the treatment of choice for compulsions, and exposure in imagination with thought stopping appears to be the treatment of choice for obsessions. The efficacy of the anti-depressant medication clomipramine in treating OCD is established more definitively than that of any other drug (Zetin & Kramer, 1992).

The second concept to be noted here is related to the phenomenon of interpreting, or misinterpreting, bodily sensations in the course of panic attacks. Because the individual is reporting the experience of certain physical symptoms, it becomes prudent for the counselor to have the client obtain a thorough physical examination in order to further understand any medical conditions that could simulate anxiety symptoms (Meichenbaum, 1995). In addition, by making this recommendation the mental health counselor demonstrates respect for the client's perceptions while offering an appropriate way to check those perceptions.

References

American Psychiatric Association. (1994). *Diagnostic and statistical manual of mental disorders* (4th ed.). Washington, DC: Author.

Barlow, D. H. (1988). *Anxiety and its disorders.* New York: Guilford.

Laraia, M. T., Stuart, G. W., & Best, C. L. (1989). Behavioral treatment of panic-related disorders: A review. *Archives of Psychiatric Nursing, 3,* 125-133.

Meichenbaum, D. (1995, October). *Cognitive behavioral treatment of anxiety and depressive disorders in adults.* Workshop packet. North Carolina Psychological Foundation Fall Conference, Durham, NC.

Schatzberg, A. F., & Ballenger, J. C. (1991). Decisions for the clinician in the treatment of panic disorder: When to treat, which treatment to use, and how long to treat. *Journal of Clinical Psychiatry, 52,* (2, suppl) 26-31.

Zetin, M., & Kramer, M. A. (1992). Obsessive-compulsive disorder. *Hospital and Community Psychiatry, 43,* 689-699.

Patricia Polanski, M.Ed., NCC is a doctoral student in the Counseling and Counselor Education program at the University of North Carolina at Greensboro.

CHAPTER FORTY–SEVEN

The DSM-IV Somatoform Disorders

Kathy Short Phillips & Carmen R. Pyles

Often encountered in general medical settings, the DSM-IV (APA, 1994) Somatoform Disorders are characterized by the presence of physical symptoms which suggest a general medical condition. These symptoms, however, are not fully explained by a medical condition, the direct effects of a substance, or another mental disorder. Even in the absence of a diagnosable general medical condition, these symptoms, which are not intentionally produced, cause significant distress or impairment in important areas of an individual's functioning. Although grouped together, these disorders do not necessarily share etiological or mechanical components. The DSM-IV Somatoform Disorders include Somatization Disorder,Undifferentiated Somatoform Disorder, Conversion Disorder, Pain Disorder, Hypochondriasis, Body Dysmorphic Disorder, and Somatoform Disorder Not Otherwise Specified.

Somatization Disorder

Individuals diagnosed with Somatoform Disorder exhibit a pattern of multiple somatic complaints for which medical treatment is sought. Complaints generally begin before the age of 30 and continue for many years, without reported symptoms. Other diagnostic criteria involve the nature of reported symptoms. The associated pain is generally related to at least four different bodily sites or functions. At least two gastrointestinal symptoms (other than pain) must be reported; nausea and bloating are common. There must be at least one symptom associated with sexual intercourse or reproduction, other than pain. Finally, there must be at least one pseudoneurological symptom or deficit which suggests a neurological condition not limited to pain. These may include conversion symptoms such as impaired coordination or balance, paralysis or localized weakness, throat problems, aphonia, urinary retention, hallucinations, loss of sensory perceptions, seizures, dissociative symptoms, or loss of consciousness other than fainting.

Although general medical conditions exist concurrently with Somatization Disorder, the following distinguishing features suggest a diagnosis of the latter: involvement of multiple organ systems, and early onset and chronic course without substantiating medical or laboratory evidence. Whenever a general medical condition is found to coexist with Somatization Disorder, the complaints and impairment are excessive.

There are a number of implications for caregivers concerning Somatization Disorder. The exaggeration and recurrence of symptoms, along with anxiety and depressive mood, should alert mental health counselors and medical personnel to the possibility of Somatization Disorder. Thorough review of medical treatments and hospitalizations generally reveal a distinct pattern of frequent somatic complaints. Individuals with Somatization Disorder often seek medical treatment from several physicians concurrently, and may undergo a variety of unnecessary medical procedures, including exploratory surgery. Several other disorders frequently associated with Somatization Disorder are Major Depression, Panic Disorder, Substance-Related Disorders, and Personality Disorders.

Undifferentiated Somatoform Disorder

Undifferentiated Somatoform Disorder is diagnosed when one or more physical complaints persist for at least six months. The disturbance exhibits the other common characteristics of Somatoform Disorders, and is not better accounted for by another mental disorder, including other Somatoform Disorders. This disorder is often diagnosed when the full criteria of another Somatoform Disorder or general medical condition are not met. Commonly reported physical symptoms associated with Undifferentiated Somatoform Disorder include fatigue, appetite loss, and gastrointestinal and urinary complaints.

Conversion Disorder

The diagnosis of Conversion Disorder is made when an individual presents with symptoms or deficits affecting voluntary motor or sensory function that suggest, but are not fully explained by, a neurological or other general medical condition. These pseudoneurological symptoms are not due to substance use, do not occur exclusively during another Somatization Disorder, and are not better accounted for by another mental disorder. The Conversion Disorder diagnosis is not made if symptoms are limited to pain or sexual dysfunction, or demonstrate a culturally sanctioned experience. Conversion symptoms are specified by the following subtypes: With Motor Symptom or Deficit, With Sensory Symptom or Deficit, With Seizures or Convulsions, and With Mixed Presentation.

Conversion symptoms tend to follow an individual's conceptualization of a condition and are often inconsistent. For example, "paralysis" may disappear during a moment of inattention with apparent normal muscle tone and reflexes. Since conversion symptoms do not conform to known anatomical pathways and physiological mechanisms, there are typically no objective signs or supporting medical tests.

Interestingly, however, individuals who are more knowledgeable of the medical field tend to exhibit symptoms which closely resemble neurological or general medical conditions. Medically naive individuals and those of rural populations and lower socioeconomic status report Conversion Disorder at a higher rate, with more implausible symptoms.

One criteria for diagnosing Conversion Disorder is the association of psychological factors. For example, conflict or other stressors tend to initiate or exacerbate the symptoms or deficits. Although the DSM-IV (APA, 1994) criteria are not specific regarding psychological constructs, anxiety reduction and the evasion of responsibility have been hypothesized as unconscious motives underlying conversion symptoms.

The diagnosis of Conversion Disorder in individuals should be made cautiously, or provisionally. General medical conditions are sometimes discovered years after Conversion Disorder is diagnosed. For example, neurological conditions, such as multiple sclerosis, myasthenia gravis, and idiopathic or substance-induced dystonia are often misdiagnosed as Conversion Disorder. However, both neurological and general medical conditions may coexist with Conversion Disorder.

To correctly diagnose Conversion Disorder, therefore, a thorough medical evaluation is essential. A history of unexplained somatic complaints or dissociative symptoms are strong indicators of Conversion Disorder, along with a relative lack of concern ("la belle indifference") over the presenting symptoms.

Pain Disorder

Pain Disorder is unlike other Somatoform Disorders because the client is truly experiencing pain in one or more anatomical sites. The client's unintentional pain results in extreme distress or impairment in social and occupational functioning. Problems with family and friends are common. Psychological factors play a large role in the onset, severity, exacerbation, or maintenance of the pain. The pain becomes a major focus of the individual's life, which may result in substantial use of medications to cope with the pain and daily life activities. Attempts to treat the pain may cause additional problems and more pain; e.g., use of nonsteroidal anti-inflammatory drugs resulting in gastrointestinal distress.

There are three subtypes of Pain Disorder:

(1) Pain Disorder associated with psychological factors,
(2) Pain Disorder associated with both psychological factors and a general medical condition and
(3) Pain Disorder with a general medical condition.

The latter subtype is not considered a mental illness and is diagnosed on Axis III. Pain Disorder can be further diagnosed with acute and chronic specifiers.

Hypochondriasis

A preoccupation with fears of having, or the idea that one has, a serious disease is the main feature of Hypochondriasis. The individual manifests in his or her mind one or more bodily signs or symptoms of a particular disease. When a physician thoroughly examines such a client, a general medical condition that would account for the person's concerns about the disease is not found although a coexisting general medical condition may be present. Other symptoms include impairment in social, occupational, or other important areas of functioning. Mental health counselors should specify *With Poor Insight* if during the episode the person does not recognize that their concern about the disease is unreasonable. Differential diagnoses typically include Generalized Anxiety Disorder, Obsessive-Compulsive Disorder, Panic Disorder, a Major Depressive Episode, Separation Anxiety, or another Somatoform Disorder.

Body Dysmorphic Disorder

Body Dysmorphic Disorder is characterized by a preoccupation with a defect in appearance that is either imagined or barely observable and results in extremely unreasonable concern. The individual is often markedly distressed over the 'deformity' and often finds it difficult to control his or her preoccupation. Common complaints include imagined or slight flaws on the face or head such as hair thinning, acne, scars, and facial asymmetry. This disorder also is characterized by frequent mirror checking, excessive grooming behavior, and may occupy hours of the person's time. Anxiety may cause avoidance of work and social situations and may result in extreme isolation. Social Phobia, Obsessive Compulsive Disorder and Major Depressive Disorder are often associated with this illness. Differential diagnoses may include Anorexia Nervosa and Avoidant Personality.

Somatoform Disorder NOS

Finally, Somatoform Disorder Not Otherwise Specified is a category that includes disorders with somatoform symptoms that do not meet the criteria for any of the other disorders in this section. For example, the disorder Pseudocyesis is diagnosed when a person falsely believes that she is pregnant. She may have physical signs of pregnancy such as abdominal enlargement, reduced menstrual flow, amenorrhea, and labor pains at the expected delivery date. Other examples of Somatoform Disorder NOS include disorders involving non-psychotic, hypochondriacal symptoms of less than six months duration, or disorders that involve unexplained physical complaints of less than six months which are clearly not due to another mental disorder.

References

American Psychiatric Association. (1994). *Diagnostic and statistical manual of Mental disorders* (4th ed.). Washington, DC: Author.

Andreasen, N.C., & Black, D.W. (1995). *Introductory textbook of psychiatry* (2nd ed.). Iowa City, IA: American Psychiatric Press.

Folks, D.G., Ford, C.V., & Houck, C.A. (1990). Somatoform disorders, factitious disorders, and malingering, In A. Stoudemire (Ed.), *Clinical psychiatry for medical students* (pp. 237-268). Philadelphia, PA: Lippincott Company.

Iezzi, A., & Adams, H.E. (1993). Somatoform and factitious disorders. In R. E. Hales, S. C. Yudofsky, & J. A. Talbott (Eds.), *The American psychiatric press textbook of psychiatry* (2nd ed.)(pp. 298-309). Washington, DC: American Psychiatric Press.

Kellner, R. (Ed.).(1989). Somatoform and factitious disorders. *A task force report of the American Psychiatric Association (vols. 1-3 & index vol.)* (pp. 2119-2182). Washington, DC: American Psychiatric Association.

Smith, G.R. (1991). *Somatization disorders in the medical setting.* Washington, DC: American Psychiatric Press.

Kathy Short Phillips and Carmen R. Pyles are graduate students in the Department of Counseling and Educational Development at the University of North Carolina at Greensboro.

CHAPTER FORTY–EIGHT

The DSM-IV Dissociative Disorders

Max Marie McIntosh

The category Dissociative Disorders in the DSM-IV (APA, 1994) contains the following disorders: Dissociative Amnesia, Dissociative Fugue, Dissociative Identity Disorder, Depersonalization Disorder, and Dissociative Disorder Not Otherwise Specified.

Dissociation is a disruption in the normally integrated functions of consciousness, memory, identity, or perception of the environment (APA, p. 477). The disturbance may be sudden or gradual, transient or chronic.

Dissociative Amnesia

Dissociative Amnesia involves one or more episodes of inability to recall important personal information that is too extensive to be explained by ordinary forgetfulness. The information forgotten is usually of a stressful or traumatic nature and the memory impairment is reversible. One epidemiological study found that Dissociative Amnesia was the most common dissociative disorder in a random sample of the general population, with a lifetime prevalence of 7.0% (Ross, 1991). It can occur in any age group and usually presents as a retrospective gap in memory.

There are five different types of amnesia: localized, selective, generalized, continuous, and systematized. In the most common types, localized and selective amnesia, memories from a circumscribed time period (often following a profoundly disturbing event) are unable to be recalled. In localized amnesia, no memories of the lost time period can be recalled, whereas in selective amnesia, some but not all of the events of that time period can be recalled. *Generalized amnesia*, in which the person is unable to recall any personal history at all, is rarer. Continuous amnesia is generalized amnesia with a disruption in the ongoing process of memory storage, so that the client is unable to recall any events of either the past or the present. *Systematized amnesia* is a loss of memory confined only to very specific types of information, such as those memories relating to a particular person, one's family, or a specific location or activity, again frequently associated with an overwhelming life event.

Amnesia can also occur as a consequence of neurological conditions such as epilepsy, brain injury, delirium, or dementia, general medical conditions, and substance or medication effects. Dissociative Amnesia is also among the diagnostic criteria for Dissociative Fugue, Dissociative Identity Disorder, Dissociative Disorder Not Otherwise Specified, Somatization Disorder, Acute Stress Disorder, and Posttraumatic Stress Disorder. These mental disorders, along with general neurological or medical causes, must be ruled out in order to diagnose Dissociative Amnesia (APA, 1994).

Dissociative Fugue

Dissociative Fugue is characterized by sudden and unexpected travel away from one's customary place of daily activities, and is accompanied by an inability to recall some or all of one's past, confusion about personal identity, or the adoption of a new identity. The onset is usually related to overwhelming stress or trauma, and recovery is rapid, although Dissociative Amnesia may persist. Dissociative Fugue is most frequently found in adults and is much less common than Dissociative Amnesia, with an estimated prevalence rate of only 0.2% in the general population. It may be more common, however, in settings of war or other highly violent and socially disruptive incidents (Putnam, 1985). As with Dissociative Amnesia, it is important to distinguish Dissociative Fugue from similar symptoms caused by neurological, medical, or other psychiatric conditions and substance abuse or medication effects. Because Dissociative Fugue incorporates the symptoms of both Dissociative Amnesia and Depersonalization Disorder, these should not be diagnosed concurrently (APA, 1994).

Dissociative Amnesia and Dissociative Fugue are treated similarly, using a trauma framework which assumes the individual took flight or dissociated memories were cognitively or affectively intolerable (Loewenstein, 1996). In the crucial first phase of treatment, the client is assisted in achieving enough safety and stability to face the second phase of retrieving and processing the forgotten memories. In the final phase, resolution is achieved when the previously dissociated material is integrated into normal life experiences. The mental health counselor can be instrumental in providing group therapy, psycho-education, and individual counseling for clients with these disorders. Although hypnosis and even drug-facilitated interviews may be used by some clinicians, these techniques are controversial because of the potentials for both memory contamination and further traumatization by premature recovery of memories.

Dissociative Identity Disorder

Dissociative Identity Disorder (DID), formerly Multiple Personality Disorder in the DSM-III, is characterized by the existence of two or more distinct identities or personality states, each with its own relatively enduring pattern of perceiving, relating to, and thinking about the self and the environment. At least two of these identities must recurrently take control of the person's behavior and the person is also unable to recall important personal information as in Dissociative Amnesia. Identity, memory, affect, sensation, behavior, consciousness, or a combination of any of these may be dissociated (APA, 1994).

The typical client with Dissociative Identity Disorder is a female in her 20's or 30's with a long history of involvement in the mental health, social service, medical, and legal systems (Ross, 1997). Previous diagnoses may include Somatization Disorder, Posttraumatic Stress Disorder or other Anxiety Disorders, Eating Disorders, Borderline or other Personality Disorders, Mood Disorders, Schizophrenia, and Substance-Related Disorders. Although some of these diagnoses, particularly Schizophrenia and Bipolar Disorder, may be erroneous, researchers have found co-morbidity rates above 60% for Mood Disorders, Anxiety Disorders, Somatization Disorders, and Substance Abuse (Ross, 1997). The Dissociative Identity Disorder diagnosis tends to be surrounded by controversy in light of its recent sharp rise in reported cases and the high hypnotizability and suggestibility of these clients.

The prognosis for clients with Dissociative Identity Disorder is surprisingly good given the apparent severity of the disorder. DID rarely remits spontaneously and is usually not resolved in a treatment that fails to address it directly (Kluft, 1996). Although few well-controlled studies of treatment outcome exist, some clinicians estimate that approximately two-thirds of these clients can attain a stable integration or fusion of personalities, with an average length of treatment of three to five years (Ross, 1997). Because "the basic principle of the treatment of DID is that it is the treatment of a person," (Ross, 1997, p. 264) the mental health counselor is an ideal treatment provider. Counseling's emphasis on healthy development, collaboration with the client, developing trust and a positive treatment alliance, building on client strengths, improving communication and life management skills, and respect for the client are all integral to treatment of this disorder (Ross, 1997). Treatment approaches include, but are not limited to, cognitive, behavioral, psychodynamic, and ego state therapy, hypnosis, skill-building in emotional containment, coping strategies, communication and relationship management, expressive therapies (such as art, movement, dance, sand tray, occupational, and recreation therapy), psycho-educational and other group therapies, and even limited use of psychopharmacology for temporary symptom control.

Depersonalization Disorder

The essential feature of Depersonalization Disorder is persistent and recurrent episodes of a feeling of detachment or estrangement from one's self. Although reality testing is intact, such persons may feel as if they are outside their body, living in a dream or movie, or that they have become an automaton. Derealization, the sense that the external world is strange or unreal, is common as well. Because depersonalization is a common experience, the disorder should be diagnosed, as with any other DSM-IV disorder, only if there is marked distress or impairment in functioning (1994). Depersonalization is also the third most common reported psychiatric symptom and is found in Schizophrenia, Panic Disorder, Phobias, Acute or Posttraumatic Stress Disorder, other Dissociative Disorders, Borderline Personality Disorder, other mental disorders, and general medical, neurological, or substance-induced conditions (Cattell, 1966). The presence of any of these disorders precludes a diagnosis of Depersonalization Disorder. Depersonalization Disorder by itself is exceedingly rare and is often accompanied by depression and suicidal behavior (Coons, 1996).

Treatment efficacy research results for Depersonalization Disorder are inadequate because of the disorder's rarity and tendency to remit spontaneously. Popular approaches include behavior therapy, reality therapy, and individual counseling focused on improving self-esteem. Any accompanying depression and suicidality also must be addressed. As some success has been reported using selective serotonin re-uptake inhibitors (SSRIs, e.g. fluoxetine), the mental health counselor may wish to consider referral to a physician for a medication trial (Hollander et al., 1990).

Dissociative Disorder Not Otherwise Specified

Dissociative Disorder Not Otherwise Specified is characterized by the presence of a dissociative symptom that does not meet the criteria for any specific Dissociative Disorder. Examples include presentations similar to Dissociative Identity Disorder in which either amnesia or the presence of distinct personality states is absent; culture-specific dissociative trances; or dissociation subsequent to brainwashing or similar prolonged, intense, coercive persuasion.

Treatment Depends on the Etiology

In summary, the mental health counselor can be significantly helpful to clients with Dissociative Disorders and knowledge of these disorders should be an integral component of the mental health counselor's clinical preparation.

References

American Psychiatric Association. (1994). *Diagnosis and statistical manual of mental disorders* (4th ed.). Washington, DC: Author.

Cattell, J. P. (1966). Depersonalization phenomena. In S. Arieti (Ed.), *American handbook of psychiatry* (pp. 766-799). New York: Basic.

Coons, P. M. (1996). Depersonalization and derealization. In L. M. Michelson & W. J. Ray (Eds.). *Handbook of dissociation: theoretical, empirical, and clinical perspectives* (pp. 291-305). New York: Plenum.

Kluft, R. P. (1996). Dissociative identity disorder. In L. M. Michelson & W. J. Ray (Eds.). *Handbook of dissociation: Theoretical, empirical, and clinical perspectives* (pp. 337-366). New York: Plenum Press.

Loewenstein, R. J. (1996). Dissociative amnesia and dissociative fugue. In L. M. Michelson & W. J. Ray (Eds.). *Handbook of dissociation: Theoretical, empirical, and clinical perspectives* (pp. 307-336). New York: Plenum.

Putnam, F. W. (1985). Dissociation as a response to extreme trauma. In R. P. Kluft (Ed.). *Childhood antecedents of multiple personality* (pp. 65-97). Washington, DC: America Psychiatric Press.

Ross, C. A. (1991). The epidemiology of multiple personality disorder and dissociation. *Psychiatric Clinics of North America, 14,* 503-517.

Ross, C. A. (1997). *Dissociative identity disorder: Diagnosis, clinical features, and treatment of multiple personality* (2nd ed.). New York: John Wiley.

Max Marie McIntosh is a graduate student in the Department of Counseling and Educational Development at the University of North Carolina at Greensboro.

CHAPTER FORTY–NINE

Sexual Dysfunctions

John C. Bandy

The DSM has gone through several revisions and publications. During that time period the classification of Sexual Dysfunction and its place in the DSM has varied as well. DSM-III had a Psychosexual Disorder section which contained four diagnoses: Gender Identity Disorders, Paraphilias, Psychosexual Disorders, and a residual class of Psychosexual Disorders that had two categories: Ego-dystonic Homosexuality, and Psychosexual Disorders Not Elsewhere Classified (APA, 1980). DSM-III-R included a Gender Identity Disorder section composed of Gender Identity Disorder of Childhood, Transsexualism Gender Identity Disorder of Adolescence or Adulthood, Non-Transsexual Type, and Gender Identity Not Otherwise Specified. DSM-III-R also had a sexual disorders section which contained Paraphilias, Sexual Dysfunctions, and other Sexual Disorders (APA, 1987). DSM-IV was published in 1994 with the Sexual Disorders divided into seven sections: Sexual Desire Disorders, Sexual Arousal Disorders, Orgasmic Disorders, Sexual Pain Disorders, Sexual Dysfunction Due to a General Medical Condition, Substance-Induced Sexual Disorder, and Sexual Dysfunction Not Otherwise Specified. These sexual dysfunctions are characterized by a disturbance in sexual desire. As varied as the dysfunctions are, so too are the therapies that mental health counselors have at hand to help their clients, including systematic desensitization and the "post-modern approach" (Lopiccolo & Friedman, 1988).

Diagnosis of Sexual Dysfunction

Sexual Desire Disorder

The Sexual Desire Disorders (SDDs) are divided into Hypoactive Sexual Desire Disorder (HSDD) and Sexual Aversion Disorder (SAD). The necessary feature of HSDD is an insufficience or absence of sexual fantasies and sexual desire. The disturbance must cause marked distress or interpersonal difficulty and the dysfunction must not be better accounted for by another DSM-IV Axis I disorder. HSDD might be global and related to all sexual behavior or may be limited to one sexual act (intercourse) by one partner. The mental health counselor should assess both partners to rule out an excessive need by one partner which might cause the other to appear hypoactive (APA, 1994).

The basic characteristic of SADs is the unwillingness to engage in, and the active avoidance of, genital sexual contact with a sexual partner. When being assessed, clients report anxiety, fear, or disgust when a sexual encounter presents itself with their partner. Two aspects of the aversion might be genital secretions or vaginal penetration. Furthermore, some individuals might have negative responses to all sexual activity, including kissing and caressing (APA, 1994).

Sexual Arousal Disorders

Sexual Arousal Disorders contain Female Sexual Arousal Disorder (FSAD) and Male Erectile Disorder (MED). FSAD is a persistent or recurrent inability to attain, or to maintain until completion of the sexual activity, an adequate lubrication-swelling response to sexual excitement (APA, 1994). This disorder may be accompanied by Sexual Desire Disorder and Female Orgasmic Disorder. MED is the perpetual or recurrent inability to achieve, or to continue until completion of the sexual activity, a satisfactory erection. Although some males may not be able to have an erection during any sexual encounter, some may report having an erection before intercourse and losing tumescence before penetration. Other males will report only having an erection during self-masturbation or when awakening (APA, 1994).

Orgasmic Disorders

The Orgasmic Disorders consist of Female Orgasmic Disorder (FOD), Male Orgasmic Disorder (MOD), and Premature Ejaculation Disorder (PED). FOD is a continuous delay in, or absence of, orgasm following a normal sexual encounter in females; MOD is the equivalent in males. The cause of the disorder is not clear. The male's body image, self-esteem, and sexual relationships may be severely affected as a result of this disorder. The essential feature of PED is the early onset of orgasm and ejaculation with minimal sexual stimulation before, on, or shortly after penetration and before the person desires it. The mental health counselor should take into account the client's age, the newness of sex, and the frequency of sexual acts (APA, 1994).

Sexual Pain Disorders

Sexual Pain Disorders consist of Dyspareunia and Vaginismus. The basic feature of Dyspareunia is genital pain associated with sexual intercourse. Usually, this disorder is treated in a general medical setting first. Genital pain during coitus may lead to sexual relation problems and sexual avoidance. The major feature of Vaginismus is the involuntary contraction of the perineal muscles surrounding the outer third of the vagina when vaginal penetration is attempted. This disorder is found usually more often in younger females who have a negative opinion of sex (APA, 1994).

Sexual Dysfunction Due to a General Medical Condition

The central feature of Sexual Dysfunction Due to a General Medical Condition is the presence of a clinically significant sexual dysfunction judged to be due exclusively to the direct physiological effects of a medical condition (APA, 1994). The sexual dysfunction must be related *solely* to a general medical dysfunction. A careful and comprehensive assessment of multiple factors is necessary to make this judgment.

Substance-Induced Sexual Dysfunction

A Substance-Induced Sexual Dysfunction is distinguished from a primary Sexual Dysfunction by "considering onset and course" (APA, 1994). Characteristics can include impaired desire, impaired arousal, impaired orgasm, or sexual pain. Substance-Induced Sexual Dysfunction is associated with intoxication with alcohol, amphetamines, cocaine, opioids, sedatives, hypnotics, and anxiolytics. Prescribed medications like anti-hypertensives, anti-depressives, and anabolic steroids also can cause this dysfunction (APA).

Treatment

There are many treatment options available to the mental health counselor in working with sexual dysfunctions. Loppicolo and Friedman (1988) advocate integrating gestalt, family of origin, and a systems approach. McCarthy (1995) has developed a cognitive-behavioral approach that focuses on understanding and changing inhibited sexual desires. Both medications and surgical interventions are used increasingly often as effective therapeutic adjuncts (Rosen & Leiblum, 1995). The key to providing therapy for clients is to match the appropriate therapy with the sexual problem. Assessing the etiology of the sexual dysfunction is complex, but is an important part of treatment. Many issues; e.g. self-esteem, depression, sexual abuse, anxiety, and physiological problems, can contribute to these disorders. Sexual dysfunction may create issues such as lowered self-esteem, depressive mood, and conflictual relationships.

References

American Psychiatric Association.(1980). *Diagnostic and statistical manual of mental disorders* (3rd ed.). Washington, DC: Author.

American Psychiatric Association. (1987). *Diagnostic and statistical manual of mental disorders* (3rd ed., Rev.). Washington, DC: Author.

American Psychiatric Association. (1994). *Diagnostic and statistical manual of mental disorders* (4th ed.). Washington, DC: Author.

Lopiccolo, J. & Friedman, J. (1988). Broad spectrum treatment of low sexual desire. In S. Leiblum & R. Rosen (Eds). *Sexual desire disorders* (pp. 107-144). New York: Guilford.

McCarthy, B. (1995). Bridges to sexual desire. *Journal of Sex Education and Therapy, 2,* 132-141.

Rosen, R., & Leiblum, S. (1995). *Case studies in sex therapy.* New York: Guilford.

CHAPTER FIFTY

Paraphilias

Kevin R. Sidden

According to the DSM-IV (APA, 1994, pp. 522-523), The essential features of a Paraphilia are recurrent, intense sexually arousing fantasies, sexual urges, or behaviors generally involving

(1) nonhuman objects,
(2) the suffering or humiliation of oneself or one's partner, or
(3) children or other nonconsenting persons that occur over a period of at least 6 months .

Paraphilia is a term used to encompass several disorders including Exhibitionism, Fetishism, Frotteurism, Pedophilia, Sexual Masochism, Sexual Sadism, Voyeurism, Transvestic Fetishism, and Paraphilia Not Otherwise Specified. An individual may be diagnosed for more than one paraphilic disorder. In addition, Gender Identity Disorder, Personality Disorders, and other sexual dysfunctions may coexist.

Exhibitionism

The major feature of Exhibitionism is exposing one's genitalia to a stranger, which may include masturbation during exposure, or the individual may fantasize about Exhibitionism while masturbating. In some cases, the individual may have a desire to surprise or shock the observer, whereas in other cases the individual fantasizes that the observer will become sexually aroused (APA, 1994).

Fetishism

In Fetishism, the major characteristic is the use of nonliving objects, which may include but are not limited to underpants, brassieres, stockings, shoes, or other wearing apparel in a sexual act. The individual frequently masturbates while holding, wearing, rubbing, or smelling the fetish object, or the individual may ask the partner to wear a object during sexual encounters (APA, 1994).

Frotteurism

Frotteurism involves touching or rubbing against a nonconsenting person for sexual arousal or pleasure. The activity usually occurs in crowded places where the individual rubs the genitals against the other's thighs and buttocks or fondles the individual's genitalia or breasts (APA, 1994).

Pedophilia

Pedophilia involves sexual activity with a prepubescent child, where the pedophile is a least sixteen years old and at least five years older than the child. The individual may derive pleasure from undressing the child, masturbating in front of the child, having direct physical contact, performing cunnilingus or fellatio, or by penetrating the child's anus, mouth, or genitalia with mouth, fingers, foreign objects, or genitalia. Some individuals may limit their activities to their relatives, some may seek gratification outside the family, and others may choose relatives as well as victims outside the family (APA, 1994).

Sexual Masochism

The paraphilic nature of Sexual Masochism involves the act of being made to suffer or to be humiliated during sexual activity with a partner or during masturbation. The suffering or humiliation may be brought about by being bound, beaten, infibulated (pricked or pierced by sharp objects), electrically shocked, defecated or urinated on during sexual activity. A potentially lethal form of Sexual Masochism is "hypoxyphilia," which is the act of oxygen deprivation during sexual activity by strangulation or suffocation (APA, 1994).

Sexual Sadism

The paraphilic nature of Sexual Sadism involves the act of deriving sexual pleasure and excitement from causing pain and suffering or by humiliating his/her partner during sexual activity. In some cases the sexual sadist may seek out non-consenting partners who are terrified of the sadistic acts, and the sexual sadist seeks total control over the victim. In other cases the individual may pair up with a consenting partner who is diagnosed with Sexual Masochism.

Transvestic Fetishism

In Transvestic Fetishism the paraphilic focus is on the wearing of clothing of the opposite gender (cross-dressing). This disorder has only been diagnosed in heterosexual and bisexual males. When cross-dressing, the male usually imagines himself as both the female and the male partner while masturbating. The degree of cross-dressing ranges from wearing one article of clothing such as a pair of panties or stockings under masculine attire, to complete cross-dressing including makeup and a mastery of feminine mannerisms and body habits. The disorder should not be diagnosed when it occurs exclusively during the course of Gender Identity Disorder (APA, 1994).

Voyeurism

Voyeurism focuses on observing an unsuspecting person while that person is naked, disrobing, or engaging in sexual activity. The observer may achieve orgasm through masturbation while observing, or after the observation the observer may achieve orgasm through masturbation while revisualizing the incident. The course of Voyeurism tends to be chronic (APA, 1994).

Paraphilia Not Otherwise Specified

The DSM-IV (APA, 1994) indicates that this category is included for coding Paraphilias that do not meet the criteria for any of the specific categories. Examples include, but are not limited to telephone scatagolia (obscene phone calls),necrophilia (corpses), partialism (exclusive focus on part of the body),zoophilia (animals),coprophilia (feces), klismaphilia (enemas), and urophilia (urine) (p. 532)

Gender Identity Disorder

Gender Identity Disorder is characterized by strong and persistent cross-gender identification (not because it is perceived to be culturally advantageous to be the opposite sex), and a persistent discomfort with one's own sex or the gender role associated with that sex. The disturbance can not be concurrent with a physical intersex condition such as androgen insensitivity syndrome or congenital adrenal hyperplasia. Individuals with the disorder generally refuse to participate in activities associated with the gender role of their sex, and they generally prefer activities associated with the opposite gender role (APA, 1994).

Gender Identity Disorder Not Otherwise Specified

This category is used for coding disorders such as,

1. Intersex conditions (e.g., androgen insensitivity syndrome or congenital adrenal hyperplasia) and accompanying gender dysphoria.
2. Transient, stress-related cross-dressing behavior.
3. Persistent preoccupation with castration or penectomy without a desire to acquire the sex characteristics of the other sex (APA, 1994, p. 538).

Sexual Disorder Not Otherwise Specified

Sexual disturbances that can not be identified as a specific Sexual Disorder, and are neither a Sexual Dysfunction nor a Paraphilia are included in the category. According to the DSM-IV (APA, 1994), examples include:

1. Marked feelings of inadequacy concerning sexual performance or other traits related to self-imposed standards of masculinity or femininity.
2. Distress about a pattern of repeated sexual relationships involving a succession of lovers who are experienced by the individual as only things to be used.
3. Persistent and marked distress about orientation (p. 538).

Treatment

The treatment of Paraphilias varies according to the specific disorder or combination of disorders of which the patient has been diagnosed. Paraphilias such as Exhibitionism, Fetishism, Voyeurism, and Transvestic Fetishism are disorders of milder severity and typically do not require extensive treatment. These disorders may be treated on an outpatient basis and individual psychotherapy is sufficient. Other paraphilias which involve violating the rights of nonconsenting persons are of a more serious nature and require more intensive inpatient therapies. Examples of these paraphilias are Frotteurism, Pedophilia, and Sexual Masochism. Traditionally, Pedophilia has been treated from a multi-modal perspective, using a combination of pharmacological medications, cognitive-behavioral therapies, and group therapies.

References

American Psychiatric Association. (1994). *Diagnostic and statistical manual of mental disorders* (4th ed). Washington, DC: Author.

Cook, M., & Howells, K. (1981). *Adult sexual interest in children.* London: Academic Press.

Gosselin, C. (1980). *Sexual variations: Fetishism, sadomasochism, and transvestism.* New York: Simon & Schuster.

Hanly, M. A. (1995). *Essential papers on masochism.* New York: New York University Press.

O'Donohue, W., & Greer, J. H. (1993). *Handbook of sexual dysfunctions: Assessment and treatment.* Needham Heights: Allyn and Bacon.

Stoller, R. J. (1985). *Presentations of gender.* New Haven: Yale University Press.

Kevin R. Sidden is a Master of Science and Educational Specialist in Marriage and Family Counseling from The University of North Carolina Greensboro.

CHAPTER FIFTY–ONE

Impulse-Control Disorders

Tricia C. Gagnon and Shawn L. Spurgeon

Impulse-Control Disorders are characterized by the inability to resist an impulse, drive, or temptation to harm oneself or to harm others. The individual usually experiences a feeling of increased tension or arousal before committing the act and relief or pleasure when the act is committed. Afterwards, feelings of guilt or self-reproach may be felt. There are six classifications of impulse disorders in the DSM-IV: Intermittent Explosive Disorder, Kleptomania, Pyromania, Pathological Gambling, Trichotillomania, and Impulse Control Disorder Not Otherwise Specified (APA, 1994).

Intermittent Explosive Disorder

The primary feature of Intermittent Explosive Disorder is the inability to effectively control and resist aggressive impulses that lead to either severe assaultive acts of violence or to property destruction. Generally speaking, there is no psychosocial stressor that precipitates or provokes the act. This diagnosis is only given after other mental disorders have been effectively ruled out; e.g., Antisocial Personality Disorder, Borderline Personality Disorder, a Psychotic Disorder, a Manic Episode, Conduct Disorder, or Attention Deficit/Hyperactivity Disorder. Also, the aggressive episode cannot be due to the physiological effects of a substance or to a General Medical Condition (APA, 1994).

The explosive episode can be perceived as a "spell" by the individual, preceded by a strong sense of tension or increased awareness, and culminating with a sense of relief. The individual also may feel upset, remorseful, or embarrassed about the aggressive act. It is important to distinguish Intermittent Explosive Disorder from purposeful behavior, or malingering. Individuals that malinger are usually trying to avoid responsibility for their behavior. Also, purposeful behavior is distinguished by the presence in the individual of some type of motivational gain in the aggressive act.

Kleptomania

Individuals who repeatedly fail to resist the urge to steal items, even though there is no personal need or monetary value in the items they are stealing, may be diagnosed with Kleptomania. There is usually a rise in subjectiveness or tension before the theft and a deep sense of pleasure, gratification, or relief when committing the theft. The stealing is not done for the sake of revenge or to express some type of anger and is not better accounted for in response to a delusion or hallucination. The thefts are not usually preplanned and no concern is given for getting apprehended.

Typically, the individual can afford to pay for the stolen items and they will often give the items away or discard them. The stealing is not better accounted for by Conduct Disorder, a Manic Episode, or by Antisocial Personality Disorder. The individual also may hoard the stolen objects and return them at a later date. Generally, individuals with this disorder will avoid stealing when immediate arrest is probable, and the stealing is done without collaboration or assistance from others. This disorder is distinguished from ordinary acts of theft or shoplifting by the fact that there are no ulterior motives that drive the act; the individual is not stealing the items for their usefulness or their monetary value. This diagnosis is only made when all the essential features and characteristics of the disorder are present (APA, 1994).

Pyromania

The essential and prevalent feature of Pyromania is the presence of multiple episodes of deliberate and purposeful fire setting. The individual may experience tension or arousal before setting the fire. He or she seems to be fascinated by, interested in, curious about, or attracted to the fire and its situational contexts. Individuals with this disorder may spend time at local fire departments, may become firefighters, and often gain pleasure by watching fires in their neighborhood, or by setting off false alarms. Any type of institution, equipment, or person associated with fire is pleasing to the individual. The individual may set fires so as to be associated with the local fire department (APA, 1994).

Individuals with this disorder usually experience some type of pleasure or gratification when setting the fire, when witnessing the effects of the fire, or when participating in the aftermath of the fire. The fire setting is not done for monetary gain, to express a sociopolitical viewpoint, to hide some other type of criminal activity, to express anger or revenge, or to enhance one's housing arrangement. The act is not committed in response to a delusion or hallucination, and it does not result from impaired judgment. If the fire setting can be better accounted for by Conduct Disorder, a Manic Episode, or by Antisocial Personality Disorder, the diagnosis of Pyromania is not made.

Pyromania must be distinguished from "communicative arson." Some individuals with mental disorders use fire setting behaviors to communicate a desire or need, usually centered around gaining a change in the nature or location of the services they are receiving. Also, the fire setting may be done by children as a part of their development; e.g., playing with matches, lighters, or fire. When the fire setting is done for profit, sabotage, revenge, or to attract attention or recognition for one's self, a diagnosis of Pyromania is not given.

Pathological Gambling

Individuals with Pathological Gambling may have distortions in thinking that include irrational beliefs, superstitions, and overconfidence. They often cannot stop themselves from gambling, feeling irritable or bored when they try to stop. They are continuously preoccupied with gambling and are constantly seeking "action" because they are frequently restless, energetic, and competitive. They may be workaholics or may wait until a deadline to begin working (APA, 1994). Due to their stressful lifestyle, and the guilt and anxiety they experience due to gambling losses, they often develop stress-related medical conditions such as ulcers, hypertension, migraines, or insomnia (Abbott, Cramer, & Sherrets, 1995). Pathological Gambling is typically chronic with gambling activity increasing during periods of stress or depression (APA).

Long-term "chasing" of one's losses is characteristic of individuals with Pathological Gambling. They feel an urgent need to undo their losses, and may feel anxious and depressed until they are able to gamble again. If they do win while gambling, they may be unable to stop. They typically increase the risks and size of their bets to obtain the same level of excitement experienced in previous wins (Abbott, et al., 1995). Individuals with Pathological Gambling may lie to concerned friends or family to conceal their gambling problem and at other times turn to them for financial help when desperate. They may lose their jobs, homes, and significant relationships as a result of their inability to control their gambling. Antisocial behavior, usually nonviolent, such as forgery, theft, or fraud may occur in order to obtain money to gamble or pay off debts. Attempted suicide is reported in 20% of individuals in treatment for Pathological Gambling. A diagnosis of Pathological Gambling is not made if gambling occurs in the course of Mania or Antisocial Personality Disorder (APA, 1994).

Trichotillomania

Individuals with Trichotillomania cannot control the impulse to pull out their own hair. They may pull hair from any place on the body, but the most common areas are the scalp, eyelashes, and eyebrows (APA, 1994). Eyelashes and eyebrows may be absent with a noticeable loss of hair on the crown of the head, with hair left only at the nape of the neck and above the ears. However, most individuals with Trichotillomania make every effort to conceal their hair loss (Rothbaum & Ninan, 1994).

Hair pulling episodes may occur briefly throughout the day, or last for hours while in a state of relaxation and distraction while watching television or reading. Hair pulling usually increases under stress, with a feeling of increased tension until the hair can be pulled (APA, 1994). Embarrassment and shame associated with their behavior and appearance cause most persons to deny and to hide their hair pulling from others except for immediate family members (Rothbaum & Ninan, 1994). Some individuals with Trichotillomania also have urges to pull other people's hair or may pull hairs from pets, dolls, carpets, and sweaters (APA).

Individuals with Trichotillomania often experience feelings of relief and comfort when pulling out their hair. Some individuals experience an "itchlike" sensation in the scalp that is only relieved by pulling their hair. Pain from pulling their hair is not usually reported by individuals with Trichotillomania (APA, 1994). Mouthing of the hair pulled and trichophagia (eating hairs) may occur (Rothbaum & Ninan, 1994). Trichophagia may cause hairballs to develop leading to abdominal pain, anemia, hematemesis, nausea, and bowel obstruction (APA).

Trichotillamania onset is usually in young adulthood. Females are diagnosed much more frequently than males. However, men could be underdiagnosed due to hair loss in men being seen as a normal occurrence.

Many children go through periods where they pull out their hair, but the behavior must last for several months before the diagnosis is given. The diagnosis is not made if the hair pulling is related to another symptom such as delusions or hallucinations, Obsessive-Compulsive Disorder, Stereotypic Movement Disorder, or Factitious Disorder (APA, 1994).

Impulse-Control Disorder Not Otherwise Specified

This diagnosis is reserved for disorders of impulse control that do not meet the criteria for a specific Impulse-Control Disorder or for another mental disorder with features involving impulse control; e.g., Substance Dependence or Paraphilia (APA, 1994).

References

Abbott, D. A. , Cramer, S. L. , & Sherrets, S. D. (1995). Pathological gambling and the family: Practice implications. *Families in Society, 76* (4), 213-219.

American Psychiatric Association. (1994). *Diagnostic and statistical manual of mental disorders* (4th ed.) . Washington, DC: Author.

Rothbaum, B.O., & Ninan, P. T. (1994). The assessment of trichotillomania. *Behaviour Research and Therapy, 32* (6), 651-662.

Tricia C. Gagnon and Shawn L. Spurgeon are graduate students at The University of North Carolina at Greensboro, Greensboro, NC.

CHAPTER FIFTY–TWO

Eating Disorders

Allison Y. Baise

Mental health and mental illness are best understood as states or points along a continuum that range from good to poor. This "spectrum" concept suggests that mental illness and mental health are not separate entities but rather are part of an ever changing process that are experienced throughout the life cycle. Like other diagnostic entities, Eating Disorders should be viewed as falling along such a spectrum.

Following this line of thinking, the spectrum along which Eating Disorders exist consists of any concern about weight, calories, diet, or figure that can be viewed as common to abnormal distortions of body image, frequent binge and purge cycles, or when the pursuit of thinness becomes so entrenched that severe restriction of food occurs. Because European and North American cultures are obsessed with size, weight, and body image, this preoccupation is perceived as normal. However, at some point, the obsession becomes pathological. Eating Disorders are now recognized as major medical and psychological problems, affecting millions of women in the United States and Europe.

The sociocultural emphasis on thinness is generally credited as a major determinant of the apparent increased incidence of Eating Disorders, especially among young women. The most common Eating Disorders found among adolescents and adults are Anorexia Nervosa and Bulimia Nervosa.

Additional Eating Disorders, not discussed, include Pica (the eating of non-nutritive substances), Rumination Disorder (regurgitation and re-chewing of food), and Obesity. Obesity is included in the *International Classification of Diseases* as a general medical condition but does not appear in the *Diagnostic and Statistical Manual Disorders: Fourth Edition* (APA, 1994) because it is not viewed as a psychological syndrome. Pica and Rumination Disorder are included in the DSM-IV section, *Feeding and Eating Disorders of Infancy or Early Childhood.*

Anorexia Nervosa

An individual who receives the diagnosis of Anorexia Nervosa can best be described as refusing to maintain a normal body weight for age and height, is extremely afraid of gaining weight, and has a significantly distorted body image. Weight loss is most commonly achieved by reduction and restriction of food intake among persons with this disorder and results in amenorrhea. In addition, these individuals may resort to purging through induced vomiting or the use of laxatives and/or diuretics. Persons with Anorexia Nervosa also may become immersed in extensive exercise to shed pounds.

Two subtypes of Anorexia Nervosa have been established by the DSM-IV. The "Restricting Type" is specified if the person has not regularly engaged in binge-eating or purging behavior during the current episode of Anorexia Nervosa. A second subtype, "Binge-Eating/Purging Type," is noted when the person has regularly engaged in binge-eating or purging behavior during the current episode of Anorexia Nervosa.

Individuals with Anorexia Nervosa have an extreme fear of becoming fat or gaining weight such that they are never completely satisfied with their weight loss, even though they may become emaciated. Their body image is so distorted that they ignore their body's signals for sustenance and may become severely malnourished.

The average age at onset of Anorexia Nervosa is 17 years and rarely occurs in individuals over the age of 40. The course and outcome of this disorder vary among individuals: some recover after a single episode, others require hospitalization to restore weight, fluid, and electrolyte imbalances, and others die if no such intervention occurs.

Bulimia Nervosa

Unlike persons with Anorexia Nervosa who are obsessed with losing weight and are substantially underweight for their age and height, individuals with Bulimia Nervosa maintain a relatively normal weight and are obsessed with not gaining additional weight. These persons also engage in binge eating on a regular basis and employ inappropriate compensatory behaviors in an attempt to counter weight gain from the previous binge.

A "binge" is defined as a period of unrestrained eating when a large amount; i.e., larger than most individuals would eat under similar circumstances of food is ingested. A binge is restricted to no more than two hours of time and would not include snacking on small amounts of food throughout the day. During a binge, a person with Bulimia Nervosa will usually consume high calories, easily ingested foods and does so in a secretive manner.

Episodic binge eating is accompanied by an awareness of an abnormal eating pattern, fear of not being able to stop eating voluntarily, with depressed mood and self-deprecating thoughts following the binges. Another feature of Bulimia Nervosa is the use of inappropriate compensatory behaviors after a binge.

The DSM-IV stipulates two subtypes of Bulimia Nervosa. If the person regularly engages in self-induced vomiting or the misuse of laxatives, diuretics, or enemas during the current episode of Bulimia Nervosa, "Purging Type" would be noted. If the individual does not regularly engage in self-induced vomiting or the misuse of laxatives, diuretics, or enemas but uses other inappropriate compensatory behaviors such as fasting or excessive exercise during the current episode of Bulimia Nervosa, "Nonpurging Type" would be noted.

It also is important to note that for a DSM-IV diagnosis of Bulimia Nervosa to be given, the binge eating and inappropriate compensatory behaviors must occur, on average, at least twice a week for three months and not during episodes of Anorexia Nervosa.

Like Anorexia Nervosa, Bulimia Nervosa usually begins in adolescence or early adulthood. The course may be intermittent, with binge eating alternating with periods of remission, or it may be chronic, with no definite periods of remission.

Associated Disorders

Research has shown that Eating Disorders are often associated with other psychological problems, such as depression, various Personality Disorders, Anxiety Disorders, and Substance-Related Disorders. The DSM-IV notes that between one-third and one-half of persons with Bulimia Nervosa also meet criteria for one or more personality disorders, most frequently Borderline Personality Disorder. Persons with Anorexia Nervosa, according to the DSM-IV, may exhibit other obsessive and compulsive symptoms, and hence, receive an additional diagnosis of Obsessive-Compulsive disorder. Thus, from a clinician's perspective, it is imperative that these secondary problems be evaluated and incorporated into a comprehensive treatment plan.

Atypical Eating Disorders

In diagnosing Eating Disorders, clinicians often can apply a DSM-IV diagnosis with ease. However, there are times when individuals may present with eating disordered characteristics that are less severe than those required for a diagnosis of Anorexia Nervosa or Bulimia Nervosa. Differentiating Eating Disorders from other disorders that involve atypical eating patterns or obsession with weight control can be difficult. Other diagnoses must be considered to rule-out other psychological or medical conditions.

Fortunately, the DSM-IV contains a *Not Otherwise Specified* (NOS) category in each of its diagnostic classes. Such a diagnosis would be warranted if the clinical features of the disorder do not meet all of the criteria for any of the disorders in a particular class, yet enough information is available to indicate a specific class of disorders. In the case of an individual presenting symptoms of an Eating Disorder that cannot be classified as Anorexia Nervosa or Bulimia Nervosa, the individual may receive a diagnosis of *Eating Disorder NOS.*

Eating Disorder NOS may include, but is not limited to the following:

- (a) a female who meets all of the criteria for Anorexia Nervosa but has regular menses,
- (b) criteria for Anorexia Nervosa are met but the individual's current weight is in the normal range,
- (c) criteria for Bulimia Nervosa are met but bingeing and inappropriate compensatory behavior patterns occur less than twice a week and for a period less than three months,
- (d) inappropriate compensatory behavior by a person of normal body weight that does not follow a binge (e.g., self-induced vomiting after consumption of a candy bar),
- (e) a pattern of chewing large amounts of food and spitting it out instead of swallowing, and
- (f) repeated episodes of binge eating not followed by inappropriate compensatory behavior.

Continuum of Prognosis

Although research shows that persons with Eating Disorders have a 60-70% recovery rate after five years, there is a proportion of these individuals who do not fully recover. With third-party payers dictating duration of treatment, the short-term treatment model proposed is insufficient for many individuals with Eating Disorders. Short-term therapies such as psychoeducational, cognitive, behavioral, and psychopharmacological assist in helping only a reported 40 -50% percent of all diagnosed cases. It is important for counselors to act as advocates for these clients. Logically, if short-term therapy has not proven to be successful for about one half of individuals with Eating Disorders, mental health counselors must push third-party payers toward allowing longer durations of treatment.

References

American Psychiatric Association. (1994). *Diagnostic and statistical manual of mental disorders* (4th ed.). Washington, DC: Author.

Garfinkel, P. E. (1982). *Anorexia nervosa: A multidimensional perspective.* New York: Brunner/Mazel.

Hawkins, R. C., Fremouw, W. J., & Clement, P. F. (1984). *The binge-purge syndrome: Diagnosis, treatment, and research.* New York: Springer.

Scott, D. (1988). *Anorexia and bulimia nervosa: Practical approaches.* Washington Square, NY: New York University Press.

Williamson, D. A. (1990). *Assessment of eating disorders: Obesity, anorexia, and bulimia nervosa.* New York:. Pergamon.

Zerbe, K. J. (1993). *The body betrayed: Women, eating disorders, and treatment.* Washington, D. C.: American Psychiatric Press.

Allison Y. Baise is a graduate student in the Department of Counseling and Educational Development at the University of North Carolina at Greensboro.

Limitations of Findings

CHAPTER FIFTY–THREE

DSM-IV: Sleep Disorders

Joseph P. Jordan

One thing taken for granted is the ability to fall asleep. It is a function of the body to provide a time to rest body and mind, and despite all attempts to deny the body sleep, we eventually have to sleep. People who have gone without sleep for a week or more, usually as a publicity stunt or as part of a study have reported dizziness, impaired concentration, irritability, hand tremors, and hallucinations (Dement, 1972., Johnson, 1969). Prolonged sleep deprivation in animals generally produces severe consequences, including death (Rechtschaffen, Gilliland, Bergmann, & Winter, 1983). When this normal body function somehow goes awry, a person can experience significant distress accompanied by extreme debilitation. When there is a problem with a person's ability to achieve, maintain, or exit from sleep, then they may be diagnosed with a sleep disorder. Sleep disorders are classified in the *Diagnostic and Statistical Manual of Mental Disorders,* Fourth Edition, DSM-IV (American Psychiatric Association [APA], 1994), and are quite varied in nature. An understanding of these various ailments will help a counselor correctly diagnose sleep disorders, while allowing for differentiation between sleep disorders, temporary sleep difficulty, and other mental illnesses.

Sleep Disorders did not appear in the DSM I or DSM-II . They were listed only as an appendix in the DSM-III and appeared for the first time as a distinct set of diagnoses in the DSM-III-R.

The sleep disorders are organized into three major sections, according to presumed etiology (DSM-IV, 1994). These include Primary Sleep Disorders, Sleep Disorder Related to Another Mental Disorder, and Other Sleep Disorder, which is further subdivided into Sleep Disorder Related to a General Medical Condition and Substance Induced Sleep Disorder. Primary sleep disorders are further divided into Dyssomnias characterized by abnormalities in the amount, quality, and timing of sleep and Parasomnias characterized by abnormal behavior or physiological events occurring in association with sleep, specific sleep stages, or sleep-wake transitions (APA, 1994).

Primary Sleep Disorders

Primary sleep disorders are those disorders that are not attributable to other factors, such as another mental disorder, a general medical condition, or an imbibed substance that may affect sleep. As noted earlier, there are two categories of primary sleep disorders, dyssomnias and parasomnias.

Dyssomnias: These are disorders of sleep initiation, maintenance, or excessive sleepiness. They include Primary Insomnia, Primary Hypersomnia, Narcolepsy, Breathing Related Sleep Disorder, Circadian Rhythm Sleep Disorder, and Dyssomnia Not Otherwise Specified (NOS). Almost all the Dyssomnias result in a lower quality of sleep (the exception is Narcolepsy) and effect functioning of the individual. They are diagnosed when the person meets certain criteria, such as decreased level of functioning within an occupational environment, a social situation, or role responsibility. A brief description of each dyssomnia follows:

Primary Insomnia: Inability to achieve restful sleep, either through being unable to fall asleep or through waking up early and being unable to fall back to sleep. Individuals must experience this for at least a month to meet the criteria for this diagnosis.

Primary Hypersomnia: Excessive sleepiness such that there is an inability to function appropriately, lasting for at least one month, evidenced by prolonged sleep episodes or daytime sleep episodes that occur almost daily. This cannot be diagnosed if there is evidence of inadequate sleep.

Narcolepsy: Sudden irresistible attacks of restful sleep, accompanied by muscle paralysis (cataplexy) and often featuring intense dreamlike images before or after the attacks. Attacks usually occur two to six times a day.

Breathing Related Sleep Disorder: Sleep disruption during the nocturnal sleep phase associated with the existence of a physical abnormality, such as obstructive sleep apnea syndrome.

Circadian Rhythm Sleep Disorder (Formerly Sleep-Wake Schedule Disorder): sleep disruption caused by environmental changes, rather than internal dysfunction. This diagnosis is associated with the inability to adapt to the demands of social interaction, perhaps due to the circadian rhythm being out of sync. There are four subtypes: delayed sleep phase; e.g., the "night owl", jet-lag type (severity is proportional to time zones crossed), shift-work type (often due to rotating shifts), and unspecified type (when another pattern of sleep-wake disturbance is noted).

Dyssomnia Not Otherwise Specified: Insomnias, hypersomnias, or circadian rhythm disturbances that do not meet criteria for any specific Dyssomnias. Examples include insomnia due to environmental conditions (noise, light, interruptions), sleepiness due to sleep deprivation, restless legs syndrome, etc. (APA, 1994).

Parasomnias: These are disorders of abnormal behavior or physiological events occurring during sleep, specific sleep stages, or sleep-wake transitions. It is a lack of control of physiological systems, particularly the autonomic nervous system, motor system, or cognitive processes. Parasomnias occur throughout the night, and often accompany specific sleep stages. Parasomnias include Nightmare Disorder, Sleep Terror Disorder, Sleepwalking Disorder, and Parasomnia Not Otherwise Specified (NOS). A brief description of each follows:

Nightmare Disorder: Repeated occurrence of dreams that produce intense fear or anxiety due to the threatening nature of the sequences contained within the dream, producing awakening and full alertness upon awakening.

Sleep Terror Disorder: Also called "night terror," this sleep disorder is manifested by abrupt awakenings from sleep, usually accompanied by a panicky scream or cry, usually occurring during the first third and the last ten minutes of sleep. Individuals cannot be comforted; they exhibit fear and have little memory of the event upon awakening.

Sleepwalking Disorder: Repeated episodes of complex motor behavior, including rising from bed and walking, usually during the first third of the night. Individuals are unresponsive to efforts at communication, and have limited recall of the occurrence. There is often a brief period of confusion or difficulty orienting, followed by full recovery of cognitive functions.

Parasomnia Not Otherwise Specified: For disturbances that are characterized by abnormal behavior or physiological events during sleep or sleep-wake transition that do not meet criteria for established Parasomnias. Examples include: REM sleep behavior disorder (motor activity during REM sleep), sleep paralysis (inability to perform voluntary movement during transition from sleep to wakefulness or before falling asleep), and other parasomnias undetectable due to substance use or a general medical condition.

Sleep Disorders Related to Another Mental Disorder

This class of sleep disorder is related either temporally or causally to another mental disorder, such as depressive disorders, bipolar disorders, or anxiety disorders. Disturbed sleep is one of the principle symptoms of endogenous depression; furthermore, changes in sleep often presage clinical improvement or relapse (Wehr, Gillin, & Goodwin, 1983). As with other sleep disorders, the hypersomnia or insomnia must

(a) have lasted at least one month,
(b) there must be significant impairment in social, occupational, or other important role functioning,
(c) it cannot be accounted for by another sleep disorder, and
(d) there is no presence of inadequate sleep.

Also, there cannot be a medical condition or substance use that may account for the disorder. Sleep disturbances are common features of mental disorders. A diagnosis of Insomnia Related to Another Mental Disorder or Hypersomnia Related to Another Mental Disorder is only made when enough impairment exists to warrant clinical attention. Clinicians must make sure that this is a predominant complaint and then be able to use specific questioning and interviewing techniques to determine if a diagnosis is in order. Insomnia Related to Another Mental Disorder is the most frequent diagnosis at sleep disorder centers constituting 35% - 50% of diagnoses

(DSM-IV, 1994). Hypersomnia Related to Another Mental Disorder is much less frequent, diagnosed about 5% of the time. In diagnosing either Insomnia related to Another Mental Disorder or Hypersomnia Related to Another Mental Disorder, one must be able to correctly identify the mental disorder causing the sleep disorder. An example would be

Insomnia Related to Bipolar I Disorder,
Single Manic Episode, Severe.

Other Sleep Disorders

The primary feature of Sleep Disorder Due to a General Medical Condition is a disturbance in sleep significant enough to require clinical attention and which can be traced to a general medical condition. It should be noted for convenience's sake, Narcolepsy and Sleep-Related Breathing Disorder are not included in this category. The clinician must first determine the presence of the general medical condition and then provide evidence (history, examination, or laboratory findings) that confirm that the sleep disorder is related to the condition. This sleep disorder has four specific subtypes, which are Insomnia Type, Hypersomnia Type, Parasomnia Type, and Mixed Type. The clinician assigns these subtypes according to which of the symptoms associated with the analogous Primary Sleep Disorder that the individual may exhibit. Note: The diagnosis of Sleep Disorder Due to a General Medical Condition, Mixed Type is used when more than one disorder is present and no one condition predominates. Also, you must include the name of the general medical condition on Axis III (e.g., Sleep Disorder Due to Chronic Obstructive Pulmonary Disease, Insomnia Type).

Substance-Induced Sleep Disorder

This sleep disorder is diagnosed when there is significant disturbance of sleep to warrant clinical attention, and there is evidence from history, physical examination, or laboratory findings that the disturbance is due to the direct physiological effects of a substance (a drug of abuse, a medication, or toxic exposure). The disorder may not be accounted for by another mental disorder that is not substance-induced, and the diagnosis cannot be made if it is observed during the course of delirium. There must be significant impairment in social, occupational, or role function responsibilities, and this diagnosis should only be made in place of Substance Withdrawal or Substance Intoxication if there is symptomology in excess of what is normally associated with Intoxication or Withdrawal syndrome. Mental Health Counselors must be careful when determining if this disorder is a result of substance use alone, or if the person began self-medicating to treat an already existing or developing sleep disorder and summarily developed a Substance-Induced Sleep Disorder. One of four subtypes may be noted: Insomnia or Hypersomnia being most prevalent, Parasomnia being less prevalent, and Mixed being used when no one subtype dominates but two or more are currently present. There are two specifiers: With Onset During Intoxication (criteria met during the intoxication phase), and With Onset During Withdrawal (criteria are met during withdrawal phase). If there is more than one substance judged to have a role in the development of the sleep disorder, both or all are mentioned. The name of the substance is mentioned at the beginning of the diagnosis (Cocaine Induced Sleep Disorder, Insomnia Type, With Onset During Intoxication) to lend clarity to the diagnosis. If the causal substance is unknown, a diagnosis of Unknown Substance-Induced Sleep Disorder may be given. Common substances that may produce this sleep disorder include: alcohol, caffeine, amphetamines and related stimulants, cocaine, opioids, sedatives, hypnotics, anxiolytics, and certain drugs prescribed for the control of hypertension.

Conclusion

The ability to obtain a good night's sleep is taken for granted by most of the population. Oftentimes, part of the treatment for mental disorders includes rest and relaxation. Sleep disorders rob people of the ability to obtain this needed rest, and can greatly complicate treatment of these disorders. Sleep disorders demand attention, both on their own and when observed in conjunction with other therapeutic issues. Awareness of the possibility of a sleep disorder and correct diagnosis of such a disorder better serves the clients of mental health counselors.

References

American Psychiatric Association. (1994). *Diagnosis and statistical manual of mental disorders* (4th ed.). Washington, DC: Author.

Dement, W. (1972). *Some must watch while some must sleep.* San Francisco: W.H. Freeman.

Johnson, L. (1969). Physiological and psychological changes following total sleep deprivation. In A. Kales (Ed.), *Sleep: Physiology & pathology* (pp. 206-220). Philadelphia: Lippincott.

Rechtschaffen, A., Gilliland, M., Bergmann, B., & Winter, J. (1983). Physiological correlates of prolonged sleep deprivation in rats. *Science, 221,* 182-184.

Wehr, T., Gillin, J., Goodwin, F. (1983). Sleep and circadian rhythms in depression. In M. Chase & E. Weitzman (Eds.), *Sleep disorders: Basic and clinical research* (pp. 195-225). Jamaica, NY: Spectrum.

Joseph P. Jordan, CSAC is a graduate student in Community Counseling in the Department of Counseling and Educational Development at The University of North Carolina at Greensboro.

CHAPTER FIFTY–FOUR

Personality Disorders in the DSM-IV

Kyra Martin-Houser & Jane G. Robertson

Personality Disorders are pervasive patterns of behavior that are developed in adolescence or early adulthood, independent of the individual's cultural orientation, and lead to impaired functioning. The Personality Disorders in the DSM-IV are categorized into three clusters based upon functional similarities. Cluster A includes the Paranoid, Schizoid, and Schizotypal Personality Disorders and describes individuals who exhibit eccentric traits. Cluster B includes the Antisocial, Borderline, Histrionic, and Narcissistic Personality Disorders. Individuals with Cluster B disorders are characteristically emotional and dramatic. Cluster C includes the Avoidant, Dependent, and Obsessive-Compulsive Personality Disorders. Individuals with these disorders have an anxious or fearful presentation. It is important to note that many individuals exhibit traits from several different personality disorders concurrently; thus, a diagnosis of Personality Disorder Not Otherwise Specified (NOS) may be appropriate (APA, 1994).

A diagnosis of a Personality Disorder should be given when an individual exhibits traits and behaviors in early adulthood which are enduring, inflexible, maladaptive, cause significant impairment in functioning, and do not occur exclusively during an episode of an Axis I disorder. Personality Disorders are coded on Axis II and great care should be taken in using these diagnoses during an episode of a Mood Disorder or an Anxiety Disorder because some defining characteristics of these disorders may mimic the symptoms of a Personality Disorder. Furthermore, a diagnosis of Personality Disorder should not be given to an individual who is experiencing substance intoxication, withdrawal, or dependency since an accurate assessment of the individual's true behavior may not be possible. When physiological effects of a general medical condition cause a persistent change in an individual's personality, a diagnosis of Personality Change Due to a General Medical Condition should be considered. It is important to note that the diagnostic categories for Personality Disorders should be viewed as a guide rather than a rigid model; consequently, clients with the same Personality Disorder should not be viewed in the same manner, and should not be given a particular diagnosis as a result (Millon, 1990).

The first disorder in Cluster A, *Paranoid Personality Disorder*, is described as a pervasive pattern of distrust where the individual perceives the actions of others as malevolent. The individual with Paranoid Personality Disorder has difficulty trusting others, believes others are deceptive, and exploitative, and has difficulties with forgiveness. This disorder is more prevalent in males and accounts for approximately 0.5-2.5% of the general population.

Schizoid Personality Disorder is characterized by a pattern of separateness from relationships and few disclosures of feelings in social situations. Also, limited familial relationships, preference for solitary activities, and flat affect may be present. This disorder occurs more frequently in males; however, consistent with the defining characteristics of this disorder, an individual with Schizoid Personality Disorder is rarely found in clinical settings.

The final disorder in Cluster A, Schizotypal Personality Disorder, is a rather stable pattern of discomfort and difficulties with interpersonal relationships. Further, delusions, limited personal relationships, unusual beliefs which influence behavior, and inappropriate affect may be present. This disorder accounts for approximately 3% of the clinical population and occurs slightly more in males.

The Cluster B diagnosis of Antisocial Personality Disorder can only be given to an individual who is at least 18 years of age and who has exhibited evidence of Conduct Disorder since age 15. Antisocial Personality Disorder is characterized by a disregard for societal norms resulting in unlawful behaviors, aggressiveness, deceitfulness, impulsivity, irresponsibility, and lack of remorse for any harm done to another person. Although this disorder may be under diagnosed in females, it occurs more frequently in males and is more common among first-degree biological relatives.

Borderline Personality Disorder (Cluster B) is much more prevalent in females and accounts for approximately 2% of the general population. Common diagnostic features include intense relationships, abandonment issues, suicidal and self-destructive behaviors, inappropriate anger, and mood instability. These maladaptive behaviors are often reinforced because factors in the borderline individual's environment inhibit the use of more effective coping mechanisms (Linehan, 1994).

Histrionic Personality Disorder (Cluster B) is a pattern of attention seeking and inappropriate provocative behavior. Individuals with this disorder are impressionable, overemphasize the intimacy of relationships, are overly dramatic, attempt to draw attention to their physical appearance, and exhibit a shallow expression of emotions. Additionally, the histrionic individual may behave according to extreme sexual stereotypes and may appear as either overly masculine or feminine.

An individual with *Narcissistic Personality Disorder* (Cluster B) presents an inflated sense of worth and requires the open admiration of those around them. These individuals are often consumed with illusions of success, power, beauty, or love and they believe that they are "special."

This belief is expressed through haughty and disdainful behaviors and a sense of entitlement. Other key traits are being exploitative, lacking empathy, and extreme envy. Persons with Narcissistic Personality Disorder may have increased difficulty in adjusting to the physical and occupational restrictions that accompany the aging process.

Individuals with *Avoidant Personality Disorder* (Cluster C) present a pervasive pattern of social inhibition, low self-esteem, and an increased sensitivity to criticism from others. There is variance in the degree that different cultures regard avoidance as appropriate, and this should be kept in mind when considering this diagnosis. Avoidant Personality Disorder is equally prevalent in both genders and it comprises bout 10% of all outpatients in mental health clinics.

The essence of *Dependent Personality Disorder* (Cluster C) is an extreme need to be taken care of, which results in submissive and helpless behavior, and undue fears of separation. These individuals have trouble making everyday decisions, doing things on their own or alone, and they need others to take responsibility for most major areas of their lives. Another trait is great difficulty in expressing disagreement with others because of the fear of losing approval. A person with this disorder will go to great lengths to get and maintain the care of others, and will desperately seek another relationship as a source of nurturance when a close relationship has ended. One must be careful to consider the amount of dependence that is considered appropriate for each gender within a specific cultural setting; furthermore, one must use great caution in applying this diagnosis to children and adolescents for whom dependent behavior may be developmentally appropriate.

Obsessive-Compulsive Personality Disorder (Cluster C) is characterized by a rigid adherence to rules, lists, schedules, and interpersonal control. These individuals are consumed with perfectionism which can interfere with productivity because overly strict standards are not met. There is a pervasive rigidity and stubbornness which is exhibited in such behaviors as being a workaholic, being inflexible on moral and ethical matters, being miserly about possessions and money, and being unwilling to delegate work. Persons with Obsessive-Compulsive Personality Disorder usually show emotion in a very controlled manner, and are generally uncomfortable around those who are emotionally expressive. In empirical studies, this disorder appears to be twice as prevalent in men than in women.

The diagnosis of *Personality Disorder Not Otherwise Specified* (NOS) should be used when an individual presents the features of several different Personality Disorders, but does not meet the criteria for diagnosis for any one Personality Disorder. There are also specific personality disorders that are not included in the Classification section of the DSM-IV, but are noted in the Other Conditions That May Be A Focus of Clinical Attention section. These Personality Disorders include Depressive Personality Disorder, and Passive-Aggressive Personality Disorder.

The development of systematic treatment approaches for Personality Disorders has lagged behind because of a lack of models of these disorders that would help to guide their treatment (Clarkin, Marziali, & Munroe-Blum, 1992). Generally, marriage counseling or group therapy may be effective for Personality Disorders. Specifically, dialectical behavior therapy (Linehan, 1993) has been one of the only therapies to undergo rigorous empirical investigations with positive results. This therapy was developed specifically for patients with Borderline Personality Disorder, and although it has been used with other populations, the generalizability of this treatment has yet to be empirically verified. Theodore Millon (1988) has suggested that the best approach is Integrative Psychotherapy or a synthesis of many different theoretical and clinical approaches that are tailored to meet the specific personological needs of the client. The goals of this therapy are to balance deficiencies in the personality by using techniques that are best suited to modify their expression in the areas that are most problematic to the client (Millon, 1990).

Resource Documents

American Psychiatric Association, (1994). *The diagnostic and statistical manual of mental disorders.* (4th ed.) Washington, DC: Author.

Clarkin, J. F., Marziali, E., & Munroe-Blum, H. (1991). Group treatments for borderline personality disorder. *Hospital and Community Psychiatry, 42,* 1038-1043.

Linehan, M., (1993). *The skills training manual for treating borderline personality disorder.* New York: Guilford.

Linehan, M., Tutek, D. A., Heard, H. L., and Armstrong, H. E. (1994). Interpersonal outcome of cognitive behavioral treatment for chronically suicidal borderline patients. *American Journal of Psychiatry, 151,* 1771-1775.

Millon, T, (1990). *Toward a new personology: An evolutionary model.* New York: John Wiley.

Millon, T, (1988). Personologic psychotherapy: Ten commandments for a post eclectic approach to integrative treatment. *Psychotherapy, 25,* 209-219.

Kyra Martin-Houser and Jane G. Robertson are graduate students in the Department of Counseling and Educational Development at the University of North Carolina at Greensboro.

CHAPTER FIFTY–FIVE

Conditions That May Be a Focus of Clinical Attention: The DSM-IV V-Codes

Claudia B. Melton and Melinda B. Miller

The DSM-IV (American Psychiatric Association, 1994), V-codes are useful in providing a better explanation of a client's symptomatology. They are often used in conjunction with another Axis I diagnosis. When used alone, it is important to note that V-codes are not typically insurance reimbursable. Diagnoses such as these, however, are vital for conveying information about a client to other professionals who may become involved in the case. In addition, use of these conditions is necessary when criteria for a formal Axis I or Axis II diagnosis are not met. Finally, the last reason for citing a V-code is if the individual has a problem that is related to a mental disorder, but the problem is significant enough to warrant independent clinical attention.

The subcategories under the heading of "Other Conditions That May Be a Focus of Clinical Attention" are: Psychological Factors Affecting Medical Conditions (psychosomatic symptoms), Medication-Induced Movement Disorders, Relational Problems, Problems Related to Abuse or Neglect, and Additional Conditions That May Be a Focus of Clinical Attention. In this chapter, the latter three subcategories will be reviewed.

Relational Problems

It has been said that all problems are relationship problems. Although simplified, there is much truth in this statement. Many problems that clinicians face are issues with another individual. As with every classification within the DSM-IV, the relational problems must cause clinically significant impairment in functioning.

It is important to note that there are many causes of relational problems between a parent and child, between partners, and between siblings. For example, if a parent remarries after a divorce and each of the partners has children, it is normal for siblings to perhaps engage in a power struggle. Therefore, it is important to remember that it is only if the problem is causing *clinically significant impairment* that it becomes a *DSM-IV* diagnosis. It also is necessary to obtain all relevant information before making a diagnosis.

There are five V-codes under this particular title:

1. Relational Problem Related to a Mental Disorder or General Medical Condition, which includes a pattern of weakened interaction that is associated with a family member's mental disorder or general medical condition.
2. Parent-Child Relational Problem, in which the clinical attention is focused on a pattern of interaction between parent and child that is analogous with clinically significant impairment in either individual or family functioning.
3. Partner-Relational Problems are characterized as difficulties of communication that are associated with clinically significant impairment in either individual or family functioning.
4. Sibling Relational Problems includes a focus of clinical attention on interactional patterns among siblings that are associated with clinically impaired functioning in individual or family functioning.
5. Relational Problem Not Otherwise Specified is the appropriate category when the focus of clinical attention is on relational problems that are not included by the above (i.e., a child's difficulties with teachers).

Problems Related to Abuse or Neglect

Child abuse is defined by Public Law 93-247 as: A physical or mental injury, sexual abuse or exploitation, negligent treatment or maltreatment of a child under the age of 18; e.g., N.C. Gen. Stat., 1989. This section of the DSM-IV focuses on abuse of individuals across all age groups and the neglect of children. In the future, neglect also may be a focus of clinical attention for the adult population (i.e., neglect of an elderly parent, neglect of an adult with mental retardation).

The V-codes are used here when the focus of clinical attention is on the perpetrator of the abuse or neglect. When the focus of attention is on the victim, the appropriate code is 995.5. There are five different V-codes listed under this heading.

1. Physical Abuse of a Child,
2. Sexual Abuse of a Child, and
3. Neglect of a Child

These are utilized when the victim is under the age of eighteen. When the victim of the abuse is an adult, the listings are

4. Physical Abuse of an Adult, and
5. Sexual Abuse of an Adult.

Additional Conditions That May Be a Focus of Clinical Attention

Noncompliance with Treatment is used when the focus of the treatment is related to the client's refusal to conform to necessary treatment. Reasons for refusal range from distress about the expense or side effects to interference with cultural and religious beliefs to the co-morbid presence of a mental disorder. If the problem is serious enough to require separate attention during the treatment process, then this condition should be noted in the client's diagnosis.

When an external incentive is the primary motive for feigning illness, then the diagnosis of *Malingering* must be applied. Malingering is often employed when the person wishes to avoid an unwanted requirement such as work, military duty, or criminal prosecution. This condition should be suspected if the client is referred by an attorney, if objective findings do not match the client's description of the problem, and if the client refuses to cooperate with treatment. Malingering differs from both Factitious Disorder and Somatoform Disorders because it requires intentional reproduction of symptomatology and receipt of external incentives.

Two V-codes exist to describe antisocial behaviors that are not the direct result of a mental disorder. Adult Antisocial Behavior, or Child or Adolescent Antisocial Behavior is assigned when the individual exhibits behaviors not severe enough to warrant the diagnosis of Antisocial

Personality Disorder, Conduct Disorder, or an Impulse-Control Disorder. In adults, this may describe the actions of some professional thieves or illegal-drug dealers. In children and adolescents, the behavior may be displayed through isolated non-patterned antisocial acts.

When a client demonstrates problems in cognitive functioning that are not severe enough to warrant the diagnosis of a mental disorder, two other possibilities exist. When a person's IQ is in the 71-84 range, the category of Borderline Intellectual Functioning may be exercised. This Axis II diagnosis may be difficult to determine when a severe mental disorder exists as well. Although not a V-code, Age-Related Cognitive Decline is found in this section as well. It is applied when a person's intellectual abilities are affected as a direct result of the aging process but do not exceed the normal limits when given the client's age. Neurological difficulties and specific mental disorders must first be ruled out prior to utilizing these diagnoses.

The condition of *Bereavement* can be given when clinical attention is focused on the reaction to a death of a loved one. Although the symptoms of Bereavement may mimic that of a Major Depressive Episode, the latter diagnosis is withheld until the individual exhibits the symptomatology for two months after the death. In addition, if hallucinations, feelings of worthlessness, marked dysfunction, or excessive guilt exist, then Bereavement should be replaced by a diagnosis such as Major Depression or Acute Stress Disorder.

The remaining six conditions refer to problems in various aspects of an individual's life. All are used when the focus of clinical attention is not due to a mental disorder, or a mental disorder does exist; when the condition is severe enough to require independent attention. The code for Academic Problem is selected when the individual presents with a pervasive pattern of underachievement or difficulties in school without the symptomatology for a Learning or Communication Disorder. In addition, Mental Retardation should be ruled out before this code is assigned. When an individual presents with problems solely involving their job or career in the absence of a mental disorder, then the condition of Occupational Problem is given. Examples of these may include job dissatisfaction or problems with career decision-making.

Identity Problem is not specifically a V-code, but it is included in this section of the DSM-IV. When a client presents with an issue concerning goals, friendship, sexual orientation, morals, or loyalties to people, then this would be the correct condition to assign. These issues must exist without the presence of a mental disorder before the counselor can determine this condition. After a person converts to a new religion or begins to question faith in their own religion, a Religious or Spiritual Problem may occur. While these may or may not be related to a specific religion, the issues faced must involve faith in order to warrant this diagnosis.

The condition of *Acculturation Problem* occurs when a person has difficulties adjusting to a culture different than the original one. This may occur when a person emigrates to a new country or when someone moves to a different part of the same country; e.g., from northern U.S. to Southern U.S. Finally, a *Phase of Life Problem* is assigned when the individual's issues revolve around a particular time of life. This may be a developmental phase or a change resulting from marriage, divorce, schooling, career, or parenthood. The primary factor for this diagnosis is the direct relationship between the symptoms and the change in life phase.

Conclusion

A variety of theoretical options exist for effective counseling of persons with V-codes. Counselors may choose to focus on the affect, behavior, or cognition of the client. In most cases, the counselor should identify the basic needs and future goals of the client. Bereavement and abuse are extremely different than borderline intellectual functioning and occupational problems, but all are conditions that may be a focus of clinical attention. It is important not to assume that clients are any less distressed because they present with these issues; they are often primary reasons for why someone seeks counseling. Although V-codes are not "true mental disorders" and may not be covered by a client's insurance or managed care plan, they may be the most appropriate diagnosis for the presenting syptomatology.

References

American Psychiatric Association (1994). *Diagnosis and statistical manual of mental disorders* (4th Ed.). Washington, DC: Author.

North Carolina General Statute. Sec. 93-247 (1989).

Claudia B. Melton and Melinda B. Miller are each pursuing the combined M.S. and Ed.S. in School Counseling at The University of North Carolina at Greensboro.

CHAPTER FIFTY-SIX

Summary and a Look to the Future

J. Scott Hinkle

Many types of counseling include mental health counseling. Community, addictions, marriage and family, gerontological, career, school, and college counselors, among others, all utilize aspects of mental health counseling. Spruill has indicated in this volume that mental health counseling is an interdisciplinary field with roots in the fields of education and counseling. A relative newcomer to the helping professions, mental health counseling has developed into a broad based discipline which is struggling for recognition and identity in the professional and consumer arenas. However, the interdisciplinary components of this definition of mental health counseling have yet to materialize within the counseling profession. In the future, mental health counseling can blossom only if it continues to evolve with the other counseling "specialties." Collaboration among the different care providers within the counseling profession is critical for the future counseling as well as the future of the mental health counseling specialty.

Clinical Competence and Mental Health Counseling

Mental health counseling is comprehensive in scope, requiring counselors to obtain competence in a variety of clinical areas. Many of these areas of expertise have been presented in this volume. Mental disorders and substance abuse are major health issues in the United States (Levin, Glasser, & Haffee, 1988) affecting nearly 45 million people. In 1990, these problems, listed in the *DSM-IV* (American Psychiatric Association [APA], 1994) were estimated to have cost the United States billions of dollars (Rice, Kelman, Miller, & Dunmeyer, 1990). Approximately 30% of the general population is at a lifetime risk of developing one of these disorders (Scottenfield, 1993). In addition, estimates suggest that from 3% to 5% of all school children may have serious behavioral or emotional disorders.

In the future, mental health counseling needs to focus more on serving the adults and children in the United States who suffer from these disorders. This does not mean abandoning a developmental model for some counselors. People experiencing these disorders may be served from a variety of perspectives, utilizing counseling methods that fit the unique circumstance and situation of the client. Furthermore, understanding a diagnosis and the associated implications is imperative to the effective delivery of mental health counseling (Hinkle, 1992). In the future it will be necessary to "speak the *DSM* language" in order for mental health counselors to have access to employment, reimbursement for services from managed care and insurance companies, and professional credibility in the market place.

Collaborating with Schools and School Counselors

Unfortunately, less than one-third to one-fifth of our country's children are identified for special education purposes and mental health treatment. Zahner, Pawelkiewicz, DeFrancesco, and Adnopoz (1992) have reported that only 11% of children at risk of mental health problems received services in a mental health setting, whereas one third of children received some services through their school (Brandenburg, Friedman, & Silver, 1990; Costello, Burns, Angold, & Leaf, 1993; Hinkle & Wells, 1995; Knitzer, Steinberg, & Fleisch,1990). It will be important, particularly for our children's sake, for mental health counselors to establish collaborative relationships with schools and school counselors.

Collaborating with Physicians

Primary care physicians are an essential part of the mental health service system (Manderscheid & Sonnenschein, 1992, 1994, 1996), and when appropriate, should be consulted. Future collaboration with physicians will only enhance the professional status of mental health counselors and improve the treatment of clients/patients who seek out their doctor for mental health care. Furthermore, such collaboration can reduce the 50% to 80% of undetected behavioral and emotional problems missed during primary care visits due to a variety of patient, doctor, and system factors (Miranda & Munoz, 1994). Obviously, such collaboration will require modifications in training models for mental health counseling.

Mental Health Counselor Education and Training

Counselors who practice mental health counseling need support at the initial stages of training. This includes competent curricular components, both didactic and experiential, as reflected in the Council for Accreditation of Counseling and Related Educational Programs (CACREP, 1994) standards, mentoring by professionals who also are competent in the practice of mental health counseling, and support following graduation (e.g., continuing education, consultation). Such preservice support and training will be critical in the future. Moreover, practicum and internship experiences in mental health counselor education and training will need to include clinical opportunities in managed care environments (Hinkle & Kline, 1996). Likewise, mental health counseling training programs will need to increase their focus on short-term treatment, as their graduates are likely to treat clients under more restrictive utilization conditions than has been traditionally the case (Dial et al., 1992).

Mental health counseling is widely acknowledged (but not necessarily accepted) by other professional disciplines, is understood by the public, and currently has a rather rigorous training regiment. In the future, the helping professionals with the most current knowledge about the human condition, the various impacts of mental disorders, and effective interventions are likely to determine how public mental health care will be delivered in the next century (see Dial et al., 1992). For mental health counselors to affect this determination and at the same time be competitive for increased wages, jobs with managed care organizations, and acceptance in the interdisciplinary health care market, they must be able to compete at a level comparable to other mental health service providers. Mental health counseling training and education models will require significant changes in the future in order for this counseling specialty to make such an impact. For example, most of the major theories in the mental health field have come from other disciplines such as psychology and psychiatry.

Mental health counselor educators of tomorrow will need to make contributions to mental health theory and treatment strategies. Mental health counseling has a valued perspective to offer, and it needs to be captured in our training, practice, and literature (Hinkle & Kline, 1996).

Utilization of the DSM-IV

Many counselor educators and supervisors believe that the *DSM-IV* rigidly follows the "medical model," even though the vast majority of the disorders listed are not attributable to known or presumed organic causes (Sue, Sue, & Sue, 1990). The *DSM* has made many noteworthy contributions to the field of mental health over the years. However, cultural formulations in the latest edition, *DSM-IV*, are lacking. Future contributions to this important area of psychodiagnosis certainly could emanate from the mental health counselor education arena.

Utilization of the *DSM-IV* has increased in mental health counselor education training, but more is needed (see Fong, 1993, 1995; Hinkle, 1992; Hohenshil, 1993; Waldo, Brotherton, & Harswill, 1993). Mental health counselor educators can help determine the course of mental health treatment by training their graduate students to be effective and efficient health providers, which in many cases includes making an accurate diagnosis. Relatedly, standards of care or treatment delineate minimum professional performance (Beamish, Granello, Granello, McSteen, & Stone, 1997), but there are few standards of care developed for the counseling profession (Granello & Witmer, 1996). Although no single counseling approach is superior to another, not all treatments are equally effective or equally ineffective (Hester & Miller, 1985). Mental health counselor educators could make major contributions to this deficiency in mental health treatment in the future.

Minority Representation and Diversity

Several authors in this volume have discussed multiculturalism in mental health counseling from a clinical perspective. Additionally, low percentages of minorities in the mental health professions is a critical concern. While the importance of cultural diversity and the presence of under-represented groups has been recognized and emphasized since the 1980s, the relatively small numbers of minorities in the mental health workforce does not reflect the composition of our clients (Dial et al., 1992). In the future, mental health counselor educators will need to make concerted efforts towards minority recruitment.

Skill-Based Training

Mental health counselor educators of tomorrow will need to shift from teaching a primarily theory-based model to a skill-based model of practice. This will enhance specific clinical competencies, and produce a range of skills from various theoretical approaches for utilization by mental health counselors (Hershenson & Power, 1987).

In 1996, the Academy of Clinical Mental Health Counseling completed a work behavior analysis for the purpose of developing a clinical examination as part of the requirements for the National Board for Certified Counselors' (1996) specialty certification in mental health counseling. This analysis reflected major themes including diagnosis and treatment planning, family and relationship counseling, and professional issues. Included in these themes were medical issues, diagnosis, crisis intervention, monitoring client progress, making appropriate referrals and follow-ups, using biopsychosocial assessment data, conducting mental status examinations, interpreting assessment results, utilizing systemic ideas in counseling, and various professional behaviors (e.g., informed consent; ethical aspects of mental health) (Hinkle & Kline, 1996). Skills in these areas need to be added to our curricula in mental health counseling.

Conclusion

Teaching mental health counseling with a focus on mental health agencies and private practice has been discussed in counselor education for almost 20 years. However, relatively few counselor education programs have sought and obtained MHC accreditation (N=16). Mental health counselor education needs to be included in more graduate programs. For this to become a reality our perceptions of mental health counseling, as well as some refinements in the CACREP standards, will be necessary (Hinkle & Kline, 1996).

References

American Psychiatric Association. (1994). *Diagnostic and statistical manual of mental disorders* (4th ed.) Washington, DC: Author.

Brandenburg, N. A., Friedman, R. M., & Silver, S. E. (1990). The epidemiology of childhood psychiatric disorders. *Journal of the American Academy of Child and Adolescent Psychiatry, 29,* 76-83.

Beamish. P. M., Granello, D. H., Granello, P. F., McSteen, P. B., & Stone, D. A. (1997). Emerging standards of care for the diagnosis and treatment of panic disorder. *Journal of Mental Health Counseling,* 99-113.

Costello, E. J., Burns, B. J., Angold, A., & Leaf, P. J. (1993). How can epidemiology improve mental health services for children and adolescents? *Journal of the American Academy of Child and Adolescent Psychiatry, 32,* 1106-1114.

Dial, T. H., Pion, G. M., Cooney, B., Kohout, K., Kaplan, K. O., Ginsberg, L., Merwin, E. I., Fox, J. C., Ginsberg, M., Staton, J., Clawson, T. W., Wildersmuth, V. A., Blankertz, L., & Hughes, R. (1992). Training of Mental Health Providers. In R. W. Manderscheid, & M. A. Sonnenschein, M. A. (Eds.). *Mental health, United States, 1992* (pp. 142-162). Washington, DC: U. S. Government Printing Office.

Fong, M. L. (1993). Teaching assessment and diagnosis within a DSM-III-R framework. *Counselor Education and Supervision, 32,* 276-286.

Fong, M. L. (1995). Assessment and DSM-IV diagnosis of personality disorders: A primer for counselors. *Journal of Counseling and Development, 73,* 635-639.

Granello, P. F., & Witmer, J. M. (1996). *Standards of care: Potential implications for the counseling profession.* Manuscript submitted for publication, Ohio University, Athens.

Hershenson, D. B., & Power, P. W. (1987). *Mental health counseling: Theory and practice.* New York: Pergamon.

Hester, R. K., & Miller, W. R. (Eds.). (1985). *Handbook of alcoholism treatment approaches: Effective alternatives.* Boston: Allyn & Bacon.

Hinkle, J. S. (1992). The DSM-IV: Prognosis and implications for mental health counselors. *Journal of Mental Health Counseling, 16,* 174-183.

Hinkle, J. S., & Kline, W. B. (1996, October). *Issues in mental health counselor education and certification: Why are we doing what we are doing?* Paper presented at the National Meeting of the Association for Counselor Education and Supervision, Portland, OR.

Hinkle, J. S., & Wells, M. E. (1995). *Family counseling in the schools: A practical guide for counselors, teachers, and psychologists.* Greensboro, NC: ERIC.

Hohenshil, T. H. (1993). Teaching the DSM-III-R in counselor education. *Counselor Education and Supervision, 32,* 267-275.

Knitzer, J., Steinberg, A., & Fleisch, B. (1990). *At the schoolhouse door: An examination of progress and policies for children with behavioral and emotional problems.* New York: Bank Street College of Education.

Levin, B. L., Glasser, J. H., & Haffee, C. L. (1988). National trends in coverage and utilization of mental health, alcohol, and substance abuse services within managed health care systems. *American Journal of Public Health, 78,* 1222-1223.

Manderscheid, R. W., & Sonnenschein, M. A. (1992). *Mental health, United States, 1992.* Washington, DC: U.S. Government.

Manderscheid, R. W., & Sonnenschein, M. A. (1994). *Mental health, United States, 1994.* Washington, DC: U.S. Government.

Manderscheid, R. W., & Sonnenschein, M. A. (1996). *Mental health, United States, 1996.* Washington, DC: U.S. Government.

Miranda, J.,& Munoz, R. (1994). Intervention for minor depression in primary care patients. *Psychosomatic Medicine, 56,* 94-96.

National Board for Certified Counselors (1996). *A work behavior analysis of mental health counselors.* Greensboro, NC: Author.

Rice, D. P., Kelman, S., Miller, L. S., & Dunmeyer, S. (1990) *The economic costs of alcohol and drug abuse and mental illness* (U.S. Department of Health and Human Services). San Francisco: University of California, Institute for Health and Aging.

Scottenfield, R. S. (1993). Psychotherapeutic approaches to dual-diagnosis patients. In W. H. Sledge & Tasman, A. (Eds.), *Clinical challenges in psychiatry* (pp. 5-36). Washington, DC: American Psychiatric Press.

Sue, D., Sue, D., & Sue, S. (1990). *Understanding abnormal behavior.* Boston: Houghton Mifflin.

Waldo, M., Brotherton, W., & Harswill, R. (1993). Integrating DSM-III-R training into school, marriage, and family and mental health counselor education. *Counselor Education and Supervision, 32,* 332-342.

Zahner, G., Pawelkiewicz, W., DeFrancesco, J.J., & Adnopoz, J. (1992). Children's mental health service needs and utilization patterns in an urban community: An epidemiological assessment. *Journal of the American Academy of Child and Adolescent Psychiatry, 31,* 951-960.

J. Scott Hinkle, NCC, CCMHC teaches at the University of North Carolina at Greensboro.

Useful Resources

WHAT EVERY SCHOOL COUNSELOR, PSYCHOLOGIST & THERAPIST NEEDS TO OFFER...

Family Counseling in the Schools

by J. Scott Hinkle

[illegible]

NEW RELEASE FROM THE AMERICAN COUNSELING ASSOCIATION

Integrating Outcome Research Into Counseling Practice and Training

An ERIC Search on Mental Health Counseling

A few selected recent resources

AN - ACCESSION NUMBER: EJ553172
AU - PERSONAL AUTHOR: Evans,-Kathy-M.
TI - TITLE: Wellness and Coping Activities of African American Counselors.
PY - PUBLICATION YEAR: 1997
JN - JOURNAL CITATION: Journal-of-Black-Psychology; v23 n1 p24-35 Feb 1997
AB - ABSTRACT: Examined physical, emotional, cognitive, and spiritual wellness activities of African American mental health counselors and behaviors they used to cope with racism. Counselors used a wide variety of wellness strategies, although counselors in school settings were less likely to engage in occupational wellness activities. Confrontation was the most common approach to racism.

AN - ACCESSION NUMBER: EJ542389
AU - PERSONAL AUTHOR: Whiston,-Susan-C.
TI - TITLE: Accountability through Action Research: Research Methods of Practitioners.
PY - PUBLICATION YEAR: 1996
JN - JOURNAL CITATION: Journal-of-Counseling-&-Development; v74 n6 p616-23 Jul-Aug 1996
AB - ABSTRACT: Summarizes how outcome research methodologies can be incorporated into counseling practice in many settings. Discusses the steps involved in performing an outcome or evaluative study, which is followed by specific information concerning instruments and techniques for use in the areas of mental health counseling, career counseling, and school counseling.

AN - ACCESSION NUMBER: EJ537289
AU - PERSONAL AUTHOR: Salisbury,-William-A.; Kinnier,-Richard-T.
TI - TITLE: Posttermination Friendship between Counselors and Clients.
PY - PUBLICATION YEAR: 1996
JN - JOURNAL CITATION: Journal-of-Counseling-&-Development; v74 n5 p495-500 Aug 1996
AB - ABSTRACT: Examines counselors' behaviors and attitudes regarding friendships and sexual relationships with former clients. Sample consisted of 96 members of the American Mental Health Counselors Association. Potential harm to the client was the most important concern expressed by the counselors. Discusses results, as well as ethical and research implications.

AN - ACCESSION NUMBER: EJ522639
AU - PERSONAL AUTHOR: Smith,-Howard-B.; Robinson,-Gail-P.
T I - TITLE: Mental Health Counseling: Past, Present, and Future.
PY - PUBLICATION YEAR: 1995
JN - JOURNAL CITATION: Journal-of-Counseling-&-Development; v74 n2 p158-62 Nov-Dec 1995
AB - ABSTRACT: Examines the significant events in the history of mental health care that have contributed to the development of a specialty within the counseling profession referred to as mental health counseling. Discusses the development of credentials for the specialty and theissues currently facing mental health counseling, and offers a perspective on directions for the future.

AN - ACCESSION NUMBER: EJ517537
AU - PERSONAL AUTHOR: Ofman,-Paul-S.; And-Others
T I - TITLE: Mental Health Response to Terrorism: The World Trade Center Bombing.
PY - PUBLICATION YEAR: 1995
JN - JOURNAL CITATION: Journal-of-Mental-Health-Counseling; v17 n3 p312-20 Jul 1995
AB - ABSTRACT: Reviews literature pertaining directly to responses to man-made disasters, with specific emphasis on emotional responses to terrorism. Summarizes the effects of the bombing of the World Trade Center on its survivors and on the wider community. Examples of mental health outreach efforts and case vignettes of brief cognitive behavior therapeutic intervention with survivors are provided.

AN - ACCESSION NUMBER: EJ517533
AU - PERSONAL AUTHOR: Thompson,-Rosemary-A.
T I - TITLE: Being Prepared for Suicide or Student Death in Schools: Strategies to Restore Equilibrium.
PY - PUBLICATION YEAR: 1995
JN - JOURNAL CITATION: Journal-of-Mental-Health-Counseling; v17 n3 p264-77 Jul 1995
AB - ABSTRACT: A workable referral system, using resources within a school and within the community, becomes important when a sudden death or suicide occurs. When managing a crisis, helping professionals need to have the means for restoring a school and community to its precrisis equilibrium. Provides specific information pertinent to developing an effective intervention plan.

AN - ACCESSION NUMBER: EJ517532
AU - PERSONAL AUTHOR: Dingman,-Robert-L.; Ginter,-Earl-J.
TI - TITLE: Disasters and Crises: The Role of Mental Health Counseling.
PY - PUBLICATION YEAR: 1995
JN - JOURNAL CITATION: Journal-of-Mental-Health-Counseling; v17 n3 p259-63 Jul 1995
AB - ABSTRACT: Provides a brief overview of events that have contributed to the development of what currently constitutes disaster-crisis mental health counseling, an area of counseling that has gained increased clinical attention and empirical focus within the field of mental health counseling.

AN - ACCESSION NUMBER: ED388883
AU - PERSONAL AUTHOR: Juhnke,-Gerald-A.
TI - TITLE: Mental Health Counseling Assessment: Broadening One's Understanding of the Client and the Clients Presenting Concerns. ERIC Digest.
PY - PUBLICATION YEAR: 1995
AB - ABSTRACT: Assessment is broader in scope than testing. Typically, assessment includes gathering and integrating information about a client in a manner that promotes effective treatment. This digest discusses how counselors can use assessment as a continuous process throughout treatment. It also reviews three common forms of assessment techniques which can be used in conjunction with testing: (1) Qualitative Assessment; (3) Behavioral Assessment; and (3) Past Records. Continuous assessment influences the direction of treatment for two reasons: (1) presenting concerns and client circumstances are not static and often need to be modified or re-ordered; and (2) assessment can aid in evaluating the efficacy of treatment. Continuous assessment allows comparisons between the client's initial baseline functioning and current functioning. Qualitative assessment techniques often consist of games and simulation exercises that are flexible, open-ended, holistic, and nonstatistical. Clients can process what they learned from the experience immediately within the counseling session. Behavior assessment looks at manifest behaviors. Emphasis is placed upon identifying antecedents to problem behaviors and consequences that reduce their frequency or eliminate them. Counselors should also utilize client's past records to identify important patterns and ineffective treatments.

AN - ACCESSION NUMBER: EJ513165
AU - PERSONAL AUTHOR: Steenbarger,-Brett-N.; LeClair,-Scott
TI - TITLE: Beyond Remediation and Development: Mental Health Counseling in Context.
PY - PUBLICATION YEAR: 1995
JN - JOURNAL CITATION: Journal-of-Mental-Health-Counseling; v17 n2 p173-87 Apr 1995
AB - ABSTRACT: Suggests that the remedial-developmental dichotomy in the counseling profession is an artifact of the profession's grounding in linear, mechanistic, and stage-based, organismic theories. Contextually based, developmental systems models are advanced as frameworks that better account for researcher and practitioner observations and bridge the conceptual gap between developmental and helping roles.

AN - ACCESSION NUMBER: EJ513157
AU - PERSONAL AUTHOR: Hall,-Alex-S.; Lin,-Meei-Ju
TI - TITLE: Theory and Practice of Children's Rights: Implications for Mental Health Counselors.
PY - PUBLICATION YEAR: 1995
JN - JOURNAL CITATION: Journal-of-Mental-Health-Counseling; v17 n1 p63-80 Jan 1995
AB - ABSTRACT: Ethical issues related to rights of children to participate fully in their own mental health treatment decisions are examined. Clarifies concepts of children's rights inrelation to legal and psychological aspects, discusses Kitchener's theory and model of moral judgment, and proposes ethical standards for moral reasoning in counseling children.

AN - ACCESSION NUMBER: ED387755
AU - PERSONAL AUTHOR: Dykeman,-Cass
TI - TITLE: An Introduction to Working Alliance Theory for Professional Counselors.
PY - PUBLICATION YEAR: 1995
AB - ABSTRACT: Few contemporary developments in psychology rival the impact of working alliance theory. This construct can predict psychotherapy outcomes to an extent unknown previously. Yet despite the importance of working alliance theory to effective psychotherapy, only a few articles on this topic have appeared in resources commonly read by professional counselors. Professional school and mental

health counselors should become familiar with working alliance theory, a transtheoretical theory dating back to the beginnings of psychotherapy practice. A key clinical revenue of working alliance research is the production of alliance "markers." Client states requiring intervention are recognized through the delineation of client behavioral clusters from the therapist's phenomenological perspective. These recognized states are referred to as process markers. The school and mental health counselor's phenomenology of working alliance can aid in the generation of valuable alliance markers. Markers, in turn, can enhance therapist training and performance. Working alliance research represents a gold mine of knowledge for the practicing counselor. It is incumbent upon counselor educators to make sure such knowledge reaches professional counselors. In addition, it is the responsibility of each counselor to seek out and apply knowledge that can increase their effectiveness and efficiency.

AN - ACCESSION NUMBER: ED387720
AU - PERSONAL AUTHOR: Feist,-Stanley-C.
TI - TITLE: Marriage & Family Counseling in Mental Health Practice.
PY - PUBLICATION YEAR: 1995
AB - ABSTRACT: Marriage and Family Therapy is an increasingly popular treatment that was almost unknown 50 years ago. Family Therapy has been multidisciplinary from the beginning, drawing practitioners from social work, psychology, psychiatry, nursing, and pastoral and mental health counseling. It is often difficult to get a whole family to arrange schedules so that all may attend therapy simultaneously. This paper briefly describes: the medical model of linear causation of emotional disorder; Family Systems Theory; components of a family system; Structural Therapy; Communications Theory; family treatment techniques; and the narrative approach. Many other theories and techniques exist in the field of family therapy that are not covered here.

AN - ACCESSION NUMBER: EJ504512
AU - PERSONAL AUTHOR: Mariani,-Matthew
TI - TITLE: Beyond Psychobabble: Careers in Psychotherapy.
PY - PUBLICATION YEAR: 1995
JN - JOURNAL CITATION: Occupational-Outlook-Quarterly; v39 n1 p12-25 Spr 1995

AB - ABSTRACT: Describes the five largest psychotherapy occupations (psychiatrist, clinical/counseling psychologist, clinical social worker, marriage and family therapist, clinical mental health counselor) and looks at training requirements, types of practices, trends, and related occupations. Lists professional associations and references for further information.